Kelvin Corcoran

Collected Poems

Books by Kelvin Corcoran

Robin Hood in the Dark Ages. Permanent Press, London & New York, 1985.
The Red and Yellow Book. Textures, London, 1986. 2nd edn, Shearsman Books, Bristol, 2019.
Qiryat Sepher. Galloping Dog Press, Newcastle upon Tyne, 1988.
TCL. Pig Press, Durham, 1989.
The Next Wave. North and South, Twickenham and Wakefield, 1990.
Lyric Lyric. Reality Street, London, 1993.
Melanie's Book. Simple Vice and West House Books, Hay-on-Wye, 1996.
When Suzy Was. Shearsman Books, Kentisbeare, 1999.
Your Thinking Tracts or Nations (illustrated by Alan Halsey). West House Books, Sheffield, 2001.
New and Selected Poems. Shearsman Books, Exeter, 2004.
Roger Hilton's Sugar. Leafe Press, Nottingham, 2005.
Backward Turning Sea. Shearsman Books, Exeter, 2008.
What Hit Them. Oystercatcher Press, Hunstanton, 2008.
Hotel Shadow. Shearsman Books, Exeter, 2010.
Words Through a Hole Where Once There Was a Chimpanzee's Face. Longbarrow Press, Swindon, 2011.
For the Greek Spring. Shearsman Books, Bristol, 2013.
Sea Table. Shearsman Books, Bristol, 2015.
A Horse That Runs: To & Fro with Wallace Stevens (with Alan Halsey). Constitutional Information, Sheffield, 2015.
Facing West. Shearsman Books, Bristol, 2017.
Not Much To Say Really. Shearsman Books & Medicine Unboxed, Bristol, 2017.
Article 50. Longbarrow Press, Sheffield, 2018.
Winterreisen (with Alan Halsey). The Knives Forks and Spoons Press, Newton-le-Willows, 2019.
Below This Level. Shearsman Books, Bristol, 2019.
Orpheus Asymmetric (illustrated by David Rees). Oystercatcher Press, 2020.
The Republic of Song. Parlor Press, Anderson, SC, 2020.
Transparent Blue of Everything (illustrated by David Rees). Muscaliet, 2023.

Lee Harwood: Not the Full Story – Six Interviews by Kelvin Corcoran, Shearsman Books, Exeter, 2008.
Lee Harwood: New Collected Poems, Shearsman Books, 2023, co-edited with Robert Sheppard.

The Writing Occurs as Song: A Kelvin Corcoran Reader. Shearsman Books, 2014, edited by Andy Brown.

Kelvin Corcoran

Collected Poems

Shearsman Books

First published in the United Kingdom in 2023 by
Shearsman Books,
PO Box 4239
Swindon
SN3 9FN

www.shearsman.com

ISBN 978-1-84861-892-3

Copyright © Kelvin Corcoran, 1985–2023
All rights reserved.

The right of Kelvin Corcoran to be identified as the author of this work
has been asserted by his Estate in accordance with the
Copyrights, Designs and Patents Act of 1988.

Contents

from Robin Hood in the Dark Ages (1985)

Deeds	17
Going to Town	19
Descartes	21
No Death	23
Robin Hood	25
Shire Politics	26
Domestic and Foreign Policy	27
Carnival	28
In Town	29
The Rise of Surgery	30
World Politics or the Digestive Tract	31
This is a Nice Poem a Nice Sausage a Nice Man	32
The Lost World	33
A Woman A Woman	34
A Slogan Will Not Suffice	35
A Statement	37

from The Red and Yellow Book (1986)

Not That Voice	41
Power Lust and Striving	42
Keep	43
At the Wedding	44
Paintings in Hospitals	45
Casual Causal	46
Of all that Nature doth entend	47
The Last Poem	49
Next	50
Radio Wittgenstein	51
Machine Days	52
My Sister Said	53
Thin as Light	54
On Hearing the Song of the Dog	56

All the Difference	57
She Sang to Herself	58
Final Thing	59
Pictures	60
The Sound at the End of Waiting	61
from The Red and Yellow Book	67

from Lyric Lyric (1993)

Lyric Lyric	75
House, Man and Water	77
Serabit el-Khadem	78
MEB	79
'Looking for the source of the chill in my bones.'	80
Frans Masereel The Idea	81
Tocharian the I-E Enclave	83
The Border	84
The Radio Said	86
He's o'er the border and awa'	87
In the Garden	88
In April	90
Music of the Altai Mountains	91
Hysteresis Loop	94
Each Station Struck One Note	95
Such Secrets	96
Index	98

from Melanie's Book (1996)

I Woke to Tell You Something	101
Radio	105
Earth at Night	106
Running Under Venus	109
Restore Us Song	114
Young Marble Giants Sleep Inside Us	117
Remember and Forget Everything	120
Athens	123

Athlone	124
Hilversum	125
Home Service	126

from When Suzy Was (1999)

Hotel Byron	129
The Book of Answers	132
At the Centre of the World	133
Is This the Breaking of My First Life?	134
How Can I Find What I've Lost?	136
In the Red Book	137
You May Well Say to Yourself — Well How Did I Get Here?	139
The Literal Poem About My Father	144
When Suzy Was	147
The God is Not a Ventriloquist	149
The Name Apollo	150
The Roadside Shrine	152
Catalogue of Answers	155

My Life With Byron (2000)

And Such Other Cudgelled and Heterodox People	167
The Ludicrous Placation of Ghosts	172
Catalogue of Ships	174
Ambelakia	175
The Objects Were Not Paid For Or Got For a Fixed Price	177
Ivy Tattoo	178
They knew what hit them	179
On Returning from the Fields	180
Early morning	181
Disclaimer: ~~Byron Never Went to Ambelakia~~	182

Against Purity (2004)

Ino	185
Myriorama	186
A Shelley Poet	189
Season of Broken Doors	192
Singing Head	194
From the Harbour	195
The Empire Stores	198
Against Purity	204
Common Measure	205
MacSweeney	207
Melanie	208
For Doug Oliver	209
Three Monologues	
Leukothia	211
Pytheas	213
The Ingliss Touriste Patient	215

Backward Turning Sea (2008)

HELEN MANIA	221
THE SUBSEQUENT WORLD VIEW	
Aphrodite riding on a goat	227
Aphrodite's Bay	228
About My Country	231
From Here According to Jenkyns	233
Visitors	234
The Harbour at Night	237
Over the calm, clear shining water	238
ROGER HILTON'S SUGAR	
Setting Out	242
The Language of Art Critics	243
The Hilton Biography – A Selection	244
The Hilton Catalogue – A Selection	245

Radio Hilton	250
Seeing Hilton	251
The St. Ives Section	256
From Botallack Out	258
The Unpainted Hiltons	263

ALEXIARES

My Journey to Euripides	270
Odes of Alexiares	275
Interview	276
Alexiares in Exile	277
From Alexiares's Separate Notebooks	285

ULYSSES IN THE CAR	290
THE ARTEMISION TUNNEL	295

Hotel Shadow

FROM WHERE SONG COMES, OR
  KEEPING THE EMPIRE IN ORDER

From Where Song Comes	305
Sing Campion Song	309
Outside	314
Reading *The Cantos*	315
From the Hen-Roost	322
A Thesis on the Ballad	326
Learning to Play the Harp	329

NEWS OF ARISTOMENES	333

THE FAMILY CARNIVAL

Apokriatika	353
A Season Below Ground	357
Hearing Mishearing Doug Oliver	359
Byron's Karagiozis	362
Epicurus Is My Neighbour	368
Madeleine's Letter to Bunting	372

ON THE XENOPHONE LABEL	377

Sea Table

WORDS THROUGH A HOLE WHERE ONCE THERE WAS A CHIMPANZEE'S FACE	399
A SHORT HISTORY OF SONG SET TO MUSIC AND ABANDONED	
Totteling State	425
Thomas Campion	426
For the Defence	427
A Thesis on the Uses of the Voice	430
Richmond Fontaine at St. Bonaventure's	433
Thomas Hardy	434
Ivor Gurney	435
Housman and Graham	437
Experimental Poetry	438
The Romantic Tradition	439
That Poetry Best Not Written	441
All the Poets	443
Ghost House	444
Elizabeth Bishop	445
The Senior Choir	446
When I First Got Geraldine	447
Peter Riley	448
Let's have the Roger, Sydney	449
Little Song Don't Fade Away	450
Sappho	451
A Nightingale Improvises	452
GLENN GOULD AND EVERYTHING	453
SEA TABLE	471

Facing West

THE ABDUCTION ZONE
- The Abduction Zone — 505
- Antiope — 512
- Dionysus — 514
- Orpheus/If I could — 522
- Footnote to the above — 527

COMMON MEASURE
- Letter to Arov Manttir — 535
- Leipzig — 542
- At the Hospital Doors — 544
- Dream Journey — 546
- Common Measure — 548
- A Greek Spring — 551
- Lee Harwood 1939–2015 — 553

RADIO ARCHILOCHOS — 559

Below This Level (2019)

DIAGNOSIS
- What the Birds Said — 589
- Run Walk Run — 590
- The White Road — 594
- Let's Leave — 596

TREATMENT
- Surgery — 599
- Uitgang, provisional — 600
- Radiotherapy — 602
- Good Science — 603
- We've bought your husband back to you… — 604

AFTERWARDS
- To Ian, Recovering — 607
- Below This Level — 608

Arrival	609
Messages Coming In	610
Across the Square	611
Singing with Chagall	612

The Republic of Song (2021)

To Write a Mythology

Rue des Hiboux	619
Biographies of the Brexiteers	622
Radio Logos	623
Mr President's New Hat	628
The Near Distance	629
The Sinking Colony Revisited in the Days of Lee Harwood	631

The Republic of Song

Come Up Come Up	637
Grahamland	640
BN	642
In the Hilton Memorial Garden	643
Having a Drink with Phil	645
The Seven Graves of Tervuren	650
Seeing the City	651
John Berryman Played the Accordion	654
The bones of them are keeping	656
Listening to Country Music	658
A Revision of Jack Spicers's *Helen: A Revision*	664
The Pleats of the Sun	666

The Museum of the Sea	671

Above Ground (2023)

As if Auguries

City Garden	689
As if Auguries	691
Crow and a Footnote	693

Of the Crows	694
The Correspondence of Objects	695
Ten Tall Youths	698
Singers	700
From Chagall	702
Preparations	704

ANOTHER COUNTRY

When Blake Returned	709
Seeing England	711
The Nansen Passport	712
Another Country	714
Drinking Songs	717
Seamarks	719

ABOUT THE SEA

At a distance count the crises	725
That Night	729
Orpheus Asymmetric	731
About the Sea	740

Afterword	752
Notes	753
Previous Comments on Kelvin Corcoran's Work	762

from

Robin Hood in the Dark Ages

Deeds

The many facets of it, the radio
like bowls of light of thickening
walls what they say neighbours
in orbit about the heart a human
world as obvious as phenomenology as
the mind becomes actual here in
the European winter I have lit
the fire we have a mineral history to burn
and we can't keep our hands off each other.

Your face that night through the windscreen
warming up, no satisfactory explanation I
have my wife my friend it is a Brandenburg
number one day occasions the gold breakfast
blue quilt, a Mexican girl talks at length
seagulls in a square garden lean into each
other on the surface horn's intaglio of happiness
sparkles the big gem of 24 hours.

*

Like the smell of nail varnish
comes in its gloss of sex occasion
to occasion a blanket lava
at the hearth, the things you do
in a plural sleep the absolute
message of perfect action each
word goes home in the deep gloss
of courage sun up open eyes
like a Germano Facetti the action
spills over the colours an extra
hard top-coat for the opening
core of Monday morning, you get there.

*

Going through these days
like Jean Dubuffet's busy life
wartime light enquiring buildings
pile white the sphinx on the needle,
clock face, a new suede jacket
handsome off the river marble air
blue distances build power houses of
common want, I'm light here January
shiny badge both ways the river
flowing too O flowers table a statement
if the heart greets even the river lights.

Going to Town

Could say heartline there
the palm's geometry of
impact speed ablaze with
a former collision does not happen here,
a contusion sinister to the line
if you see it, it's alright
despite the red space heartline
the passage of co-ordination
that your face is beauty so welcome
thank you   a perfect fit.

*

The first lights of town, the fixed stars
on the fovea shine the arc of arrival
the neighbourhood dislocation shock absorbed
each day, go forward, kouroi diastole a charge
in the blood lights to both sides
and I'll be over by eight.

*

A compositional device and the place
is all around you, unlike the market
up or down, the financial world tonight
but no change, the ports stay closed.

Along this retrospective silver laid
in the backward dark the line of attention
is relieved in the home light
you splash into town, a door closes opens.

*

In town the roads and buildings
hang in safer speeds the duration
of civic use cushions children by the way
play ahead, slow take care here
daylight corridors the heat
from the shops spills onto
the street of people and the structured
light of leaves arranges a mutual speed,
drift ease the corner lean
into each other lives meet here.

Descartes

1

Descartes came into the poem. He did not like his new job; the way the chairs, the hi-fi and the fire lean into each other. He came in, I have just cycled from Stockholm, there is a lot of road between there and here. Times Square had soured him, peeled off a few skins and measured the depth of green. It is as I thought, the valve worked loose outside Paris.

It's not as if he's Malherbe either, across the field the slant of December. Descartes couldn't give a toss for rounded edges like playing cards, a Roman resting place, a holloway, two on the way to work, the combined action of human and natural agents – like I said, he didn't notice these details. He changed my life, hat polish for a start and envy in the dark.

When he was tired, his mind elsewhere, tossing coconuts at the poet's lawn, anywhere but here, Descartes would sit and doze and fill the house with it. Brown, hairy, large. A fistful of encased piss milk, remember no memory, the mind elsewhere. The violated child, courage turns us now next the light through the leaves, this path can be traced to the Wiltshire border.

No, he would not take a walk but that dip down to the brook is the boundary of the two villages. Yes, you can go there, that's mine down to the brook. The horses of this complex geometry are curious as you go.

2

Is it raining at my back or silence
high in the end of day head Monday
waits on shiny hill the conceptual sun
rises on the circuit of new green spring.

A quick look at the Dantean stars
window open, foxes yap if the moon is full
no animal sleeps silver bangs through
the heart the field fills with light.

A short time now, the unseparated events
come together, Linda's paintings dry
in the last heat blue roots against a fire
other plants an unfixed surface of blue
light   these are the forces of victory.

3

The money is on the table
on the way out I was zipped up
dark and tight, I was Frank
O'Hara's orphan brother
planning a windy route
through the new green spring of air.

The money is road signs, turn the hard U
in love is Shakespeare's cum sweet luv
I would kiss your mouth and the secret
deep in it flesh of everything said
or will you he said well I'm glad
you're pleased by something, walking
out of a C19 novel and upstairs at speed.

No Death

Combing out your blonde
using my cold hands I read
much of the weekend, draw out
£35 a week and try on that
soft crash on the bike
flop into the snow, I turned
to the traffic arms in air laughing
a hearse passes, the private joke
beats big death and always will.

*

The watch stuck in the table
varnish tingles the base
of the spine, love under
cover is how it begins
awake in the morning
and meet the white day breathing.

*

de Kooning's face the chalk of March
on your tongue braille bird song, exciting
isn't it, he looked over the woman and
the room filled with light floats I thought
no that's not it   where then 3 o'clock and
it's spring, a face like the sun in another room.

*

You can tell it's dry the lawn's
cracking, we've got a wet axe here
a loose blade, lambswool hurts no one

he was behaving like that
the wood swelling into the head
an abstract movement, if it's language
that is the sun attendant warmth
        rising to meet it.

Robin Hood

The hot symbolism of dawn rolls out
green and lush the air falls
over my head and onto my hands
the world pops up a 3D book.

Figures without obvious support,
there goes Robin Hood green like
the dawn the jolly mind
cross hatched with windows silver
trees and cars of the opposite row
sent spinning as day to day.

There are different rooms where virtue
in a coat the colour of day
that's a nice coat, trust him
always the birds in the air
touch your face   the summer sky
fits like your favourite shirt.

Shire Politics

Driving through the dread night of shire politics
rolling the sea swell and lunatic police cars
we have you John in our ears, Gloria, fruit
and carnival, carnival and sudden death.

Intention nouns its pleonastic way
'they must learn the principle of law and order'
her blonde pressure greens in the memory,
kiss me not her, one in the box the other raving
ah fuck it Frank, run from the madding crowd.

Bach arranges the body about the instant of knowing
take a gun for example, an Italian apple
and the ocean of your cool hand
I held   and would recommend to anyone.

Domestic and Foreign Policy

At this level crustacea stick to the hull
flourish and tattoo the hills
in soft whisky light like language
the crane flies bang themselves up on the light bulbs.

The walls are built around a story of morning
in it a king is everyone rises for the work
in my pocket *Birds, Cattle, Fish & Flies*
at lunchtime too I go about
and watch the kids play football
slangy and blown up and down the sloping pitch.

Don't worry about turkey sandwiches
or previous talk, that was night
you touch all these things; a carpet of grass,
a silver currency and hand on shoulder
these tesserae of day flake off and on
a 24 hour smile, the heart keeps it warm
then there is this line   really said
'Send in the helicopters and morphine.'

Think hard but the days zero weekend
he is the red fruit of South Africa, the best of Costa Rica
I think these South American governments
are fucking with my coffee,
I am a counter too, she leans over
hair up and back   the story breaks
holes in the day darkness that doesn't.

Carnival

Wanting a really better life we go to town
but the black wind of adulterous fucking birds us,
sing well baby, the trap door opens
the sea runs a corridor of sound through
the mind behind those cheap chalets where the old die,
another runs off where the flats fall back
to reveal ropes pulled by the three mayors
of newspaper repute and small-town fecundities.

Set back from the weekend fields
the new medical centre in English light
takes of like a political campaign,
one arrow indicates forgotten exchanges
another, as big as the dark room says,
– You will not leave this room again,
the lines of the exchange tied in one fat word,
the unbelievable everything everyone wants to say
fries the wires green and yellow.

We gather the familiar corners and wide pavements
of human design where the talk fits
as sunlight moves across the fields of summer,
a generosity of children stands before their parents,
the carnival comes, local schools and brass bands
parade flour and money in the air shining
has a clean sexual click for the Vikings and girls with good legs.

In Town

In town I wear a huge cowboy hat,
my mother laughs behind me
and we walk on with the wind in our faces.

Seven births, five children and poverty,
she arrives at love, my hat flaps its wings,
my wife, my mother hold on, laughing.

The Rise of Surgery

A picture of the wound man depicts
injuries suffered by combatants,
and a map of the lighted areas of the globe
the spurious coasts and interiors of the white world.

A slit of daylight descends like glass, at the speed,
at the speech of light values zeroed in on them,
a boy and girl together with no past – let's…
thickened the blood and thinned the soldiers,
his jacket sort of Chinese but even looser.

What do you mean, how do you find it?
A basket of fruit in January,
a wasp on the coal, quite perky
a new acquisition by Max Ernst.

Tramlines of hurt score the sky, touch the hill,
clouds bloom into shops and darkness;
shopkeepers ride giant sex organs of corporate purpose
which is sport for all, brutal Toryism
or love me or leave me but don't leave me lonely.

He put his arm around the woman
but the ship was a tramp, loaded with tractors,
chemicals and ten tons of Phos B 470/H,
– Don't be wet, I'm your father.

There's a fault, lights flicker, the sea empties
and the captain came to calm them;
they saw the life jacket under his jumper,
sharp teeth like money, the fifth night of fog,
in the grip of the weed, they bow their heads.

World Politics or the Digestive Tract

In the living room of his voice, 'no more dying',
the martins have gone high in sky dark August
the lawn is grass covered, cat opens mouth
and green eyes a literal song on the radio,
that's a funny song, never grow old
the cenotaph rocketed into space.

England is free, soldiers don't they just do,
clouds of our boys precipitate the distant ocean
the African veldt has brutish men
and heroic animals tune in a major contentment,
like this cat stares and shiny
the all-over cat look, radio I was thinking
soldiers don't they just do.

I make a little space, red wine expands
the wall below chrysanthemums in a glass
in jam water pink and pinker, waiting for food
enzymes and things I can't imagine
my internal blue tubes crimp the foody air.

Here comes the woman in a green jumper,
a woman's life in her body walks about
my heart in orbit, O cat what she does for us,
woman, cat and food – my god, what a constellation,
how fast it is Linda when you're drunk,
a superabundance of the green age
love I mean you, yes in your mouth.

This is a Nice Poem a Nice Sausage a Nice Man

Delay the speed of heroic film and
the words go everywhere like cups of tea,
novels, pets and coins of an earthly issue
give I back I, the absence of politics
in a decent person, the veins of gold
varicose the slack containment
of everything we don't do here.

In magnetic August feel the rush,
he sings, 'Fall into your human hands'
a woman walks by the cinema and
the dashboard lights up like a city
a charm in this idle landscape like
an industry by Sheeler minus the machines
the afternoons click over,
stupid, you've lost all your money.

I speak in my nice voice,
so that's how you drive a car
use a phone, wear a shirt,
we're all up to this in our eyes,
– Amor Vincit Omnia
I put my shoulder to Fortuna,
I put my hand to drift in your hair,
casualty reports coming in.
Your hair is cool
human hand
hear that voice.

The Lost World

There is a lost world, the table
I touch sunlights my hand
– Do you want to go for a ride?
A film blue set square to look through
sparrows on the lawn
and children in bikinis
my heart in its place
in the calendar of light.

In English literature, said Churchill,
there are heroisms all around us
attended by Zambo our faithful servant
stuck up a beech tree like a white prick,
– Damn me, look at those apes,
this is Babylon-a-Disney
'They must learn the principle of law and order.'

Sparrows and children in bikinis
ride hello in my heart the calendar of light,
imagine a secret in yourself
of tv screen, carpet and chained hero,
called first baby, it has a perfect face
and the powers in its hands push push push.

A Woman A Woman

By the fact of a woman the baby floats
coral bones of the sea surround the house
called Monday to Monday, you do this
and that in silvery light dots
encode a broadcast of perfect action
called a life together called
Monday to Monday down the big dipper
going up in the clothes you wear
your nice trousers and aertex shirt
flowers in the jar pictures on the wall
and I'll clean the kitchen
cells hold it together, no arrows
no, a woman a woman.

A Slogan Will Not Suffice

The work of the sun, not illusion
diamonds hidden in the kitchen calendar
we pin them in the cork and shiny frame
bills and visits and mathematical stars
like a deck of marked cards.

You are already here,
the trial of love that should be love
each word against each word
down of your arm, I look, lift in my heart.

Trust the occasional radar through the dark
the cold wheel cash holds together,
it is a plot against the chickens of America
the wealth rolls off the Atlantic in neat symbols,
one dark raindrop, a semicircle of sunrays.

A pigeon wings it on hard blue March,
your money or your money and then
spring comes with obscene practices in the sky.

She saws through the bread down to the table,
slices each period of life conducted in the way
life is conducted and stored in the polar box for summer.

Eat strawberries and run away, the lungs open
the shoulder blades spread, and it smells like bread
like petals and horse shit in the massed scents of May.

At the beginning RAF boys probe the hills
farmers on tractors bravely waving, our boys in dungarees,
I walk in their film, you are in it, part of it.

– Well, captain you look bitter, hurt and drunk.
– I do? – Yes. – Well I am, just rub that for me and forget,
just bad debts from people we won't pay.

When I hear what is meant to do to me I hate it,
I'd rather the flopped hollyhock and yogurt lid,
I'd rather the adverts, there's always music for your feelings.

It's like landscape in Thomas Hardy, beside your self
under the heat of this traffic, a man will leave if you fail,
– Hello sir, it's me, Nic – on a horse taller than the hedge.

He found a dead town formerly a zero
buzzed across the helloing girl, dark a girl garden
decked in trees, families and traffic fresh from the word.

This is not Wittgenstein or a dream you could dream in sleep,
below the arrow of the town map outside the library.
You Are Here the roads travel from the varnished frame.

Around pink blocks on bleached green, the whole thing looks
nasty and fucked up, the police station, the play-with-me houses,
the churches and insanitary schools.

I think of their real colour, the same sun greens the real town,
I think of how we could have lived,
I think five aces, hit the deck or die.

A Statement

The streets crack and the hospitals smell. We are not the poor, we do not sweat under the ghost of a foreign policy. The furniture is carved out of sugar and white bread. Our fatty hearts are not cast in nylon, flog us more junk and we'll get better. Our women aren't uppity. He was a lovely baby but look at him now … this is impossible, nobody really says this – certainly not in a poem. She must be bemused at the stupidity she has authorized. This is not the book of those fears, this is a message: the poor do not exist, you do not have to bother with them nor the children of the poor, sexualised at 10, 11 and 12. The facts are known and they don't count. Where there is no vision the people perish.

from

The Red and Yellow Book

Not That Voice

the trees and grass come up for air
a man shouts through the crowd, I could
with the blackberries of that sun
but the faces wobble my head in your lap

in this other city; its little lakes and frigid ducks,
Dantes is a removal firm, the man is not a rhetorical figure
shouting at the scene of the murder, an underwater duck
is a plastic carrier full of water that surrounds it

give me that burger, that friend
I never want to leave, I mean to save your life
check trousers comma did she
touch with hands like mine

catachresis, Alabama and its moon
dark when you go, dark the bed when you come
O moon, O mad sex against the city of business men
hold hard in the lodge of our aging

Power Lust and Striving

all evidence is taped, these rats have bubonic plague
would you challenge the fleet, silver grey it sparkles
bobbing offshore I have been home all day
the ports are blocked with French farmers twenty deep

this is meat, this is your photograph
the food is fat in Panama, you sang
my own fire, my own true fire
in the exchange there is a secret message

regresses nervously along the circuit fibre of the forgotten tomb,
it is 6.30 already and gale force winds toboggan
this secret shit, did I do that and did you?
there is a golden chain of love

all day the weather rocked the house
boomed about and called February
the bomb of Spring is ticking,
the people of China do not starve

Keep

the town was tourist wrapped and ticking
the sun shone through they only dream of me,
despite going down on Wall Street
sleep and sleep for England

guilts eased but with doll figures
bigger than expected sugar and lemon granules
lift and drink as easy as selling sweets to kids,
with the engine of my performance
a clean bra and knickers in case I fall

they call women girls but only dream of me,
buttocky stable lads beam in the pre-dawn
they are handsome men in Cotswold summer
sleep and money and my steady voice
sleep and sleep for England

At the Wedding

there's a wedding and I'm waiting
with the red and yellow book,
it's big and bright
each poem a maze
the words in relief,
somebody reads and we eat, drink and dance
I check what poems to read –
the hot symbolism of dawn rolls out
green and lush the air falls
over my head and onto my hands
the world pops up a 3D book,
I remember what was happening
in the sun, attendant warmth
rising to meet it
a fat man puts his foot on the book
which can take it, it's strong
can slay its enemies
but I rescue it all the same,
the food is cleared off tables
and there's hectic dancing
    now?   as all this happens
              I am fixed on my book
              which is bright and can take it

Paintings in Hospitals

she smashed the glass and swept it up,
at home a husband of 56 year old baby fat
followed me through my life
Spring rips through the world, everything looks good
this is the fifth line, made it o.k.

– it was a petrol glass

you breathe out, I hear cooking
imagine rich people with emotional problems
it's heaven, it's probably Paul Newman
and certain domestic appliances hummed on,
I think he can deal with it

paintings in hospitals can help;
local scenes, the haywain, a good frame
or the two cartoonish kids looking at the moon,
they are folksy and sit on a bench
they are rumpled and happy

– I am not joking

Casual Causal

For a long time when reading books of philosophy I mistook
casual for causal. Philosophy seemed more entertaining
than it turned out to be and imagine how loose-limbed the
world became, even without examples.

Say twenty cubes, on each face of each cube part of one of the
six jigsaw pictures. The feel of them is good, their size, the wood
and six pictures plus hybrids. No matter how casual you are they
fit together so well, edge to edge, the wood, with a nice knock, they
always fit.

Despite the feebleness of this conceit, for a long time when reading
– what do you expect?

But still part of Ivor the Engine patrols the sea
below a girl's nose and mouth joins the snowy mountains
to something uncertain which hovers above
the Indian camp of musical instruments
torpedoing a partial jungle of just red.

Of all that Nature doth entend

He is a great magician
and handsome, everyday
I wear the clothes but
to see those you love
in the knowledge of general terms,
get your foot off mine
with explosives you can
I mean him, gold gold
in this film a bullet is an explosion of paint,
John/Juan mouth to mouth
accelerated the lines of consumption
indicate out and drop a gear
push it foot and hand.
Afraid to use the unwritten words,
bandito discovered, lost since birth
the fly buzz, never known before
go faster and that man is in trouble
what kind? Picture in the paper kind.
The what just grows up
through your body like satyriasis
in a field of hairy balls
make European foodstuffs.
Pick the tune I don't know
the inaccessible music of feeling
in a handheld world
it all goes word bang, that sadness
deep eye in head of horse
ghost train in false glasses
and there is only power,
on the trams, in the yards
talked seriously, said comrade
my/his hands shake
outside the bank of all that money

all that serge underwear
and iniquitous economics,
that face too close.
I like to look, with my fingers
no part of your body
far from another
flute music never tasted so sweet

– I wanted to take her in my arms,
she sleeps it down over the bridge
which crosses a dry river
aim your gun, answer me
heaven comes in a myth of light
of diamorphine
I hope
against all men who know.

The Last Poem

– no death is an average death

I wish I could get my voice back oh

the fields where you grew are burning

– would you like your bed jacket now?
Yes   I   think   I   will

fear no more the heat of

the last word – drink –

8.50 p.m. 9 August 1984

– we're with you mum (kiss)

in my arms, all gone
a Mannerist portrait
58 years old, all gone

Next

hardest of all thins to morning
down the petrolled ways,
see the girl ride her bike along the path
safer that way, I check the tyres,
I float in a clean shaven sky
no more to talk and hold your hand
palm against palm for the dying months,
the first person a fiction now

the dead do not talk
we are not with them

*

        one
      breath
      another
      the dark roof
      rests
      on the white walls

Radio Wittgenstein

this is Radio Wittgenstein calling
possessed of invisible splendour
and a sunny morning wind in the roses
is all the case is in a carpeted fold
safe from the living air
and the flaming circle of our days

they really use this language
they mean to do these things,
show me your leg, how it feels inside
smooth as a wedding ring, fast as a travel show
where we go fallible and unfixed

Machine Days

I follow the argument of this book
between machine days
and all that I can't believe,
the little door opens
a smell of resin and 3 o'clock dark,
the faces rush to the sides

the soil of the garden is damp
the apples come into taste and
kids in the street play guess the tv show,
there is traffic or there isn't
there is nothing in the paper,
just faces, just writing

My Sister Said

it's like my body twisting round
crying in me, twisting me round
when it rains, I think of her
                  in all that mud

Thin as Light

By the window in an easy chair
spectral grey and thin as light
her eyes fixed alive on her grandchildren.

*

The newly dead look dead so soon,
her black black hair
over the gone face,
not my mother then.

*

Two steps down

He didn't visit very often
spent time and money
in the pub, a small place
below the level of the pavement.

Monday is pension day,
Thursday spent out, penitential flowers.
'Have you seen dad or anybody?'
'Take two steps down, you'll find him.'

*

Home for the last time, out of the hospital, home because one of us would always be there. She sat in her chair, legs propped, never asleep. All night I listened to her breathing and gave the elixir every four hours. Unable to lie down, pressure sores, legs swollen, lungs filling up.

Eyes calm and holding hands she said – When I had so many kids people said I was stupid, but they're not saying that now. Later, when I wasn't there – Oh he does make a fuss of me.

In the morning we watched *Tarzan* and then the visitors came.

On Hearing the Song of the Dog

A heaving landscape is ornamented;
Pegasus shrieking leaps from a hill
as cupids dance slapstick in a ring
and two others, impaled against a stormy sky,
drop rigid roses and other equipment.
'I don't mind really, I can understand
why people confuse fiction with reality
but I'm not a bit like Mavis Riley.'

This exchange can exclude all civilian lines,
out across the map of western Europe
the suck of the sand, the literal surf
the diamonds of my waking wash my feet.
We are all in this, we saw films on what to do,
food riots, that sort of stuff.

At night the third and perfect body,
what mind behind those eyes?
Which woman, which man?
The Miró blue of the night
lit from beneath by the street and houses of us
and the dark trees of the hold we have.

All the Difference

We were a high spirited crew aboard the Melusia,
in the dark mountains rivers run
rivers of gold, cool and bright
stuffed with gold and babbling oh my
it makes all the difference.

Some of us do not like princes
nor women paid to sweat it out in furs and leather,
it makes all the difference what you do,
most striking of all are the women of the valley
such noble girls before the white man,
the celebrants at a pig feast
who build schools on asbestos tips.

You are on this island in deep water,
the corporate tricks and reluctant decisions
in the voices of the land that time forgot;
walking about, in the bar, on the air, in the shops
the revolting confidence of ownership,
each turns a page of English history
it fingers you and gets it wrong.

She Sang to Herself

In the angry dark
her house fades;
she sang to herself
she made cakes
in the kitchen
with plants at the window,
the easy talk all gone.

The dead take us with them
but we are not the same,
it's cruel enough
in this darkness
the face that fits my face
gone, my name unmade.

Final Thing

I was with my mother when she died, by the bed in the corner of the ward. Quiet after visiting time, her brother and sister and my sisters. The doctor had said at mid-day, 'It won't be long now, she'll soon be free of it.'

I went up town to buy the ginger beer she wanted, small bottles with screwtops. My final thing for you, and until this last day you held the glass yourself. In the teeth of death a human act.

The day before I'd been called back to the hospital to get rid of my father, drunk and talking about euthanasia. Only the medically qualified understand alcoholics. He left noisily but she was beyond embarrassment then.

I sat on one side holding her hand, her sister on the other. Through six months she was gentle and kind to us all. I could feel no strength in her hot and cold hands.

Her shallow breathing stopped, stopped, in suddenly, taking the chin and lower face as well. Not her face then. I watched the last pulse in her neck, kissed her forehead and said, 'We're with you mum.' Then the Sister said, 'She's gone, she's at peace now.'

I was with my mother when – after so long it seemed hurried.

> A gentle woman of great strength
> she raised five children in love.

Pictures

The moral climate I had in mind is not
natural. It is the product of a particular
architecture, a fascist band, a slave market
is a community of men – of a sort.

The book had no pictures or conversations in it.
It was of no interest at all, she thought.

Todtnauberg, the Black Forest
8 April 1926
Edmund and Martin.

Here's another card,
one of my favourites,
see you on the 17th
Rothko Black on Maroon.

From each dark corner
and unoccupied house
came the howl of the dogs
unlike words but of the solid night.

Ten water colours made from that star.
It was an engraving after Moorland
except for a hole kicked through the centre.

The Sound at the End of Waiting

Through the jammed layers of separate intentions
in the city of lead and gold,
solid as carbon and the shining air
with the wipers fused across the slab of day
just no time ashes the shoulder pain
stuck up the councillor's piratised bus route.

Breathe out and think of the word – relax,
under the apparent coral reef
hit and miss music starts all over the place,
factual, certain of itself and anxious;
the brutality of facts in the box of delights
will open bright in your face.

Then it all breaks down like Muybridge,
traffic and trees stuck in grey and white;
the passive geometry isn't a picture
it's there, what the papers say in solid air
one morning imposed on another,
at the next junction the sky condenses.

*

He lived in the forest and thought language life,
he knew crowds of faces that were themselves,
that did not float, but were held in falling everyday.
At the end of five, tired and chopped into segments,
weak in the chest and falling forward
his hands full of the night at the end of the garden.

The that he felt spelt hunger, the forest and
the forest of lights, cars, holidays, faces –
hunger was the imprint, the clearing of Tuesday maybe.

To refine to simple terms meant loss,
you could buy it but the shops were often closed,
only puns rang the till in the towns of the great inflation.

He knew books of pictures and gems of green and red,
they made a story which lit up his face;
a secret aquarium, a secret forest in hand-held words.
Imagine the whole field by any light,
each day glimmers in miniature on the calendar
a series of Palmer landscapes flick over and fit one on the other.

Stray conversations, chairs he sat in and string,
the empty never empty of itself – but string?
Disgusting in this bar, so much like the wreck of the anthill.

Work on the Rhine dykes taught him nothing,
just mud, just cement of a new order of feeling
as the pincers of Russia and America close in.

The sky was vast and blue with a do-what-you-will consistency,
along the road you expect the sea, choppy, fresh and populated,
but the authentic man has clean hands and is resolved,
a barbarian with a pure dialect
– it makes all the difference what you do.

>   This has gone wrong, what escapes
>   the sun or dry wall of coveted rooms
>   and the commerce up town, I don't know.
>   Digging the heat from the rolling sea
>   or cold fronts clipping across our sky space,
>   how can I get him for what he said?
>   Although it's January I'm warm
>   and joining the dots; it's Economics,
>   the current repressive intelligence
>   or a runaway train full of children

        or duck and ducklings fat on the pond.
        Each day transparent, tangible and involved
        we walk abroad on the air supported
        and it's bin liners and Ready Brek I want,
        the politics of more than one country
        the many lives tied at your hand.
        Walk in this impossible knowledge
        but definite as the printed word,
        the body as starting point in the philosophy of flesh.

Across the way in the dark there are boundaries,
polished paving stones laid along the path,
horizon of moon, streetlights, trees and houses
lit from below, it's not hylozoic, it's ours;
we walk to the late open off-licence
and you blonde every monochrome street of new year's eve.

*

The shapes and colours of the green world
wrapped in the town map on warm, middle tint paper
as the crowds of Saturday heightened with body colour
people a golden and mirrored shopping arcade.
Hi, my name's Tracey, I'm a student of phenomenology.
Telescoped arches belly up to ultramarine skies.
We need to see the five days it cost,
we need to see human obligations.

Hi, I'm Tracey the shapes and colours of the green world,
sepia mixed with gum then glazed, flaked off and didn't last.
You don't look at people's faces closely enough.

*

Above the garages the January moon rises,
guess how old he was when he wrote
'Ode to Michael Goldberg ('s Birth and other Births)'?
It's cold out there but I'm warm in here,
the east coast under snow and intensified policing
ice snakes up the roads across the country.
We the common people have ancestors and blood,
moon smack in my face launches into snowy clouds
as 27 years ago Frank in winter early spring.

I pull back the curtain, the crust on my head cracks,
the metallic light of morning and night coming
picks up the tarmac and ascending windows;
a lovely blue like a freezer flaking off an aria sky.
We have blood and I have you on the carpet
I shall enter in under that arch
more gentle than July before an early death
or, as if, in the very heart of loss
the steady voice of Alec Guinness says,
'…on the very next day', what you want to hear
and were about to say.

That voice remains like a dream when you wake
as the mayor of your home town in the shining day,
where your family and friends are alive again
in the first house of a perfect childhood;
the red and blue triangular sails of the yachts
slip down the river of familiar afternoons
between seemingly fields of sprouts and chrysanthemums,
and on the far side a reasonably shaped hill
holds a railway line for black and green locomotives.

I stared from the back-step, it was exactly like this;
she piled up the ironing, sang to herself,
looked at me and care was in the world.

I dreamt of a rowing boat that rocked me skyward,
I didn't want to float into that anaesthesia,
bring me back out of thin air,
spread straight from the knife it ends the story.

*

Snow falling in pop songs dumb dumb,
what do I do tomorrow whilst little shapes
falling skid a rubber car down canals
with horrible echoes all over the rock,
two lines of traffic brake, cannot hold that shape,
how do tomorrow when others jigsaw talk,
his teeth in your mouth
snow falling on the whole world, crepuscular and infected,
the light wheel flutters in my hands,
this is it – with no control you carry on.
If that's the case I'm leaving.

Double pearl, fire and ruby bear her name,
how did it start snow falling?
Mountainous sky of non-verbal weather
experienced antibiotics in nervous tracks,
across the sky opens snow and out falls
a complete town, the powder of light, the many lives.

Why don't you lift the piano lid to play that tune?
It's not a piano, it's a poor metaphor,
see my fingers presentive,
presentive fingers playing a metaphor
like polar bears dive from glaciers to fish
or my foot arch curls with secret warmth;
the final continent beyond analogy
here are the poor, they have number,
the adults with worn hands of too much care.

The sky hits your head, it's so cold
a door slams in your chest,
shock settles like breath in the garden,
chestnut leaves falling on the grave of Martin Heidegger.
That wave held be careful how you drive
foam engineering, a lorry takes a corner
a string of red lights comes on
against the iron hills age
ancient Europe, those people up there
that face looking out for me.

from The Red and Yellow Book

The house fronts flip over
subterranean rivers surface in
public fountains of gods and tortured horses,
brown and rabid near the rapist's carpark
the grand sweep of the municipal offices,
see the hand moving, its trick
the truth has made us free.

*

Clouds pile up in the sky
anvil   lemon   cicatrix
with the industrial revolution
marriage, divorce and public health.
William, it was English poetry too,
in the circle of our blood
blinking like moles through the other side of winter,
in the fields of Peterloo
in the valley thick with corn
the kind man reads a world revealed.
Honey flows in the sky
piles of soap and hot bread
in the streets smell the earth,
bright buds clean as bullets
the polished cars and public lies,
they are what they do.

*

To find the western path
I breakfasted swords big sun
              gates of and
at first breath   bird song

happy in the stupid heart,
the fool with his finger on the trigger
no further forward for men and women,
hot days of rubbish letters
surface to surface arrows
telekinesis and country music
spark across the imperial world.

*

Rain on April streets and cars,
the occupation forces hold the populists' gazebo;
no sweet moderation shines in Port Albion.
Walls of sound of sea made them soft and witless;
hamsters in perspex balls
daffodils and socket sets
markets crash and banks roar,
they dream wealth creation in elected bodies
and we all fall down.

*

Another life in a sparrow's wing
spreads above the prisoners,
running through the desert
they leave coils of rope and clouds of red dust;
having modified their experience
the look of the sentence and the title
emanated a spell – shazam –
the bristling globe, the shores of men and women
silk descending folds around
the piano keys nervous itch
as Jackson Pollack trees scratch the sky
balloons absorb each other, the green garages
and unknown pedestrians in an opera of no pain.

*

Just look, *In-der-Welt-sein*
but nowhere to park the car,
it rains local newspaper lies
about a town nobody lives in,
it means a fistful of mush or
darkness in the kitchen on tottering legs.
In seed time learn the beautiful history,
I must wash my hair
I must be happy
                the first dictionary
had only four words
I will tell you what they are,
you will live a better life.

*

Open your hands, let them go
there's no going back to that world,
this room has many pictures
I think of the beginning book
silver tried in a furnace of earth
up to the elbows shines in words,
before meanings the restraint is all
as Spring rattles its couplings
birds fornicate in bare trees
the light flicks a switch in their eyes
fuses blowing everywhere,
the dark earth and its smell
grows onyx, carnelian, quartz
the fifth and greatest monarchy;
I know you in my hands
the level streets of a life before us.

*

Day into day, night into night speaks
far off and exceeding deep
in all the houses that are lived in
broad sunlight through the park.
I buy a pineapple at the Chinese grocers
warm that house, it's Greek to you,
a woman is wearing pink trousers
she walks in morning and legs
opens shop doors, the happy actors on blocks
write sky on a banner above the street,
they pretend everything is O.K.
a street in the sky, the real sky
in blue capitals the language of delivery.

*

Around all all
the need to say
what it is to wake with you
not one touch
can I say
or measure
you naked
seem just from the sun
always and
waking find you
hold delight
a shape inside
each other
we walk in
day to day
not one word
can speak the lustre
of that touch
I breathe you

the dumb speak
the secret body
of one life
leaving only
a verbal substance
on our fingers.

from

Lyric Lyric

Lyric Lyric

The helicopter cuts cold air,
I work in London but live here
shredding light on frigid grass,
my animals eat and grow:
shattered in an obscure tongue
lyrical ballads endure.

Fog rolling over square fields,
I go the straight song
square music drives me,
it lacks only notes, words;
the compact town's design
fixes real business spread.

Paired down to working parts,
breeze blocks and depletion
scabbed across the land:
the human meaning
out of the dark dream
breathing immediate words.

*

So, you can travel to one place and think of
another, looking for a school of sound seeing
lines of red lights. In the dream of it a car
leaving a Roman town takes off over the snowy
hill road, bounces, rolls and lands in the ditch.
The driver flaps away on bent legs.

It was hard for me to make the connection
between the very apparent economic activity

and purpose. It's an exercise in manufacturing the common book; erasing blue lines, glueing carbon traces and holes. Lyric Lyric, show your hand.

House, Man and Water

I could write through the table, cursively gouge down to the hieroglyphs living in our capitals. B, E and M are some of my favourites: house, man and water. Dusted with logic and sand I set them right against gentlemen thieves burning in the east. The dirt piles up at the back, tradition blocking the stairs and the light at the bottom of the stairwell.
– Are you alright down there Linda? Is the baby alright?
– Is that smell December outside the window damp and rotting into latent spring?

The tunnel down is steady, the trees overhead let fall unfixed statements. If I have run carefully, watching my tread along the dark stream, then all things will settle into all things and I should arrive at absolute normal breathing the air of a new speech. Look at the sea, its immense rolling indifference. I love it.

It shapes the words into packed cars, children, medieval stripped pine garden tools, tight jeans and living spaces. It's entirely sincere and doesn't feel like a fetish. There's a substance to my neighbours that you can't see through. It doesn't look like economics. Are they agents? Are you? Circle each precious name. Everything inside is mine, it took me years … All that stolen time never to be returned. Then whoosh, the centre dysfunctions, an accident or failed organ. Everything gone. Look at the sea.

Serabit el-Khadem

In the turquoise mines
at Serabit el-Khadem
our Lady of Turquoise
letters the first alphabet,
ten years to read one word.

Lady of Turquoise
in the river country
freshen our mouths,
around this garden
we know everything.

Blackbird sings days end
glazed light rays spring,
money burns the path
sex turned inside out
delight lay before us.

How can we ever, that carpet,
I shall pin the dumb song moment,
familiar shapes inscribe
man, woman, driving home
return me word by word.

MEB

My father waits at the gates of the Midlands Electricity Board for the forgotten sandwiches. A small, strong man anxious to get back inside out of the rain. I remember this on the edge of town where the river ran through water meadows and layered silence in live trees. The woods rose to a story sky behind factories and industrial plots and the grey road shone like a dark mirror. Here's your sandwiches dad. How much the drinking as percentage of the packet? Drilled with holes, sealed, and then unsealed before home. A bitter man, a rum man, an anything man in fact.

M   the wave sparkles
       burning the time
       drawn back to land

E   man with downcast arms,
       Ireland, India, Burma, England
       at the gates to nowhere

B   house given up, empty
       dosshouse, boarding,
       no home kept without her

'Looking for the source of the chill in my bones.'
　　—Jack Spicer

I took advice, travelled north
and jumped into the ocean off Cape Wrath,
ocean is an expected word I think,
a vast body of water sloshing about,
endless, deep and cold,
giant stacks aloft spinning the unfixed sky.

I had a conversation there,
piano music and no sleep,
a vast body – nothing said nothing;
I listened and spoke, tidal washed
submarine rubbish, like here discarded:
imperishable plastic, gulls and jaded wrecks.

If there was a figure in command
he was not there, he had no shape,
as water is in water we walk through,
against the laws of erosion
a slow current sang.
　　　　If I were the King of Ireland
　　　　and held love that was not power
　　　　but destroys all the same.
I see you falling
across the seabed
a band of light, insane.

Fran Masereel The Idea

The man sat at an empty table,
his mind enmeshed in a web.
She's already there, perfect,
naked, light emblazons her.

Her beauty is undimmed,
no man can handle it.
Fornication and commerce
continue unabated.

Lettered, sent abroad,
translated, manifold, athletic;
against perverts and capital
her beauty is undimmed.

*

Off the public corridor
a room of rotting paper
shaped into blocks, printed
in the Schiele typeface.

She read the sign
and hit the wall
with a flat palm,
three times evenly.

What do you want?
A photograph?
Rain, burning eyes, music
sports the clouds of May.

*

This is the Chinese notebook, black boards,
almost olive green in this light,
red leather spine and corners
with September falling, today stilled
without a ripple.
Are the lines too narrow for my needs?
Is the pasted cover wobbly?
Giraffe Jiangsu China notebook.
Delivery and frost in the enclosed garden,
a private thought he thought, but was mistaken.
A scatter of sparrows flew from the tall pine,
every way all at once, a strange medicinal air
settling on my days.

*

Stones, roots, the river course
my traffic singing.
I lean on these words
face against the blind.

Low sound rises there
sliced into sense,
heat rolls across town
against sleep, your absence.

The wind has blown this way
all summer long,
– rendering what?
Sunlight probing mortar.

Tocharian the I-E Enclave

They say there is, along the silk route,
a life away, another language like ours,
used by people unlike us.

Its way is lined with hoardings
across the figure mountains real mountains
that will kill you if you stay out too long.

A few lights come on in the darkness,
yellow squares draw in the day,
it is absolutely normal.

We watch the cars, shop for leather shoes,
check the post and think of a reply,
begin a working day eating English breakfast.

It's only a sustained analogy
I've never been there of course,
I'm right here telling you.

We live east of the Altai mountains,
oases cities in the steppeland,
we light our streets, pipe music all night.

Imagine the postmark, the stamps,
our busy trade in visions,
outside is only arid and nomads.

If you speak like us say so.

The Border

Mapped around the border
of what can be said about
the mind of the government,
which is to say nothing,
petrol air ribbons overlay
the dim plain burning,
a shopping arcade of mirrors
spattered with marble grain.
Reflected in unexamined action
we queue revenues decline
with dark and hollow mouths
nothing will ever fill.

*

The first-person fiction held it,
for a few lines I held it
in my hand, show your hand,
come out of that open air.
I thought I heard the many name
the miles between two points,
as if thinking would help
slung like a net to catch the day askew;
the ready-made roads converge
where you go a-burning the contacts.
It's hard enough under the sky
and in all these other places
lights fixed and moving
an uncertain grid of fields.
Without a dream, you knew just what
came out of that open air.

*

Do you think I am trying to make this difficult?
You are not watching the disintegration of
anything, where the first push went opening sound
reduced to the scabby politics of acquaintance.
Stuff it. The ripped voice makes us free.

The Radio Said

The road travels
through flat, white fields
and into the sun
an ordinary day.

Fruit in the bowl
from the free trade drift,
the Taklamakan desert.
– Go in and you won't come out.

Beside the stream
we waited all winter,
pink, muddy snow water
the news breaking.

In the narrow pass
smell bad meat, poppies,
children eating junk
trashed at every station.

The houses, the schools
the cost of basic food,
it must stop,
call the legation, vanish.

The radio said

– You see her now,
she's walking towards you,
your eyes click
it must be audible.

It's the end of everything.

He's o'er the border and awa'

Which border? Any you like,
in fact, I don't know him,
just by post, names
almost exactly, any border.

It comes out in bits
you make it that way,
a taste in the mouth
like youth, at night, the static.

Wind rises solid night
against the window,
'the city … seen as though
in an isometric plan.'

And then it's spring
as the shops close,
still light the air calls
there's another place to go.

This window, this machine, this weather,
this window machine weather
the March wind table leaps
up against the wall voice.

Fauns and trees agitate
tearing at the sky,
the conspiracy of your body
next to me at night.

In the Garden

The garden surrounds me blowing
these disconnected, separate powers
through the air space. Who owns it?
Glitzy helicopters come and go
in the Spring drift above the town.
The centre traffic free, barricaded,
tubular sections of concrete sewer pipes
await the arrival of the prime minister;
all day all day this grating noise
shreds the sky in filmy strips.

Washed up on non-specific virus
lethargy spreads like a weather front,
I see a small child crouch eye to eye with a tulip,
in a moment of stillness stick her fingers in the cup,
the flies and bees start up again
weaving the square of green and trees,
the world is all the case.

There's a lot I want to say in this voice,
tilt my face to the sun
and work from the centre of what is.
Say some Chaucer to us, the young girls said,
imagine that music begins afresh.
Outside April rain through sunlight
shines the fields and beaming hills.
Say some Chaucer to us.
And all the other traffic vanished
whan that Aprill with his shoures soote.

I read in the dust one morning
– He is helping to distribute the crops. –

I work all day to earn the money
to buy the things I work all day. Fullstop.
You know that tune, I bought my love a fridge,
now there's nothing we won't do.

Three hundred yards away, over a barrier and flower beds,
a jerky grey midget walks her goons;
dressed up power gone in the mouth.
Shame on you. Shame on you. Shame on you.

In April

In April park weather this morning
young couples in flash sports gear
play tennis behind a chainlink fence,
slogans and grunts playing for keeps.

The sun gleamed bright on the slide
down which Madeleine slid,
her performance applauded by two drunks,
a man a woman with cider bottle.

You could do this in real time,
the sun shining on the playground
at the centre of all these powers.

The low wall of upturned logs
surrounds magnificent love – *Do again, do again*,
the fall cushioned with soft wood shavings.

Music of the Altai Mountains

Comes to us from a distance,
it's not ours but an air surrounds us
in broken, ambiguous clouds;
a voice sings four sounds simultaneously
longing for the real to start up
in classic loose cut denim;
the hills are alive, you're not fooling anyone.

The song continued a day and night,
face-up, clearing out the house,
absorbing shapes of rain and shine
the stars and remote traffic,
transcribing the garden father's talk,
a fox at the rubbish, a car door slam.

All you see is drawn into that closure,
there's no technique there,
no interior, instrumental light for bearings;
you think you're trading with the enemy,
the inhabitants armed to the teeth
with the culture they despise,
look straight at you and ask one question.

*

I think it's your eyes that do it,
alive like the sky flaking away
forms such as never were in nature,
these words made for your mouth
name and strip the margin
between here and the blue folder.

We go up town for clothes,
working over the white table
in purposeful music and movement,
sends these loaded terms, your steady look
out of the window into Spring take-off,
the west everywhere reeling.

It looms behind plate glass
wrapped and cushioned in lace,
rank and pink, the perfumed heart.
What can you do with it?
In this heat on the bespattered pavement.
What?   I was walking   and you

Walk by the river in darkness,
where the water flows with ease.

*

At night an air of leaves spills
like waves of thought in darkness,
scribbles care without sight of that face;
her hand touches moving inside;
I feel the drink hit the spot
and the roads spark into the hills.
It could be a scheme, it could be a country song,
the news is out all over town,
it's my business, a bright pattern of cracks
the white light shoots and floods our lives.

That morning cars came out of the sun,
I couldn't measure the speeds,
careering subjects released from rhetoric
smacked up against the white wall.
The birds flip from branch to branch,

their funny watery cries all around
splash and blend in garden heat.
Splayed out under the big one
I saw that morning remote traffic arrive,
real, unexceptional vehicles.

Hysteresis Loop

You will have noticed that we are using
a different set of symbols in circuit
diagrams to represent logic gates. These
changes have been made to agree with
those symbols found in manufacturer's logic.

As he lowered himself into the bath,
imagining he would soak out the drink,
steam rose and released tobacco fumes
caught in his head from last night's pub.
Get out. Get out. You resinous demons.

It was the time of end pieces,
the time of folding away the truth table
from which they had eaten
and scored into its surface
a name that belongs to something else.

Leave the car under the last light,
in casual regard, don't turn away,
I can see your face in the islands of the street
about which the air of June turns
and darkness pools the thought of day.

Each Station Struck One Note

John, that passionate man, in his action tower
held like a thought over London mapped
lights living patches to the hidden river,
an underwater bass singing its heart out.
The books are safe away in his generous hands,
a thousand anonymous musicians go dumb
waiting for one book only to appear
in this floating room behind the glass.

I woke up on the two-lane section, roving
westward into rain county literary guide,
the cheek of it unfolding, a thing to say
I woke imagining each station struck one note
passing at speed heard in sequence;
all at once, a static song laid out to home
intones little pressure changes in the ear,
drop down, leaning forward, open mouthed.

What am I doing here flying over England?
At a nasty tilt green fields and Conservative clubs
flatten out like a grid to the Irish Sea;
off the road there are houses where children live
and the heads of the republics return to the centre.
The country looks like a picture of itself,
state the name for it, petty towns and news shows
drawn in the wake of a commercial van.

Such Secrets

In blue September between blue bands
I write and drink, thinking of money,
thinking inside the physical forms of words
for the pleasures of reification.

The solid book of pictures opens like a new country,
bevelled streets run to a silver point
arranging the space in days, you do it with your hands
as if you would be given such secrets.

At seven there was a purpling of the screen,
– the field is the land of our dreams –
because it was a poem, I read it twice
in the light of the hotel T.V. that morning.

We shall hide in their coastal waters,
listen to their rock and roll then sail away
without them knowing, see gulls slip
from the bank of clouds to the south.

On this other edge, head to the ground, the sky rips
clean away and Atlantic light steps out of the sea,
a line of white rocks, sharp white fingers working
for me to pick about in exactly the right spot.

Circles of influence surround the city,
quaint clumps of trees and hills show the way,
a river forms a lake below the shaded mountains,
indicators sweep the land pointing to the trouble.

It looks like a model of system collapse,
moving into the heart of the state;

who knows what's said, the stations light up,
sigint listening out for you.

The bright ones learn Japanese and Arabic
running up the walls of banks, shops and palaces;
the rhythm of neglect, step out of it
through the door into the house talking.

Index

In the end you might find an index
my eyes on Spring's season of love,
season of gaps in the grey air
just flicks through the green pages,
the ghosts say what you don't say
those people locked up without cause,
their hands are empty, their mouths are empty.
Against ironic commentary
the poem a hymn to the republic,
my name and all that history I suppose
a dream book called correspondence
was whatever what was happening
and who driven from the capital
under a sky of stupid messages,
sound tunnels lined with hoardings
the ruined traffic spirals
I would make go the other way.

Melanie's Book

I Woke to Tell You Something

Snow has fallen all night
whiteness blurs the street
muffling incoming calls,
you can't get out even if you wanted to.

I woke to tell you something
dreaming of the baby
half formed under the driven sky
the blizzard turns about.

All our names made vague
block the roads out of town,
a tangle of limbs, two lives
caught in the drift of speech.

In the snow all over England
we look for the candid word.

*

February sun burns low in the sky,
second sight glazed by refraction
punches a hole in the white world
admitting fields of gleaming snow.

The black road like a river
rushes in from both sides talking,
goes on and on to the first moment
falling backwards into lyric.

Through a hedge of bright ignorance,
cutting out the shape already lived with,
the dark engraved capital

half buried in that narrow space
echoes the message landscape
walking with you to the house.

*

Driving through town Saturday morning
this winter's credit squeeze
makes unaccustomed space all around,
- how can you lose, so bright and cheery?

Soon all of this will be library pictures,
like the war of library pictures
strikes the coded air, incoming then gone,
each day reconstructed.

You mustn't know any of this;
the roar of prayers and aircraft,
sirens sound in Jerusalem, Jerusalem the golden,
the war zone burning Sumeria.

Use the correct form of expression;
the war is good and bad for business.

*

Wait for the light under a canopy of leaves
casual music burning the crisis,
time to get literal, the man said to the man
message comes out all the same.

Estate by estate, family by family,
the poor turned invisible,
in the hard blue sky above the stadium
currencies vanish, nations appear.

Saturation coverage tells you nothing
I was thinking in the water, on my knees,
the new year rolling across the park
you already know it's poetry.

Men walk like this, women walk like that;
our sense of purpose would stun the traffic.

*

Portland Plymouth London Irish Sea
severe gale force nine
funnelled through the channel
roaring at the window.

Who sang the song that went
forget the past, trust to speed,
waiting for the one sign
big sky fairing in the west?

The harbour landscaped out of memory
reappears ranch style,
like a thought that won't shift
battered in and out of dream.

All day its tinny music keeps us warm;
all night we float on darker sound.

*

Awake out of the window I saw
the dark towers of the women,
a grainy woodcut against the glow of the city
spread out like a fresh map.

The north door opens, only one word,
we find the body difficult to speak;
corridors of sea flooding the streets,
the great stink of it just around the corner.

This is not the voice of an actor
making the word nation an embarrassment,
politicians praising other politicians;
wash of salt staining the lot.

Radio

The family radio was smaller than the fat battery attached to it. We kept it in a tin; twanging Duane Eddy, the Shadows and assassinations echoed out of a metallic past. Its casing was sky-blue with a silver plastic grid over the small speaker. The transparent circular tuner had a serrated edge for a better grip. A blood red line picked out Athens, Moscow, Luxembourg, Athlone. O city city. Turning. Turning.

Earth at Night

My arsonist neighbour lights another fire
dirtying the end of summer, Moscow burns,
smoke thickens, ignore the words, listen to the tone.
Can you cope with this in a golfing suit?

The room fills with smoke and all sense evacuates,
- If I stood up straight the line would be unimpeded,
and longer than all the seasons rising above the white desk;
he lost the inward walk, promenading frames at an exhibition.

Variously orchestrated the moon rests on the hill,
the air is softer than a hidden message;
the airwaves carrying Russian music, American poetry.
We'll conspire to forget the world whatever it says.

There are moments of Biblical rhetoric here
above the loaded tray, telephone, assumed narrative;
I would rather talk to you in the light,
not rub anger into it at 2 o'clock, 3 o'clock.

We float away from England, mapping the brittle voices;
our house at night is full of noise, ringed by fire,
if this is what happens I feel cheated,
and nocturnal animals pull at the rubbish for love.

If I stood up straight the line would be unimpeded.

*

Earth at night is an uneven smear of lights;
America, Europe, parts of Asia, the Gulf,
fires burning in rural tracts cash the crop;

it's homely, a light left on in the dark.
Earth at night is the pattern of money,
a squid fleet off Japan, gas flares at sea.

Below red cliffs in the narrow channel
the days pile up in line astern,
stupid in the mouth of the good time.
The trade route takes you anywhere,
along the streets of a new nation
imagine the film of all these faces.

In our lives country music is literal,
sounding out the low place of compromise
the money sets in all our hands;
we turn into the darker wave,
we touch the ground and keep the deal;
a river of silk pours over the desert.

*

Clematis float outside the window,
watery stars riding the air.
I hope you read this soon, written over, thick with dust,
I hope you see the free state rising,
not just a green place with good sport
for English power to set its foot.

*

The bosses have all gone for the season,
one block of light falls across the corridor
quite after business, don't walk away from love.
Curvy T house martins bomb the gardens,
that's all my life in the bowl of summer,
– I am out of the way of it at present.

I am drunk thinking about you,
the birds twittering a hole in the sky,
their sharp black beaks drilling
the other side where everything happens,
like the single song from your red mouth.
What happened to you? (I mean who?)

*

There was much fatuous surprise
at the endurance of the right,
its invention of the common view
and resurgence in the hearts supposedly sung for.

The shift workers didn't wait for the reconstructed ballads,
leaning against a wall, you just want noise out of your ears,
hands out of filth, one breath of fresh air,
we're happy stupid in the garden, wrapped in thin profit.

I thought it was my life, my family.

Running Under Venus

I run into the cool morning
rooks study the rubble of the pavilion,
a motorbike buried in the hedge,
the day laid out in swift decline.

Disintegrate the myth of speed
was all she said, a blown code,
the white and staring sky
rises behind the glowing houses.

The recession is over/deepening
the new estate on the edge,
securing its inhabitants
breaking bargains in a ring.

Running under Venus
straight into the ditch,
a white hole burnt in everything I see,
face flat to the cold ground.

*

In the middle of the journey
the straightway lost
we came to a dark wood.

Pine needles for bed
branches spread across a sky without depth,
you felt the earth swallow you whole.

Your cry startled a bird,
your breathing the beat of wings,
April sun ascending.

We came to a dark wood.

*

There I'm thinking with my hands
and the room's flying over the city,
over the bridge, the parks and zippy motorway
your open face floating before me.

Every time I see you
something happens and I can't speak,
like birds in the air
calling and calling your name out.

That will do in plain speech
against what we don't know,
the burning traffic takes us
wrecked on the far side.

The aerial words wait,
unequal to your next breath.

*

Night rushes in at the car window
lighted houses and cold miles westward.

Later in the hotel we hear
voices going home drift away
and an owl calling over the border
over the dark hills and rivers.

There your face is changing above me,
love pours into us and we cross a threshold
writing a page from Melanie's Book,
– nobody has loved me the way you do.

*

Inanna Queen of Heaven and Earth,
everything flows from you
you go to hell for your lover.

– You're the Queen of Heaven and Earth,
 I thought you'd want to know.
– You know how to stop a girl eating her breakfast don't you.

*

Out into the white morning
we were surprised to see other people alive
going about their normal business
for we know this world is uninhabited.

*

The river rose in the night
flooding the winter fields,
a slow thought emerges
frozen by morning.

All this landscape stuff?
Just ice age mud and trees;
I suppose I live here now,
unpeopled more or less.

At night we burn,
I look into your face
and the world's made dark
in the music of your red mouth.

Thy faire vertues move me
not to use one word for another,
perfect sexual beauty
say my name over and over.

*

Moonlight pales the dark river
revealing the banks where lives are broken,
the distant hills emerge as negatives
and the sky's gone to another country.

My brother's name in Babylon
and if you kill me, he'll kill you.
I am not there between one town and the next,
the fields laid out for spring.

*

Look when I take my hand from you
how white it is   shining shining
I once held love in that hand.

*

Driving with him at night
she sees the road running parallel
known only by the lights of other cars
and thinks – my life is perfect.

*

I see you float on quilted water
another room somewhere,
head back, right thigh resting on the left,
as it to take a step.

Turning in your sleep
lifted by the dark wave
silver hoops catch the light
I want you   I want you   I want you.

*

In the middle of the journey,
the straightway lost,
we came to a dark wood.

Pine needles for bed,
branches spread across a sky without depth
you felt the earth swallow you whole.

Your cry startled a bird,
your breathing the beat of wings
April sun ascending.

We came to a dark wood.

Restore Us Song

Restore us song on Sion Hill,
it would be Saturday lodged against the note
– insert after April poem.

As the crow flies over the 14 wires of the street
weather caught messages,
artefact, lime tree, the first place will out.

Then I knew what I couldn't face
at the dark end of the street,
the great awakening.

Restore us song on Sion Hill.

*

One night we walked across town under the blown stars, with all the damage at our backs it does not come well arranged. Dark houses piled up; try lust, pride and covetousness. Try closing the door on that lot. Domestic gardens alive with those animals.

We saw the fox eyeing cars, staring into the moment of impact and then sauntering off to leave a fox shaped hole in the air for all the traffic in the world to drive through.

Dark houses piled up. Close the door. The fox stepping in and out of life in front of us.

*

Around midnight a drunk sings
the timing all wrong or right
modal song obscure innocent
waking medieval sleep.

*

I bet you can tell where I'm from.
Can I talk to you a minute?
I've got no one to talk to, you have.
Have you been shopping darling?
I can see.
Look at this medal my mother gave me.
Look. I never knew her.

*

In the dream I was driving down a narrow lane to an English village where I was born, or through a dangerous and disputed border country.

The lane narrowed with overhanging trees and the hedgerows pressed in. I was lost and stuck with no way of returning. She beckoned me the way through. The colossus of earlier poems, dead now for nine years. All proportion is thrown.

She kindly takes the car and drives me through the tunnel of trees, the car is hers now. Her worn hand rests on me and I shrink. She reaches through the windscreen, which dissolves, and removes obstacles from our path.

She stands looking at me as I leave the car. I'm exactly in the right place to set out across the open hills. Then I know love is not a metaphor. Her love surrounds me. It has only one name as I leave, turning to tell you as you wake.

*

One star rose this morning
weather walked over the slates,
from here you see every day

the air drawn circuit of birds
and light falls from the hills
moored at the back of the set.

Spring rushes into summer
floating dense green at the windows
flooding along the road,
one way the park, the other town,
Odeon in red at the centre.

I walk towards the eastern gates,
early traffic, dark transparent artifice
thinking to find the poem,
thinking to find the big way forward;
I begin to write the book of all that happened,
I wake now writing the book of all that happened.

Young Marble Giants Sleep Inside Us

Cruising away from England at 33,000 feet
we saw you and waved but you didn't look up,
playing in a bright green square
your faces rise fresh in my mind.

In the dream of falling, I wanted to jump,
rush into the circuit of states and sculptured coasts
the real map of the air of desire,
dense like the language we spoke.

Saying yes you would, so we jumped
bouncing off the wing into the blue harbour
watching ourselves fall into Cyprus,
into the poppies of the necropolis outside Paphos.

Oh set your arms around me,
hold on and let the wave lift us to the shore.

*

A white ship scratched on a black pillar,
the sea retreated out of memory, the sea,
sky salt marsh sky, slow abstract disc rising.

Then separate islands, the white ship sighted.

The Aegean, a metaphor, (thinking it's) blue
literal (not a metaphor) the sun's path over
dot and dash waves, the polished sliding depth.

Crowded with dark messages.

*

By the harbour an offshore island,
out of the air above the waves
Theseus abandoned Ariadne,
previously geometric, previously unknown,
you take a step down into the sanctuary.

Eating the fig in the shade of the well
we were drunk with seeing,
– One time you could smell what the boats brought in,
slice a tomato and smell it,
like that, on the other side of the street.

Beyond the causeway, out of the sun,
the swimmer can see the submerged town,
collapsed doorways, shining paths
step through marbled light, on the blue threshold
into deeper pressure I heard – Hello Boy.

The sea rolled over our heads,
the thought of the next island or another person
ended here: the body of water crashing about us
delivered one word – love,
and a terrible fight it was too.

*

On tracks through the dark hills
the sea wave bands all around us,
the blue domed white chapels
and the unimagined cubist town
rise up as night lifts us into the sky.

*

Young marble giants sleep inside us,
that virtue which fills the body with itself,
limbs and head emerging from stone
if only I could, as if to take a step.
O you islands of men and women.

The free state does not come well arranged,
falling through the air of transmission
at every station we talk it over,
you've come to this place and it's inhabited,
at this hour all the radios play.

Terraces rise to the summit,
grit and the smell of thyme blown in your face;
the ten street lights of Kastro Hora
shine in a constellation under the stars,
Ouranos shines down in darkness to the sea.

Remember and Forget Everything

At night the dark presence of
the trees by the side of the road
over us the whole country
turning into winter.

Melanie, you know where we are,
the way back home
past where the girls live,
this is the literal poem of

Night the dark trees
just here my sleeping girls
and where we go
rain shining the road.

Let's use the small map,
its anthropomorphic spaces
coloured for the ordinary day
to save our lives.

*

I would trace the airblue print
by the window in the high, white room,
collect the days on this narrow table
a bright promontory above the town
launched like a metaphor into nothing.

Traffic bears us back into lyric,
into this explicit personal experience,
I would restore the working model;
we see the shops stacked and go to work,

the shabby families rise and fall.

My family's reduced in the cold ground,
the old man bowed his head to listen; oh let go, let go.
She's selling the book of my country's impoverishment,
in all those channels meaning money.
You must outlive the misery of it.

I hope you're keeping some kind of record,
I'm going random in Lavater in fact,
a strange land before the songs,
in the fields of archaic sculpture
the pure body entirely present.

You must remember and forget everything;
tracts of the homeland reassigned,
memory taken from us into other hands,
the republic all gone, all,
don't fuss over terms, get into position.

*

The nation's only there at night,
dark map cast on the air
station by station the names restored
lighting the shape of another country,
the pure body entirely present.

Zion, a way of behaving, remember,
and those earthly stars, the next town
imagined as elements in the statement,
every item underfoot in the early hours,
the ghost furniture and all that happened.

When you wake and open your eyes
transparent days rise to the surface,

each part aligned on the grid,
etched on the face of the unworked block
today's already horizontal light.

Shares fall in the Asian morning,
fears fall to earth and burn us;
numberless they clamour at the glass,
cathedral clouds roll in from the west
the sky opens to drench us to the skin.

Will you wake and open your eyes
or are you away in the big truth
sailing the white ship to those islands?
– Pull the sheet off your face boy, you said,
the day is up and running.

Athens

I saw an abstract concept of human form
outside in the rain of Monday
turning cold with Autumn.

I saw you across the room
your good legs under the table,
the sky opening our senses
everyday this absolute music plays.

In the blue field carved from the block
without loss of reason your life appears,
you can get personal about it or not.

Hands reach out and lights map
dark streets and familiar traffic,
in this unimagined town I imagine
I see your eyes, your face, your colour.

Athlone

This afternoon a summer wind
revealed the underside of leaves,
fields in waves all the way home
made green light to swim through.

I was the boy again, it was my picture,
look at these colours,
it was the summer rolling out
and the personal dead lying down.

There are things not said in poetry,
the personal dead and the lying down light,
this casual breeze all over England
and the boy I was afraid to meet gone.

Nothing is lost in all that time,
it's my daughter saying, – Look my picture.

Hilversum

Saxon mouth, telling us how to live,
over the scabby allotments back there
but for the warmth in the name
even my sister, what do you expect?

It leaps from the long table into your face;
at 1.20 dread wind slips into town,
at 1.20 total loss holds me.
There's no stepping back from here.

Standing outside the house
I thought we were dark bodies
walking through the light of facing windows,
another family lives there now.

It means don't believe the broadcast,
the time of your life or.

Home Service

Driving away from there
ground fog ankle deep in meadows
live radio cast before us,
the car packed with trophies.

Westward into big sky
deep in the dark fold,
ghosts drift over the fields
each boundary lined with snow.

Night silence gone down the tunnel
our view is immediate landscape,
the wealth of supermarkets
exploding for sheer enterprise.

The external narration is nothing.
Stop. Unload. I know where this can go.

When Suzy Was

A Book of Answers

'No clear case of disobedience to a specifically
solicited oracular response is recorded.'

Hotel Byron

From Hotel Byron the wind slips over red tiled roofs
bearing us back into port, one more day.
The red and black banners of the KKE
stretched tight as sails above each street,
– they think Lenin lives still in Moscow,
nobody tells them, so they think it still.

Above the sea, a village of old people,
– You Italiani? America? No, Anglos.
No bakery here, at night the dark sea speaks;
no pirates, no Turks, no baker.

Our faces sunk in Saronic blue,
we suffered confusion, the last car fading.
Small boats scud and arc across the bay of light
and you make those shapes with your mouth that I love.

*

Laconic

Kranai   Marathonisi   isle of fennel
one fisherman   the still waters of Githyon
the sun rising

Kranai, Helen said, so
tell me now and I won't ask again
and with morning they sailed into myth.

*

The choir of many voices sing
my heart is broken, oh
the bird flies from the clearing.

How one sound, all my life I've heard
our mouths close around many shapes
possessed by death, by vengeance song.

Deepest octosyllabic land
oh my heart is, the sea rages
make me see what's in front of my face.

*

In the fast channel of Despotikon
I married the sea, the gold circle sank
to surface in a dream all night.
Out of corrugated light; give it back.

Its white absence aches on my finger,
stolen from sense to the seabed.
If I could work it out
I would know you again.

There is:
the apparent surface of the water;
the light in the body of the water;
the unknown ground under the water.

It sank because it was an object.
It cannot be lost, love has no weight.
It sank into irretrievable regret.
Give it back.

*

By Monday, at the end of the world,
falling in the dizzy air of Cape Matapan,
the lighthouse, the cornflowers alight like blue sparks,
no birds calling the last step down
drowns us into the submarine cave called hell.
You can get into hell. It's not literature.

Each separate light a white path on the sliding waves.

At the end of the world, ships pass bound for Crete,
blue devices low in the water following a strange trade.
We lost track of days and the meaning of number,
heads empty to the waves speaking the first language of sense;
island to island white spume ripples the shore,
a whole country rising up in free association.

The Book of Answers

We sat at the truth table in the quiet house and I told Lee about The Book of Answers, as a way to try to think about what is always there: the alphabet, an etched model of silence that speaks. (Nonnus) My conceit to make the physical condition of language, the arrangement of the struts, curves and sounds, the form of discovered truth. Completely simple questions. To think about what is always there: reification as a type of behaviour in the moment of the poem.

We took the short walk to the sea,
turn left from Lee's house and it's there;
a silvery band across the end of the street
the sea charge sparkling in the air
in the bright almost early Spring day.

Lee pinned his answers to its open door:
to measure the medication between pain and clear thought;
to listen to the radio;
to do more each day;
to read Lynette Roberts;
and by April to be out and about across the hills.

At the Centre of the World

this is all there is, the blue
upon blue of layered mountains
to the sea below Parnassos

Apollo and the wooded valley
at the centre of the world
all thought is thought about something

one column of smoke rises
the radio plays, I want nothing
the substance of light surrounds the hills

*

That night snow fell softly
then morning walked on white mountains,
Melanie slept dreaming of snow
and the world turned into Spring.

*

We found a real meadow and breathed in its smell,
right out above the sea, a meadow of tall grasses
April poppies and daisies lifted up into the sky.
Wading out on a promontory of absolute Spring
through tall grasses, blue and distant mountains,
under the eyes of the serene empire.

*

Beyond the white church the sun depicts
the hills of the Argolid and Tiryns;
exact light, presentive and miraculous.
Seferis waking with a marble head in his hands.

Is This the Breaking of My First Life?

Yes: Monday cracks across a grey enamel sky.
No: Monday cracks across etc.
A fragmentation pattern called the backward calendar,
reduced to naught, a circle in a red square.

*

I stood at my mother's grave
a door closed for ten years,
the remembered town arrayed
I see her black hair still.

A river crawls around the place
liquid shit sets the tone,
one step back on narrow streets
faces bloat and shops topple.

Bright stations of the Tory economy
flicker misplaced rhetoric,
clay is soon washed off the hands
but its dark punctuation drills the field.

*

At the long table the sun rises
in the face of the-lyric-gone-orchestral-syndrome;
the lines lushed out with strings
as in make the page sing or die.

On the other side a value system shines
at first light, the literal myth;
we shall be joined again
and the boy leave home in early traffic.

One by one the characters exit
by ambulance, dispute or indifference,
though many walk off into nothing
you must allow the discontinuous past.

A step away from this room
the clothes fit, they're even comfortable,
the cars speed around the one-way all night
speaking the memory substance meaning.

Bound tight like a circuit
the latest models flake off in your hands,
my parents' voices buried in the wall,
one word set free would flatten the house.

How Can I Find What I've Lost?

Apollo Hylates, Apollo of the laurel, the myrtle,
the sea lifts us gently onto yellow rocks:
Apollo Hylates, Apollo of the laurel, the myrtle,
the sea lifts us gently.

*

A radio picture from the tower
reforms inside your life
in the moment of the poem, light
at first a line.

My daughters lolling on me, their weight,
their substance against me is heaven;
they speak dolphin language in their sleep,
awake in the land where names are feelings.

I remember the single leaf,
a bright flame
lifting the blue hills of morning
against the window's inner darkness.

Black hair cut into the nape of the neck,
low lights, a silver hoop
smooth from scapula to breast;
let the morning lift us gently.

In the Red Book

I'd like to write one poem but darkness is down,
just one word – the water's running against me;
fingers tied in knots and eyes gone
filled heavily to the shape you see,
but one spark, lie down you stupid bugger, lie down.

*

We kept to coastal routes, in sight of meaning
around the shores of the various world.
Held in a disc of swimming light, miles away,
a picture of the park; under spreading oak
the exiles relax at last, their children playing.

I remember in the red book a diagram,
trade patterns put food in our mouths;
those people from across the great green
at that level of sophistication inventing surplus:
you are dedicated to trade and you to magic.

Carving this seal in carnelian, a fingertip across,
dolphin accompanying other fish, will ruin my sight
– and you to magic, just different work
in a disc of swimming light.
Look. All the trees gone for ships.

Ash   Elm   Boxwood   Maple
     the pollen levels sing from a pit
Olive   Vine   and   Fig
     the land is rising to meet you
In the red book I am a small axe.

*

The fleet sailed from Stonypath;
the Temple, Precipice, Sphink and Fortune,
away for the Gulf boys, on the morning away:
scattering salt on the white world
all bright and sparkling in its wake.

You May Say To Yourself –
Well How Did I Get Here?

1

There are four pictures by Mr. Halsey
I would begin by looking at,
this small, bright green field
the history of the world as grapheme,
scratching out a living.

A great ambition for the first truth
directs the order of our seeing,
in several scripts magical animals jump and fly;
the clay temple rises from A to Z,
a face adorned the sun in that age.

In the roots of our bright field,
Jane Harrison is singing
face to face with the fact,
the substance of the god is a social custom;
a worrying thought given the state of things.

But with the phoenix we're lost in quotation,
each term enfolded in real time
the surface will not give,
even if you set about it with a mallet;
the animals sit in a circle and sing.

2

This picture makes a form of habitation
yet the whole view is without image;
a microcosm of London, the fault running to the north.
From a distance, and several generations,
it's the British Empire reconstructed,
pink patches tattooed on a turquoise world.

From here Alan it's an echoing green,
around an altar of piled earth
figures beat home truths out of one another,
then run off to invent civilization:
– this river will do, scratch some shapes in that clay.
I saw the face of g-d, and these are his words.

Remember, at the turn of the line you must turn
or fall into unframed darkness.
We could bury that thought in a labyrinth,
draw power from the streets and squares of the new city
and watch the two dimensional hands of the poor
flutter across the real extension of wealth.

3

Here we're above ground, in the over world
sun streaming upon us;
it could be the olive groves around Amfissa,
a green wave rolling to Delphi
making an inland sea of perfect forms,
the thought itself sings in your head.

Cretans, or Egyptians, from across the great green,
merchants on their way elsewhere,
unpack their cargo of lightmeters, archetypes, plumblines
spilling out over the shore;
their boat, or Shelley's or Byron's, stands off in the bay.
They think a woman looks down on them.

We discover another giant here:
whose face is the sun with radiant glory bright;
whose twin arms the horizon above us newly born;
whose body, half buried in the earth, we walk on
capitals in the undergrowth,
where still words rise anacoluthic.

Breath perfect, spoken across the clearing,
we follow the curve of our lives inland;
a theatre of sound shaped from the block.
Above ground in sweet air and presentive light
I would bring you asphodel and vanilla
and kiss your mouth as the world turns to Spring.

4

A ditch marked by three red flags
and brown steps down into the earth

the name of Artu (Arthur?)

the name silver, in the river flowing

circular fortifications, spokes in a wheel
around a centre of power

Baron Politique, his titles
printed in gilt

a blue stairway into the sky

*

From Europe, the grey machine,
the waves flicker and flatten;
squares of light in national colours
roll in on the morning air.

You find it in the blind leap
held for one moment,
night fabric brushing your face
before thought hits the ground.

I feel you let go, breathing out
in the sea of sleep,
we hear the Bird-King
we understand the speech of birds.

Climbing the blue stairway,
step by step into the sky
rewarded in a series,
as though returning across a lake.

*

We see the satellite image of a mythology
drawn live from the air by benign science,
its postholes and apparent shape laid out for us;
our lives moving inside its circuit
the perfect calendar of the living and the dead:
how your favourite clothes fit,
how the set of your mouth makes me feel,
the shops we like and the way we go to work.

*

Here is written what, in the bottom left,
a Runic script?   a run on the bank?
I'm facing true north Alan, tell me.

At night walking along the headland,
the small Celtic fields at each boundary
brimming with light, the greater sea.

The water is wide I can't get o'er
the letters are, the colours run blue
on the other side I can't.

The seasons on earth I remember
each moment, the taste of wind and rain and sun
the goodness in your heart breaking

and the dead I love in the dance of their bodies again.

The Literal Poem About My Father

There's nothing like music,
certainly nothing like the music in Enniscorthy,
cracked and sobbing republican songs
sung in the face of the Black and Tans.

Those murdering bastards from Glasgow slums,
for what they did to the priests,
nothing like the tuneless drone from upstairs
and a curse on the morning for what they did.

Each night we breathed a drunk's mythology,
the English officer and sweet colleen;
the drone's in the air around me still
though he's in the ground nine months now.

When my mother was dying I was strong,
I hit first and faced him down
all my years buoyed up against him,
but for all that it's like he never was.

An alcoholic given to violence;
a thief; an abuser of his children;
an arsonist who was finally sectioned:
each term I secure for clarity.

Where's that Johnny Corcoran,
the little Irish man with all the kids?
He is gone, gone, gone,
four daughters and a son angry with a dead man.
Gone, gone, gone.

*

Again I think I drive the old road
but it's the open landscape design
and the memory is stronger and physical.
This is where the old road was,
the look of the trees, the nearby village
– it's not there, the place is changed,
and the people at the end of it gone.

Out there, field upon field of darkness
I don't want to be out in
but on the narrow rise of the old road;
descending into the next town
the pool of light of streets and houses
I think I drive towards,
each time along the flattened route.

*

I thought I saw my father
walking towards me on the street,
though he's dead ten months now.

It was another man in the crowd
but he looked as I remember him:
short, compact and fixed;
a trouble to my mother and sisters.

I catch my breath before the truth,
watch him go and fall in the dust.

*

Lee I was thinking of what you said
driving to the next town
through September rain and landscaped roads,

there's no end of things,
the good is the fact you're writing.

I think the trees in the wet fields
lean the way of the coming truth,
to return by instruments, by earthly stars
mapping out a restored country
as darkness falls in each fold.

My children talk themselves into dreams,
our hands deep in the sea of glass,
we rush to the edge of the known world
where the road ends in air.

When Suzy Was

If I look up from here
glancing off the picture David sent
I can see Skorpios across the water,
owned by Onassis, empty and unvisited.

At night navigation buoys burn
five fixed points in a line,
the island is a picture of death,
a dark thought in broad daylight.

Hermes, psychopompos, took the man down,
rising beyond the private island
the Pindus mountains make no comment,
drowned in miraculous light.

*

For the dead I love to dance in their bodies again
the house is too small in fact,
the decor rustic haute bourgeoisie
– death turns a delicate ankle
it looks like his veins need stripping:
"We could do a deal…" I think not,
climb over the counter, forget the books.

The trick of separating them from their lives
gets underway before I arrive,
numberless they clamour at the window:
this one thinks if only he could arrange the letters
it would make all the difference; it won't,
the matrix of dots but motes in the air.
When Suzy was a skeleton she went rattle rattle rattle.

What strikes me is how flat it all looks,
despite four grown men going mental
pressing their faces into the room,
and they become four deaths: mine.
The books bake in an oven
in a frenzy of vowels sans sense;
don't pretend you hear distant music.

*

It's futile to confuse my girls' fatal serial song,
the empty island of a dead plutocrat
and the printing house dance;
mountains and islands rising from the sea.

In the village an old woman stares into Madeleine's eyes,
she wants to hold the young girl's face,
it is a marvel to her, she shapes the air between us;
they're face to face and the air is still.

When Suzy was a nothing, a nothing…

In fact the dead have names;
my mother, my father,
Stuart, who died aged 22,
my two brothers who died as babies.

They buzz like nobody's business,
they flicker against the tiny panes
– let us in, let us in;
invisible everywhere in the picture.

She used to go like this this this

The God Is Not a Ventriloquist

I'd thought to make this book a version of the oracular process, to find out what is always there in the making of the poem; ambiguity, bounding like Koretas's goats across the high meadows of language in the Spring of the god's returning.

Imagine the inquiry as the unearthing of the poem. The descent into the *adyton*, coughing up fumes to the Pythia's raving; revelation for others to make sense of afterwards. As Pausanias says, "…when she descends into the place of the prophecy, she does not take with her any kind of skill or talent." So, I thought myself well-qualified.

Holding a cord to the omphalos, and in the other hand laurel, she is possessed by the young god. The god's words are incoherent; at what point, and by whom, the meaning was fixed is unclear. The priest as exegete delivers the answer to the inquirer. I see the ritual, in all its versions, as a blueprint for introspection at the centre of the world – the thought of it. Three impersonal figures hold as functions of the making mind: inquirer, possessed and exegete as one.

Though I'd thought to make this book
I don't know … in the place of calling up
let the wheeling sky come down,
wash these hands and cleanse all fault.
I am the brother of the snake,
I spit laurel between my teeth.

The Name Apollo

Apollo, god of words, accept my song,
let it rise like an arrow
the voice and flight of birds
[unblown and pure into the sky]

strike out into nothing,
into the [empty] air of spring
and satyrs enter, in revel, saying whatever:
I know another returns, I know

by the ivy tattooed on my arm
[the silver foil] the pigeon feather,
the flight and voice of…

You don't wrap it in mystery, in proscription
Apollo … I do the work of vision…

*

I came down from the northern forests;
furs, wax, honey and slaves:
they took me to their coastal cities,
merchants, craftsmen of the wonderful art,
from the inland sea to the ocean.

They took me for their own
to those islands I was borne;
her arms around a single tree
in a soft meadow split asunder
in the centre, miracle of light.

In my bones the white north sleeps,
each winter I return there:
they are children in the garden
making magic with stones
and hidden designs in my name.

*

I was the chosen boy, both parents alive,
no touch of death, in the place named for me
a boy leading boys.

Dressed in laurel, dressed in light
the waking dream of spring
parades from door to door.

I took the year from the earth,
the flight and voice of vision,
made a hole in the ground speak.

The Roadside Shrine

1

As if by arrangement four figures are spaced evenly in the foreground of the photograph; a road sign, an old man seated on a bench, an empty bench and a shrine. The road runs around the southern slopes of Parnassos. The view drops into the deep river valley, make one mistake and you die. Beyond, the mountain wall of silence rises out of the frame as you stand with your back to Delphi.

The road sign is a red circle with a red diagonal through an old fashioned car horn, more like a bugle, meaning prohibited – don't touch it. The silhouette of the old man is at rest. Hat back, walking stick propped, he looks into the valley but not, the angle of his head suggests, at the sanctuary of Athena below.

Next to the empty bench, the roadside shrine is a blue display case on stilts, topped with an open fretwork cupola and cross. With glass on four sides and the mechanism on top, it could be a crane operated lucky dip machine – the tension in the claw set so that nothing of substance can be lifted. The air-blue wooden sides are weathered, the door oil stained.

You stand with your back to the sanctuary. The road is empty on a morning in Spring. Scattered with scrub and gorse, the white mountain rises.

2

The candid mountain shines
through the blue fretwork dome,
the shrine glides over the valley
a broken television on the air.

Tangled scrub surrounds the case
visible through glass on every side,
blown and spiky, a promise of life
against the dead contents exhibited.

Inside, a cameo of the patriarch
stares above a box of matches;
in the centre, a framed Christ,
casts a picture within the picture.

It looks as if sea and sky
meet in line with his shoulders,
an ouzo glass of oil on water
stands in front of him.

To the side a plastic Coke bottle
ready to refuel the flame;
in all this sky and mountain
interior darkness absorbs the light.

3

In this case all we have is the succession
of deities and the memory of uncreated light,
the faded grey blue of the central figure
– a young unbearded Robert Powell cum Byzantine androgyny,
the panama halo and gaze of utter blankness
in the face of the sun as great iconoclast.

To open a window in the sky, the copy must be perfect,
as in, 'When you see your brother or sister, you see God.'
or, 'The best icon of God is the human person.'
We should praise iconodules, in particular St. John Damascene;

'…for the flower of painting makes me look,
charms my eyes as does a flowering meadow…'

The Coke bottle, fixed in plastic, does not shine,
a corruption of Samuelson's 1916 classic;
the figure dull and thickened out,
'aggressively female' as Loewy said, it sells plenty,
but in the wrong way here;
the label script full-frontal and invisible.

In the ouzo glass, viscous sunlight glows amber,
appears to ignite the oil without burning the wick;
light catches on the right of the frame
lending definition to its cheap detail:
neither effect is proof of anything
but the great Spring day rising on Parnassos.

Catalogue of Answers

a white-painted bull
on a floral background

*

In a single wave the civic windows
turned silver and the sky collapsed
into the hollow bowl of new industries:
that's the Eden burning song, I think,
it's all in the plan, here's your part
– you stop, you go etc. then you're finished.

As the black streets freeze
make this absolute information sing,
against number, against knowing;
let Lucy come among us and
gather morning into reason,
send music music straight into the sky.

*

there is no poetry in this room
though in the backyard
my Beckett tree flourishes

*

mistress of the animals
tree goddess…
snake goddess [with] us
sea goddess
one with…

[mother] goddess
lover
she is *kourotrophos*
she carries the young god
in her arms, Zeus
      boy of boys.

*

walking home through town
traffic checked and faltered
I saw the river running
clear lyric swirl of glass

*

The red sun rests on Alan's hill,
across the Wye making rings and fish,
facing the big view from inside
the west pours in where he works,
lifting light in every page.

Nameless Shelley elaborates the margin,
opens a door in the cabin of air,
just to the left of where you sit
transcribed in the ash, in the lee,
hails the sun to rise again.

The hills go on and on to the sea Alan,
where darkness waits for one boat.

*

The catalogue is a dark book,
deep margins frame each figure:

there is only one copy,
everything is revealed.

*

The dream of the lute went like this. I was sitting
on the doorstep trying to play the lute, trying to
make the wires sing. A tall woman leaned out from a
toppling black and white cottage and called me over.

She said, – Look – and turned the lute over.
– You need to cover the back with felt, preferably
green felt, around the hole for the sound; and make
sure a tube is fitted, like cannelloni in fact,
but bigger. (Oh Sigmund)

And then you will play the lute.
And it will sound like the river.

*

In the bright vision there are magical animals
and indistinct human figures. That man is armed.
Below us fish swim a crowded sea and to the right,
away from the page, Asia is a model of the world
around its red function.

Look: the birdman steps into the green field site.
All about him the blatant geometry of planning
cuts in; an axe throws light on the issue. If any
straight bearing is finally a powerline we should
leave now. The tectonic plates grind against each
other at the committee stage. We should leave.

*

Oh Oh I am north, a frozen mapp. Shrunk to
the core in my tiny house, under a sky of
icefloes, tinkling.
Let the yellow flower rise, let it radiate
something. Feed me you sub-atomic, half-life
zoomorph.
From the door of St. Magnus the men of Orkney
went mad for Egypt, roaring an alphabet of
hot triangles across the great green.

*

(the catalogue is a dark book
its cover a white-painted bull
dancing on a floral background)

*

A series of empiricist hymns
before linear thought; the absolute literal
in rock crystal, amethyst, agate:
scattered in palatial rubble.

Each stone a model of candour;
the wheat, the barley, oats, wine and honey,
string of figs and other fruit
shooting up from the earth into your hands.

In a flood of light, the living tree,
we walk to the water as one body:
the goddess steps from the boat
in rock crystal, amethyst, agate.

*

On these short days the roads are frozen solid,
no-one moves in a nation seen as traffic plan;
at the ice station we imagine the flightpath grid,
the god of frost grinning.

Incoming control, packed like cold affronts,
government by insult out of spite:
from every house a line of music soars,
thin hope scales the glass sky.

To unsay one thing fit to sing, most probably,
turning each sheet of ice,
scratching black words to sing or else
give it up for the lusty sparrows.

Full of fight, sure of breath and mighty,
a scatter in the frigid tree.
Sing up, sing up, you querulous sods;
burn the branch to make spring come.

*

Standing on the road outside the house
I sing music for yelling, I can't stop;
against the big west prevailer I see
the back garden full of children.

The low sky fits over tunnels of winter,
unlike the ceilings of rock-cut tombs,
painted blue, blue as heaven;
then burnt out to be reused.

No one is there, even ghosts die;
in the dark river streetlights doused,

around the house night takes the estate:
we vanish into tenantless air.

*

Woke around three this morning
to the yelp of foxes mating
somewhere between the backyard and Chinese restaurant,
ululating in strict measure, under moonlight.
Retake the republic of feeling,
such cities and temples beyond the art of Phidias
and from the anarchy of dreaming sleep,
retake the republic of feeling.

*

I found her in Myrtos
sleeping by the Libyan Sea
by lemon groves and burning rock,
with sixteen different words for blue.

My village goddess;
her elongated head and neck,
her accentuated breasts,
her blank and dreaming face.

Worn and naked in my hands
all of eight inches tall,
she carries a water jug
out of red earth.

*

To Thyestes,
unguent boiler of Pylos,

above the ocean of air
and the great trading sea,
spices for the unguent;
coriander, ginger grass,
wine and honey.

*

she can dim the morning light
she makes me talk
she gives me my life
she can fuck me anytime she likes

*

I know I pursue the impossible archaeology
of the restored family album,
most of it sold for drink
– wedding photographs for the frames,
their bed, the radio, her clothes:
our belonging particles somewhere.
What we can tell of their lives is by what's left.
The old man sleeping on the floor,
on the eiderdown with two pillows
exactly where the bed would have been.
From a great height we stare down
into the pit of generation: look,
the framed cast of a man asleep.

*

they thought they saw
in the meadow by the sea
a white bull dancing

*

That morning sweet birds
made small pools of sound,
one music   a message
from the waking god.

Kastalios said, where we go
they are like us and unlike us,
we will barter with them
and keep safe in coastal waters.

What we see as islands
are the peaks of a lost landscape
the seaways open at first light,
who can read this waveform model?

We did nothing to make it happen,
the big dolphin hit the deck;
first fear, then radiance
– after that the ship was not ours.

Kastalios spoke out,
we followed the bounding youth
as if dancing, inland,
we forgot our homes, our wives.

*

The field of understanding, Pound said,
and how to extend it, imperial measure:
tin from Spain, copper from Cyprus
with gold from Egypt as payment,
to run the arms race against Hittites.

The field of understanding, but not
an equation as yet resolved,
as metallurgists did not say to the great Wanax
when, one bright and focused morning,
subsistence became surplus to feed experts.

*

static singing the arc of days
losing all trace, I touch
the alphabet of knowing shapes,
the dark substance of a music to make you free

as if the coast of a continent
rises into view on an undreamt day

ascending on a child's breath
the noisy birds, Siobhan said
they're so noisy, they want to speak
people language like us

*

another night, tunnelling
only nocturnal systems for sound,
drunks, traffic, domestic machines,
dropping a rope into the cave

dreaming of external light
the marble quarry, a white field,
a promontory over the sea,
figures waiting in the ground to rise

stone axe, obsidian, emery
enough to shape gods

My Life With Byron

And Such Other Cudgelled and Heterodox People

Climbing the liquid stairs of drink
we go   are you there Alan
in the English good night
where Byron glides unwritten.

*

Across empty England tilting under cloud
towards a new order and petrol thirst,
trees lift like visions at the margins of fields;
an innocent history passing with ease
as if the rural poor lined the road, waving.

Blasted through a slot together landscape,
with no essential link between these lives
– easy as speed, didn't feel a thing –
dead winding gear, wooded fields, barracks towns,
figures moving together in a film.

To answer the young lord's questions:
we can commit a whole country to its prisons,
depopulate and lay waste all around us and
restore Sherwood forest as an asylum for outlaws;
in the English good night, where Byron glides unwritten.

*

In the cold eye of the lake
light dissolves around the trees,
a boy, free as a fish, dives
dreaming of the sea.

*

Lyres on earth cast like nets
to catch the living god
but to stand beneath these walls
and fall into those hands is terror.

The beginning is music, a strange thing;
in the shade of power we found ruin and delight,
crossing Paynim shores, Earth's central line,
through an invisible door.

Over the dark sliding wave
into half the world unknown,
with liquid nerves in charged air
we sought the god of birds.

Saw the blue cape afar
said his heart, tamed to its cage
all summer long;
milord is dreaming an island of light.

*

'I ran to the end of the wooden pier… the dear fellow
pulled off his cap and wav'd it… God bless him for a gallant
spirit and a kind one.'

*

After an interval of years, this composition to one far and firm;
events left me for imaginary objects, an imaginary England.
Do you remember when we were out with the Luddites,
from airy hall about the county, about the forest and villages?

But buzz buzz eager nations, not with human thought,
no new land nor fair republic, no deep sea music sounding.
Events left me in the umbrage of green shade,
my dear Hobhouse, return to that country.

In that completed state words are things,
the electric chain we darkly bind about ourselves.
From this tower of days I see the pathless woods
and the waters washing empires away.

*

excuse the scrawl, fresh morning at daybreak
boat starting for Kalamo … blue upon blue these mountains,
the Turkish fleet gone, the blockade removed

the air fresh but not sharp, we sailed together,
the song we sang was – a nation to be made,
when the waves divided us we made signals
firing pistols and carbines, tomorrow we meet at Missolonghi

if at the head of some one hundred boys
of the belt and of the blade, that I may
(calculate the cost of keeping one man in the field for one month
        the sale of the Rochdale manor?)
we bore up again for the same port

excuse the scrawl ..
frosty morning that means to be of promise,
that I may get the Greeks to keep the field

the final port or [word torn out with seal]
who will stick with the Greeks now?
the Lemprière dictionary quotation Gentlemen

or those who do not dissemble faults or virtues?
(when I was in the habit)
I reserved such things for verse

*

Aboard the Florida in an oblong packing case lined with tin,
organs and intestines in earthenware jars
– *this heart should be unmoved* –

The case stamped with seals of the provisional government,
painted black and submerged in a barrel of spirits
– *worm, canker, grief* –

Hobhouse went aboard at London Dock Buoy,
the undertakers were draining the barrel
– *life blood strike home* –

Though assured 'it had all the freshness and firmness of life',
he declined this last view of his friend
but later identified him by his foot.

And John Clare, wandering down Oxford Street,
saw the funeral train and a girl sighed – *poor LB* –.

*

To answer the young lord's questions.

Saturday night at the trough
they talk about technology,
new magic make you work harder,
their veins corrupted to mud.

I can hardly make the words out,
I never saw such things in the provinces of Turkey;
men sacrificed for cheap exports,
for spider-work to bloat others.

The magistrates assembled,
troops ransacked homes around Newstead;
men, guilty of poverty, wanting to dig
but another owns the spade.

This mob enabled you to defy the world;
the poor pitched against the poor
must learn flexible work and slut-time,
must learn global economy.

Capital tips off the edge of the world
to strike the old deal still in place,
a life above ground or boundless waste;
here we go, here we go, here we go.

Breakers of frames, iconoclasts incandescent,
let me be among you about the county;
snap their heads awake
with the politics of paradise.

The Ludicrous Placation of Ghosts

Beyond my hand and the round eye of light,
Byron, Jane Harrison and my mother
stand in the mist of Niagara Falls.

They stare at the wall of water falling,
decked out in the tourist's black poncho,
the water falling a thousand feet.

In the great rush she looks at me
with such courtesy for the living,
then steps into the beaded air for ever.

*

His shoes were black and shiny,
he danced across the Irish Sea in 1946.

Spic and span drill in the holy orphanage and British Army;
I'm not making up a word of this.

How wide's the Irish Sea?
How deep the coastal shelf?

*

They will not eat blonde food,
think of Dumuzi, his snake hands
            his final descent,
– dig a trench to the west of the tomb –

They will break a contract of shadows,
they long for morning air, on the street,
to walk and let them live in us,
— *look along it to the west,*
pour down water as purification, then myrrh —

Some sounds some burdens can release,
— *do not name the dead —*
some sounds some burdens can release,
— *but they will have blood —*

They know there's nothing like the world,
they cannot make up one word of it.

Catalogue of Ships

Aboard the Princess Elizabeth, the Lisbon packet
for the Vathek theme park.

Aboard the frigate Hyperion,
big sun bright sea the land of.

Aboard the Townshend packet,
Captain Bucket at your service.

Aboard the Spider for Prevesa,
Missolonghi over the water, low in the mouth.

Aboard the Pylades, quick step to Smyrna.
Aboard the Salsette, salt it for the Hellespont.

Aboard the Hydra, transport ship
stuffed with Elgin's plunder.

Aboard the Volage, sweet frigate.
Aboard the schooner Bolivar, oh my Bolivar.

Aboard the Hercules for Cephalonia,
an unnamed mystico, an unnamed bombard, fit for song.

Aboard the Florida, down the blackhole
all the way to Hucknall Torkard

Where Cain stands in a spotlight
and nothing flows from liquid space.

I walk with dust in peopled darkness – come.

Ambelakia

All afternoon the birds of Ambelakia sing
and the air is the shape of itself
rising in one breath to Olympus and Ossa;
that light should have substance and sound.

The Common Company of Ambelakia founded 1778,
founded on madder, sheep blood and method,
the red dyed cotton of the first co-operative.
'We have decided to renew our company,
spreading a table for all … in the dress of communication…'

Schools   Libraries   Hospitals   Mansions   Welfare

In 1811 Ali Pasha, sociopath and maverick,
admirer of Byron's ears, raided the village.
By 1820, with the rise of Manchester as king,
the fall of the Bank of Vienna and the war of greater powers,
the beneficent society collapsed.

Remember the Common Company of Ambelakia,
the first industrial co-operative.
Remember schools; libraries; hospitals; mansions; welfare.

*

The painted ceilings and walls of the houses
depicted real and imagined cities,
young girls gazed down from balconies
and the world abounded with birds and flowers,
as the high meadows with aconite, anemone and cyclamen.

The full moon is high tonight,
the spring sky milky with stars;
other villages cast like sparks
shine out across the valleys.

The Objects Were Not Paid For
or Got For a Fixed Price (Elgin)

As they lowered the last metope marble rain fell on their faces,
'Telos.' The Disdar stepped into history and with him the five   (Clarke)
girls crying for their sister, the ravished one, ready for shipment
in the lower town, filling the air with lamentations.   (Douglas)

The events dictate a mythology of fact and we wait for the girl
to return in Spring. 'Milor explored in the bowels of the earth to
dig them up.' Milor stole gods to that coast of no return, to the (Benizelos)
shadow world below this light; the triumph of Eng-a-lish classicism. (Byron)

Milor ripped the Panathenaic frieze from the walls of the cella
where the goddess dwelt. It is the procession of all her people
translated into stone and she the city incarnate. 'To realise its
meaning we must always think it back into its place.'   (Harrison)

Of the money Elgin received half repaid to the government in debt;
the objects thus an integral part of the British Museum collection. (Smith)

Ivy Tattoo

The ivy on the wall lifts in one wave
as summer flares into the sky,
a pattern of streets, a map of pleasure
rising deep in the green cell.

If it pours in over our eyes and mouths
light flooding through limbs,
the young green hands
hold us breathing under water.

Then a door opens deep in the cell,
you hear the music of all your life:
to go in is dangerous,
to turn away is dangerous.

Brother to the snake, in winter riot born,
let me bear your tattoo;
light splashing from leaf to leaf,
glossy cups scandent for the god.

They knew what hit them

They knew what hit them
out on the coast
            sky black with ash
            earthquake
            tidal wave
            fire.

They knew
a crowd on Harbour Street
white stones bordered by blue
a crowd in one wave
sacrifice   to get at the life again.

If this is a poem
about the death of
the one the many
there must have been children sleeping
in sweet abandonment
as the unknown sailed into the harbour
and the world stopped.

Even the air of the high peaks
thick with ash   bitter mouth
even the blood dead   they knew.

On Returning from the Fields

Late at night another station fades in,
late late, when only security lights burn;
this is the news, another station,
Orpheus ascending in ritual intervals.

From the archives of Radio Sofia
a language I don't have,
Yanka Rupinka, Kalinka Vulcheva
– sung on returning from the fields.

Nerve stripping voice, unearthly scale,
my whole life pouring back to me
at ground zero, I hear it fade out in
a table song by different means.

Early morning

Early morning frost this morning,
white ghost packing blue fields away,
turning from night, these counties
run to the capital, pale horse racing.

Thinking your dark body asleep in my hands,
thinking big sun raging
from a slab of marble sea,
anaesthetised by Duveen out of Elgin.

But to wake on Ossa in spring,
at each step a grove, a secret stream,
the air rings under an endless sky
waiting for a figure to appear.

In delight a door opens in the air,
we see the whole of Thessaly rising.

Disclaimer: Byron Never Went To Ambeiakia

'I saw before me in the vivid occupation of the people of that place
a living notion of the world made good, a species of heresy, a society
unfallen – just suppose this were known in England – the very thing I
had traversed the theatre of war to find, here…'

He saw the Common Company of Ambelakia working,
the houses, the schools, the three hundred workshops,
he saw Shelley plain and the technology of genius.

As polyphonic bird song filled the air
he saw Ali Pasha's troops rise out of the Vale of Tempi,
indifferent men climbing the foothills of Ossa.

To exact murder, taxes, arbitrary arrest,
invisible powers of empire on their backs,
he saw the same beset the Nottingham weavers.

He saw the enormous condescension of posterity
rise up and he retreated into the house of George Mavros,
all thought and poise gone.

Milord knocked clean off his box.

Against Purity

Ino

By the well of Thalami, Ino my bride,
come out of your house, come out in the night,
with ship gods as well as land gods,
with bronze statues on the island
in the open air of Pephnos,
with the whiter than usual ants.

The owls swoop down
on dark wires sure as death,
hunting in pairs, back and forth
threading the night.

My mind empties around the tower
of Kapetanios Christeas and into the sea;
my old neighbour sings at night,
her imperfect beautiful voice
rises for no-one or the moon, Ino, for no-one,
or the dark ocean wrapped around the world.

Myriorama

By the houses of the living
and the houses of the dead
congregation of flames burn.

A door opened in the ground
releases the great blackness,
first light unfurled the sky.

Keeper of the chambered sea,
they say that in the sea…
the story is widespread.

Details vary along the coast,
but the baby Ino, was a god?
– out of a box from the sea.

       *

Under the bronze mountains spring walks,
girls follow in translation
one moment in the garden tracing Lusieri.

Blinds make bars across the page,
errant note? No, I remember the bliss
of the lines, my eyes opening on them.

Byron's estates in Eng-a-land
annexed to the big idea,
[*exeunt* the peasantry through every possible landscape]

I cast the cards of the myriorama
for musing swains and lacustrine vistas,
traffic jams and haunted bedrooms.

Turner asking Elgin for £400 p.a.
– I have been obliged to be a little barbarous –
and the Cretan fish eating all Lusieri's pictures.

Ten men line up to shoot Judas for Easter,
Nicolo dancing on the ruins of empire,
Nicolo dancing on broken stones and harbours.

Yannis Ritsos is free.

*

As we came out of the mountains
the moment not day or night,
music surrounded us.

Out of the silence of the gorge
through walls of rock and air,
we walked in a tunnel of sound.

Long-song synthesised unearthly,
swirl of sea and Taygetos
shatters into goat bells.

Reforms into music of the passes,
random harmonics, goat stink
rises up to us earth song replete.

*

This is Radio Free Byron on the shortwave
broadcasting to the English shires: wake up.
We urge war against the west, against Fletcher;
the Maniots are the men for me, they will do the deed.

Wake up you boys and girls, you sneak careerists,
forget the English Bores co-option of Ashbery,
the discontinuous prose continues;
this is the big poem of right belief – immaculate

That black speck veering across your sky space
above the town where you live,
riding cold fronts off the map,
homing in, set at zero, is your death

With this magnifying glass in both hands
I burn sunspots on the calendar,
burn for canonic, burn for garland on your head,
so each day comes up fresh with a hole in it.

*

Running the high meadows
day and night in the skin of a lynx
the bloody meniscus sticks.

Swallows roll in mountain air,
pop music, something emotional, defiant,
reaches into the same blue quarter.

Yannis Ritsos is free.

A Shelley Poet

12 July 1822 from the harbour Agios Dimitrios

Calm languid sea on every side
the air as though resting above
one fishing boat
               sails out of the gulf
leaving a long, subtle wake.

        *

and then nothing

the same etc sleep

        *

at night a boat came in
battered, sails gone
from another world by the looks,
the Ariel
two men and a boy

        *

They came ashore next morning and greeted Kapetanios Christeas.
They are a Shelley poet, Cpt Williams and a boy Vivian,
the Shelley recites Sophocles and revolution very excited,
we have it here already, saying life of triumph and something after
      a big storm.

The Shelley jumps about like a boy,
Christeas looks at him puzzled
in the great morning of the world.

        *

He read Hellas to us, we sat around the tower,
he looks at us and says the final chorus was right,
the rest was bluster rhetoric with something about our fig tree
– which was not his to give for it anyway.
Christeas liked the fighting parts
and made the shouts of victory victory.

The Shelley dug his hands into the red soil
and held the white rocks in the shade of mimosa,
he looks at the sea everyday and will not leave.

The Shelley in earth twisting and turning,
came out from under that language
unblinking to get it right.

Empires crack
        the snake renews itself
green and mighty spring returns.

        *

The sea made noise all night,
mountains of water falling on the harbour;
I went to look in the morning,
the confused messages flooding the horizon
and the light changing depth.
Here we sit like birds in the wilderness.

        *

I am alive on Cape Sublime,
the sea and mountains blend in song
this place was once called Pephnos.

Around the tower and into the deep,
mistress of many voices
walked into the water.

Out of the shining I saw her then
keeper of the chambered sea,
white goddess who saved me.

Here there is no shadow
in the sky, no authority
rising to dull the lens of light.

Here I am, this way boy,
swim to me, into my arms.

Season of Broken Doors

between Ag. Nic and Ag. Dim
near the dry river bed

above Kalamata to?
small white
J quotes Coke, Krischios outside

road to Neohori – 2
old rusty and new deluxe

between Saidona and Kastania
white cross black cross photo

road out of K
cross on top, after Exohori sign

as 6 Ag. Bapbapa

30/3 between Argos and Tripoli
the mountain road, no toll
white flowers everywhere

*

I found boxes scattered along the roads,
secret, earthbound constellations;
their contents would make Cornell blush
weathering into a new coherence.

*

Jesus quotes Coke
by the river bed Salinitsa,
a fusebox burning.

The sides are rusty
– stick your tongue on it,
taste salt, lemon, blood.

This machine of objects
blooms tectonic
on the fault of right belief.

At the end of exile
you open the door and
the circuit of air ignites.

*

My family home stands above the western portal,
the one gate of Monemvasia; my obviously heroic head
stares at empty sea lanes striking liars dumb.

I look at weeds, trinkets, strangers,
passing into the erosion I feel; if one word escaped
I would shatter in a new diaspora.

But listen you stones, you politicians:
Yannis Ritsos is free.

Singing Head

Bodies of a man and child
off Lesvos, earlier in the same channel
three young girls.

No Sappho
No Aeschylus
No singing head afloat.

Afghan banknotes in their pockets,
they are thrown overboard or the boats sink;
they cannot swim and the lifejackets fail,
some have never seen the sea before.

No Sappho
No Aeschylus
No singing head afloat.

From the Harbour

We spring out of the box of winter,
that curling cloud, a letter – Chalcolithic,
that girl leaning towards you,
that shadow in your cup – is from my hand.

I wait at the door to your house, ivy tattooing the wall,
spurge blooms on the hill behind me;
I swept down from Thrace and the narrow pass
from blueprint villages in Anatolia to this warm water port.

Where is my sister now?
the light in slices shot through your thinking dark,
and the sky cracking over the whole world.
My sister? – trumpets calling from the water.

I swept down, my birds in random green go mad,
on to this landing strip between mountain and sea,
into this natural amphitheatre
I set my foot for riot to follow.

The ground returns my tread, the chambered earth, and she steps ashore.

    *

I found a plastic bull on the beach,
toy Zeus fronting the waves erect
with bleached hide and shrivelled horn
– if he grins girls, you're over his back
crashing towards a bed of luxury, where it all begins.

He has the look of you about him Byron,
the set of his head and lordly gaze,
though I forget we are both dead
I think you would like him,
he bellows sweet amphionic odes.

Let's walk him along the cape,
spring begins again with his snort;
we danced all our lives to his delicate step,
to the beat of his blood, even now
as old as we are, descending in shadows.

Yours, Shiloh

*

Those stories, those songs were television to us
except alive on air they wrapped us in their signal,
except that we ran it and it was real
in the grain of the wave as we cleared the harbour.

So, like birds in the wilderness, we are its variations,
making the picture atomised, the republic of light,
and the sea shaping a tunnel of sound
as long and slow as summer around the western shore.

*

After his victory at Actium Octavius founded Nicopolis,
a blighted shithole befitting his political soul:
call him Blair, Bush, Sharon or Milošević,
those who are wired to the world, who cannot set ambition aside.

Of Antony an old man said, he was glued to her,
a lover's soul lives in the body of his mistress
and she set sail for the Peloponnese;
off Tainaron her women reunited them.

They spoke and afterwards did sup and lie together;
across the dark calm of the sea Antony said,
– we are keeping company with famous ghosts,
Helen and Paris sailed this way to their final sortie.

Let's glide to the cave below the headland
and paddle in the mouth of hell, hand in hand
we'll walk the streets of our burning city
and gather the asphodel of our sweet defeat.

*

Stack the myriorama vertically,
each card suspended apart
a spatial landscape made temporal,
olive tree blown white in the wind.

Seeds, insects crowd the air,
oil from the boatyard bleeds into concrete,
at night Kurds come ashore
we help them on if we can.

The walls flake into the sea,
palimpsest, underwriter
of this harbour between worlds
opening its broken arms.

The Empire Stores

A reading of Alan Halsey's *Dante's Barber Shop (De Vulgari Eloquentia)*

'How can we sing King Alpha's song in a strange land?' (The Melodians)

1

We closed down the Empire Stores in the bay,
we don't shop there now, only for our imaging
of the map of others and zero longitude fancy,
globally patched, then a rising tide at your door.

Or the ineluctable, brimful culture piled up
lettering every street, heaps of incoming names,
and even this is not my thinking,
see all this dirt fair clogs my eyes.

Be clear: we reject the old but new holy war,
the demographics of canonic fodder, new but old flags
– these colours don't fade;
give me rivers of dirt and bring my poets back to life.

It's those conversations I want, you speak
Oh England on slick rails to the dumb chamber;
put your ear to the ground, your hands in the air,
there's a chance archival unity won't rise and shine you.

If what follows is a metaphor then this is no poem
– Caspian oil sucked across the Stans to Karachi;
it's not a silvery zero tube but ignition:
make the ordinary language good or die.

2

With grammar stocks rising on song
he sat opposite me at the big event;
– cosy up to them and push their hot buttons,
triangulate the Blairprint and common thought.

When Shelley arrived out of the ever living past
he checked in at the King Otto, Byron next door;
he saw dark figures rise before the liberals,
how the few valued the many and bought the government.

They dribbled conscience on the accounts,
we stare at the glaze mostly, eyes glued to the past
cold filtered through a grovel image voodoo,
clean up and apply to Concept House.

What scene unfolds in that domed snow shaker?
White boys on the road, zoot suits and patronage,
a limited view of human nature
in a medium of implacable pessimism.

To make us the object of such devotion
the secret voice print is calling,
in rank order, men, women, family groups,
our faces tipped into the light and locked.

3

If we could write an archaeology of the soul,
unable to speak in a barcode dancing,
the little birdies would sing for St. Valentine
with big light raining on a Vatican elsewhere.

But we came dark cloud boiling from white north
drawn by the smell of luxury goods;
the journey knocked narrative out of our poetry,
even pedants see it vanish as lives unravel.

See the red, the golden threads tied in secret knots,
slipped from your pommel into Scythian scrub;
the religious spillage in our wake is trash:
what other authority do you dream?

Such ingenuity we had kept those ships afloat,
allowed our parents to eat in that war;
she said learning English would make her free
and the perfect sentence dismantled Ilium.

To begin again, the girls coming and going
set their feet in the meadow,
in the red, the golden day, the invention of fair writing
in the meadow by the sea.

4

One day the secrets of the present war will be out,
— let's have a positive idea on the topic Capitano,
I'm ready, I'm taking down the boss words,
I is dredging it up the homeland tunnel.

Give me the spoken order like balm in the air.
Give me the holy father dumb in Gilead.
Give me trade ban and big starry eyed kids.
Give me a cypher on two legs, clueless.

Anything but watching it live on t.v.
It's not a cure for pain, that day, that morphine song,
you already know the colours, the palm tree cutouts,
sound off, text up – in B ghd t d y.

Talk to this wooden face, Marydoll, prissy lips,
they have tunnels under the desert, intricate and rich;
awaiting glory elevated in the sky garden,
the poverty of public discourse goes unsaid.

Who wrote the history of truth telling? What's the ratio?
Without Shelley, MacSweeney and little TC?
Ye boys of England, from the midlands and the north,
clean up the abattoirs and each chartered grave.

5

Jerusalem the Golden shipped up in the south east,
in the Valley of Dawn they believe what they like;
see the mansions on the hills, barred and empty
– last time I looked, the variable script disintegrated.

We made deep pools of all our anxieties,
hungry mouth at the bottom of the well said nought;
plans for the real world in the language of beasts,
a distilled purity, contra natura, abhorrent.

Come dance with me Joanna, Ioanna Southcott,
Ioanna big mouth, the sun is always rising
in the riff riff valley of Don Van Vliet,
I was miles away myself, under a sky thick with migrating souls.

Do you think for one minute this dub dub over tracking
out of the ever living past très moderne?
Wake up, the room is full; Shelley and Ric and young MacSweeney,
dying for want of intelligent talk.

And what will happen to any of us?
Speechless boy of a speechless tribe,
see the nation of morning, nation of supple creatures
beneath the pretty page of a kind empire.

6

Shelley took wing, wrapped up Lundy Fastnet,
sent thought balloons across the Bristol Channel
to the slave trade capital, a power of no good,
astride its Palladian funding stream.

He was my aerial in that broadcast
on the ever living short wave, anagrammatical;
court historians swing on the rim of the imperium,
snorting stipends, vamping up the Empire News.

Our Boys March Along Candlelit Streets
Babylon Falls To The West – Byblos Taken
Child Prostitutes Lie Down In Alleyways
Make A New Home In King Alpha's Land

Shelley took wing on that day,
migratory birds homing in joined the dots;
in one moment radar spelt it out,
the lost art of traffic control, welfare, moderation.

I was miles away myself and rushing back,
at the same time the pigeons of Assuit rise
and the white wings of our common books open
lifting into the common light one word.

Against Purity

Out of sight at the boundary
blue hills and magical trees
mock and dance in around,
the greater life flashing in the sky.

Somewhere believe or singing her
a field god rises, hungry,
close to the ground, eyes like smoke,
singing her those particles wake.

They say that they say that sometimes
she's seen in the neighbourhood.

*

I see things out in the fields,
the word heliotrope in blood;
in the faces of our children
the road's a dark river.

I see things in the other room,
Melanie's dream speaking
the old women click clack,
blind in a circle oblivious.

They say that they say
she forced her way into the room,
she broke the circle, slit the cloth
of the empty air where the dead spin round.

Common Measure

Lifted away on England's heat wave
into an earlier dawn rising over Asia;
imagine a city as microcircuit,
the whiz and pop of hot lights and money.

I remember common measure, 4/3 4/3 or 8/6,
how Burns shapes the stanza's second part,
the emerging truth where everything fits
rushing past us both, my fair, my lovely charmer.

The lights of Moscow cartwheel and further east
the dust of lights descending;
the business will go elsewhere,
across the world turned upside down.

4/3 4/3 or 8/6, common measure
sings up from every street on Earth.

*

On the top of this column
the English peck at the pool, float, make plans;
the sky sweats, ripped red over Kowloon
with a line from W.S. Graham in Argyle Street:
We. Know. Nothing. About. These. Lives.

The boy made good into a ghost
sleeps on cardboard at the ferry terminal,
a bottle of water at his head;
he's released from the metaphor
in red and gold script, not exactly pictures.

The island night spangles names
bouncing over the South China Sea,
workmen shout, sink steel pillars in mud;
a market opens its mouth: big teeth, big hunger.

My students amend their texts in Cantonese:
juxtaposition   copse   pump room.

    *

They cross the river from the mainland,
flower sellers, contract killers
to Macau of the casinos
in the morning of the world.

Our driver today is Alan
– the Republic there, the new causeway,
low camouflage hills
under abstractions of poured concrete.

We see the bones of the Japanese saints,
Xavier's scapula, teeth etc
on red cushions in cases,
to be returned to Hiroshima.

Asia is lit up and shopping.
Who knows what will happen?
The big names sparkle;
made in China, made in U.S.A.

Rowing across on the morning
flower laden boats, drawn up on this side.

MacSweeney

Here's a jar of honey for you;
we stand the beehives in the fields of borage,
the pollen's rich, the yields are high
from the bright blue flowers you knew.

Morning light spreads across the floor
despite liars in public places,
lapis miners get to work in Badaskhan
and wind lifts the ivy on the wall.

I walked out into the street,
we all moved together in a film;
faces lit from below, easily engaged,
and the blue Autumn sky falling away.

As if we said forever, buildings rise in air,
lives going in and out of them
and that would be above ground,
my girls growing up for instance.

The valley of the assassins has been extended
and escaped our rhetoric;
I'll pour the honey in the ground,
you rise up and spit the pearls in their faces.

The pollen's rich, the yields are high
from the bright blue flowers you knew.

Melanie

Melanie I've been thinking about when we first met. How in all that trauma to ourselves and others, you would feed me the best soup, the best scrambled eggs, and then send me away. You were thinking what to do I think.

My obsession with you began then; each part, each limb, your mouth, your skin – each part of you, and you wanted to be wrapped around me entirely; an impossible hunger we couldn't understand and had never known before.

Mighty and literal, love burns the world to leave only your face above me in the dark room. I didn't know what was happening; driving back and forth by hidden reference points, flares in a sea reduced to one day, uncharted. Your face, my eyes on your face.

For Doug Oliver

I saw Doug Oliver last night
standing in the shadow of the tower,
Christeas's tower guarding the harbour.

He was not in line at the ditch
and did not need to drink,
he was listening attentive, invisible.

The black sea filled his eyes,
he walked with Shelley unconfined
along the sea lanes of perfect sound.

He turned his good ear to the waveform;
his words, his maps and theories of song
released on the air unencumbered.

I heard the dialogue with Alice begin,
a woman came into the room a woman
back and forth flooding the paths under the sea.

I heard it all for the first time,
pretty weeds streamed from their hands,
bodies in sea light walking in one another.

*

And sucked down into the oracle of the drowned,
into the dry cave, backlit psychorama and honey glow,
the echoed rise and fall of the waves
beats this moment and the next to the breathing of the sea;
he stands on the dry powder floor of this cave,
Peak District manifold, Apollonian on this shore.

But the dead can only speak through us,
around here the living feed the grave,
talk, share food and pour out their hearts
unblinking with love in the mortal fact,
the secret monologue broadcast,
I'm talking to my mother though 18 years dead.

So if I wait for Doug to speak, my teacher, my poet,
I imagine I'll wait for ever,
even in this dry cave, in honey light,
wrapped in the murmur of the sea, of bees;
in the honeycombed tunnels running to Matapan,
you hear Doug speak in a land made unstrange.

*

Look the owls swoop and dive from the tower for you,
alive in their dialogue of death;
I was thinking Alice of the life shared
and the lamentation of its ending,
their flight sounding in your ear, patterned and lethal,
their beautiful trajectories alight
against the black wall of mountain darkness.

Poetry is the way we think and speak here;
in one moment wingbeat instants take flight
over the gulf under the eyes of the serene empire,
to Methoni and Koroni in the darkening west
and the unpeopled cities of the sea.

Three Monologues

Leukothia

I am Leukothia, goddess of calm waters,
from the depths I watch the chambers of the sea;
I am companion to Poseidon,
call me mistress of good voyaging.

In my mortal story I was Ino,
daughter of Cadmus, lover then wife of Athamas,
sister of Semele the mother of Dionysus;
my other sister dismembered the fool Pentheus.

I saved the boy god, dressed the darling as a girl;
Hera drove me to madness and death for it and
my perfect dive into those arms,
in that world I breathe water.

Now I speak truth in dreams from the well,
the dark well house of Thalami;
whatever the villagers ask is revealed,
a wet hole in the earth speaking.

In the spring they carry me out to their fields;
they ripple and wave for me,
men tightening sinews in my name;
they honour me with their blood and fucking.

They say of me, they say of me
but who is speaking, do you think,
out of the well's dark mouth?
Even their dreams echo my voice.

But I long for the earth, the waving corn,
the boy god of my village standing up;
then in one moment the wave rises
turning limbs in vaulted light.

      *

So I do what I can to save them,
they come from Albania, Iraq, India;
they walk, hide in containers and small boats.
I save them if I can, thinking of the voyage;
they come from Romania, Afghanistan, Iran;
from darkness to darkness, I lift them up.

They are not the first to journey this way,
I remember the Pelasgian and the Minyan,
and the great flood to the west, the new America;
the endless weeping at doors and harbours,
enough to make starvation seem a luxury;
I remember Europa and the white turbine.

Think about what they want to escape,
to face danger and at best indifference;
show me Kurdistan on a map,
show me the remittance economies of faith;
he is not my brother, she is not my sister,
from darkness to darkness I lift them up.

      *

I am Leukothia, opening my arms to you,
the wave rises, turning limbs in vaulted light,
I hold you in my hands one moment
magnified before the white crash.

Pytheas

I am Pytheas of Massalia,
I sit and watch and drink.

When I speak I am not believed,
I will die on this dockside in the sun.

I watch the ships sail away and return,
captive in thought circumscribed by Strabo.

*

I sailed into a greater knowledge,
driven by a curiosity stronger than any trade wind;
I saw all the things and places I tell you.
I did not follow a picture of the world,
whether from Miletus or Egypt: I looked,
I saw the invisible Isle of the Pritani.

I talked and bartered my way across Armorica
to the sea at the supposed edge of the world;
the trade in knowledge was local,
what Agde knew of Carcasso and Carcasso of Gironde;
I joined each link with my own hands,
then took ship from Ushant to the Tin Islands.

I cast my words like rope to secure the boat,
pulled into harbours for which you had no names;
we stuffed our boxes with gold and silver coins,
perfume, coloured glass and exotic trinkets.
We were hungry for tin, the magical alloy,
to run the arms race against Carthage.

Has the world changed much at all? I doubt it.
Are there still elites and prestige goods?
Consider who wants you not to find out for yourself,
add it up, exchange outside theogeny;
for immediate and dangerous knowledge
I swapped gifts with strangers and stepped ashore.

The great ocean put the chill in my bones,
I stood on the promontory called Belerion
bright and shining one, after 95 nautical miles;
this single fact dismantles your geography.
I crossed the land bridge to their market,
saw the Pritani work the tin in clever ways.

The painted ones called it Albion,
Apollo flies at the back of their sun;
island by island and further inland by foot,
the flightpaths, alignments, circles of stone,
rectangular fields and riches buried for gods;
after 95 nautical miles I measured it.

*

I wait in this room over the drink shop,
Winter wraps a cloak around the harbour.

Water flops against the empty quay
and light in waves spreads across my ceiling.

My dry bones whisper the great ocean,
open the box, a knucklebone of tin.

The Ingliss Touriste Patient

What do you mean too late? Is he in danger?

And I was afraid and thought I would die,
lifting off the table, only the ceiling above me
and the vertiginous air for your voice Melanie.
– Yesterday you should bring him, you must
be like sleep now, you must go to the hospital.

Next to Yorta, unconscious – ella Yorta, ella ella,
wake up wake up my daughter, my child;
Yorta – Aorta – Iota not caring one jot,
there's something wrong with a letter,
a letter is unconscious, a letter is Maria's daughter
next to Aorta, mine, something is wrong with the invisible.

Stand up.
Close your eyes.
Stand feet together.
You have the hurt problem.

I was there and not there,
under the great weight of the water
with the silver jackals and companions of the sea
suspended by a taste for the shape they once had;
diamonds of light dance over them,
they sit in a circle shining and grin,
– Look at me, look at these anchors, look at these roots,
– Down here the mind is overcome.

And I was there and not there,
wheeled off to brain scan land.

Where is my wife? Will I come back here? Where is she please?
Που είναι η γυναίκα μου; Θα έρθω πάλι εδώ; Σας παρακαλώ πείτε
    μου που είναι;
She's with the gypsies from the big camp
sliding along the corridors, riding hips,
I was back in the cardboard town by the airport,
– Where do they come from?
– From here, they come from here.
Sliding along the dark corridors,
her hand holding up the baby's head to light the world.

Gracious Maria found us cold water;
she sat by her daughter all night,
drowsy Yorta recovering, Yorta the beautiful,
and Melanie thanked her for her help,
– Oh but we are all people, yes.

I was there and not there:
Pound in the olive grove raging,
a ghost white man waving a broken branch
in the perfect climate for the human nervous system;
the olive tree blown green and white and
the air like a lens for the Earth given a fair chance;
Pound went down to the ship, Europa, the wreckage,
raging, raging at the innocent ants of my harbour,
its arms open to the various world.

I was there and not there with my wife and my mother;
we stared at a small television at our feet, the size of a dark footlight;
it was the emergency services concert,
– firemen, bare-chested, singing *Bohemian Rhapsody*,
which was not to my taste;
we stood around the dark hole at our feet,
companionable and variously entertained.

My head was away and singing:
an' war'ly cares an' war'ly men/May a' gae tapsalteerie, O
my girls wait by the sea, longing for the waves,
green grow the rashes, O standing up so straight.

My head was away and singing:
all night I saw with my eyes closed
squares of blue black landscape,
thinking my eyes were open,
villages and tracks, cisterns, temples, bus lanes and hospitals;
a series of design features made for civilisation
before it was named; and talking and water channels,
a mythology rising at every turn, local, particular and useful.
At last with my eyes open in the new day,
surprised not to see the landscapes imprinted on the world,
checking again and again, I was ready.

From Cambos, the air heavy with eucalyptus rolled over the car,
sweet pine and burnt dust off Taygetos drenched the road
and through Kardamyli jasmine in waves fell upon us;
so you kept driving and I lay down and the full moon
made its path across the water and I was there.

Backward Turning Sea

Helen Mania

Yannis told us of the alternative escape route,
Helen and Paris making chariot wheel tracks in Thalami
down to the harbour at Pephnos.

Spartans left waiting at Kranai,
mouths open, bored before the myth
– look at those sparks, like stars eh?

They spent their first night here,
fell upon one another, spent
until the sun came over Taygetos.

Helen set foot on board, trumpets sound
over water, sewing in the grain
the ships of all the world in her wake.

*

Helen didn't want the trouble
safe behind those walls
the army of the fertile plain said so.

I looked at Marathonisi, plotted
the chariot tracks crashing down
from Thalami to Pephnos and the sea.

Helen didn't want it to happen,
then love like Paris arrived.

I looked at the serene harbour
isle of fennel, empty blue mirror,
Helen was not there nor in Egypt.

Honey melting the other side of Taygetos that night.

*

We need a name for this war,
economics won't move our heroes;
plunder is nearer to it but
join our trade war won't swing it.

We need to make it personal.
Control of grain ships through the straights
and increased tax revenue? I think not;
if we had a woman abducted for instance.

In the future they'll see through us,
as if we would turn the world upside down
for a Spartan girl who warmed up the house guest?
Menelaus' hot wife gone wrong.

*

I set my foot in the track
greased slot to smashed Ilium,
one way ride to bliss or exile.

Night of stars, night of revelation
silver jackal sniffing around the door,
storm came smoking off Taygetos.

The house became a boat and
the great green flooded her mind
the island, her dream, floated out to Paris.

Snakes and figs littered the yard.

That morning Helen threw aside the carpet of stars,
that morning Helen stepped aboard.

*

I kept my Spartan girl wrapped up,
hidden under a pile of cloaks
for this languid, sexual periplus.

We drew bright lines across the water
phosphor alphabet dissolving clues,
we lipsticked the mouth of hell below Tainaron.

Even so she could not be dimmed,
she shone so fair like a bowl of light
desire lifted us like the tide.

Up from the inky black a message,
where fish pick the bones clean and
fields of seaweed denote a continent.

We turned the world upside down:
Menelaus – Where are your divisions now? Stop.
– Your squad cars and riches? Stop.

I left of my own freewill and cannot stop. Stop.

She lay in the boat burning, my beacon,
shaped by heaven,
they built temples in her wake.

*

Who would believe it over a girl?
despite our endless back and forth,

Io, Europa, Medea and the sassy east?
Moonstruck lovers is all we need.

We could get the Egyptian priests on our side,
build a temple to the goddess stranger;
variation as a post-something aesthetic,
she was a ghost above the Skaian gates etc.

I have it now: our brother's loss is our cause.
Make sure you don't catch them,
clear all the harbours down to Matapan;
it's Priam's turn for regime change.

*

We fled in the hour of the furnace
Helen a black outline in the blast
dark one, I see only your face.

Swing the pendulum myth
another woman, another man sail eastward
pass Kythira, ploughing the grain.

Aphrodite came swanning out
attendant gods swim in her wake,
their mouths shaping O O in the eddies.

Oh Helen I loved every woman
to have you, Mr Meat Me, the fool
to find you deep in darkness.

*

My lord they have flown;
I have posted guards to the passes

but who can outrun love?
I'll stick the barb into Menelaus.

I think I hear armour clashing by night,
see smart bomb snapshots of Trojan bunkers;
saturation red hits the air in waves,
reconstructed it's just as real.

Draw up the list of ships
and tilt our western powers into the east;
we can lead our little princes
into the divided meadows of Aphrodite.

*

Helen you are not to blame,
your smoky heart faced the east
the colour rising inside you.

She ascends the steps above the gate,
Helen, the cicadas whisper unearthly,
the sky fuses around the shape of a girl.

Politicians made silent as stone,
remember hope, scratch at lust,
the word wanton dry in their mouths.

She steps forward parting the air
into the live broadcast
wrapped around the world.

She steps forward, pictures the boat
parting the waves, the field of men below,
what? the dream of? the plains of Argos?

She wanted to see her brothers
on the island of Pephnos, they stand in the waves,
guarding the safe passage of her escape.

She steps forward, it is Helen
ascending, her shape makes a window
in the air for the breathless sky.

*

We saw the sun burn the high meadows
the rain drench the white roots
the wind fuck the come hither waves.

We ran up the goat tracks, breathless
between spurge and aconite and mallow.

Helen you have undone the world
I taste your looks, touch your colour
you were always there, my radiant lexicon.

See how our boat dips and rises
to our shared step aboard
noses out of Pephnos over the endless sea.

We lie together in the seabed
just rippling the light with our breath.

The Subsequent World View

Aphrodite, riding on a goat
keeps me here, anchored in song.

Aphrodite's Bay

I walked in the favour of the gods
the children calling from the water
once out of the bay of the Libyan Sea.

You Egyptians from over there
who can work the gold like us?
make trade in gifts, copper and staples?

We are dripping with this blue
we will prosper for ever
the children call in their drowned language.

There's no dignity wading ashore
the stones roll under foot
and you stagger through endless need.

At that moment, face to face,
sea around your feet, sky falling away,
you must choose, abacus or knife.

*

I was in the market of market town on Saturday
when I found her in daylight – from where?
Across the Caspian, Anatolia, Sumerian dark wave
against the backdrop of Birmingham bargain stall,
over my head in the tide of singing birds.

Looky, look at this, where'd they get that?
How did that get here and what is your name?
I am not from here, my name transpontine,
I step over the silver thread between two worlds,
I walk to you across water and open the door.

Red dust of Asia perfumed my feet,
the golden hordes at my back look around
their horses nickering for fresh water;
I come from the founders of towns and trade,
I rise up from boom and bust harvests.

I led the way from rickety kids to shining surplus,
I focused the mirage of the blueprint town
across the high tableland, made specialists spring,
dreaming a design to catch the whole world;
our turbine ploughing to the western shore.

*

Today the lesson is English grammar.
It is dangerous to swim in Aphrodite's bay.
Repeat.

Why since then everybody wants to die?
It is the third world war already I think,
bit by bit, what is happening, this music.

Everybody so running to die – why?
You see this aria of Tosca, if they did,
maybe it would make them ok.

And it is dangerous to swim in Aphrodite's bay;
the razor shells will cut your feet,
the currents around the rocks are unpredictable.

Though the water is milky and clings to the skin
like a second body that slides and fits around your own,
long after you have returned to shore.

Today English grammar is heroic film;
the black and white harbour before money arrived,
western coiffure on Levantine heads.

At night I watched the ships unload:
the dovecotes, trinkets and sex toys,
the belief in mythology as fact.

And finally, more than we bargained for,
objectivity in Babylon
brought to book on the banks of the Euphrates.

About My Country

At Actium Octavian invented the West,
half-arsed imperator of the risen state
launched naval blockade, trade sanctions;
those terms rolling over us like white breakers.

*

Around Saddam's Kevlar hat
they gather in dark circles,
stuck on a pole, pre-emptive spite
twisting about in the breeze.

William Blake calls in despair and rubbish,
rubbish is not the answer;
to make this song twenty years,
another city at hand, lit up.

Until we have built between the wars
the syllables of the temple
speaking psalms from the sky,
though Mars is raw on all our heads.

*

They have dug up the bones of Opicinus,
he has photographed the sky above Mogadishu
ambition resting its left foot on Jerusalem;
he is their map maker, surveyor of the oily waters
so that they can ride the Vulva Oceanis.

Those white breakers falling on us, to make the world invisible.
You have been duped by Wahhabi cowboys and Yanky Rapturists.
You were not even a pause in the plan drawn up before election.

You must think of the good to others abandoned by such vanity.
You must think of the schools, hospitals and homes of a better nation.

*

We knew before Alexander told us
we would arrive in the valley of song,
through familiar villages and secret passes
to find our doubles living like we live.

Inscribed in the mountain air above us
we came to see they were the real people,
we their hungry shadows on the wind
in the valley of song of how we could have lived.

From Here According to Jenkyns

From here according to Jenkyns
Sappho entered the western lyric;
I can see the coast of Asia minor,
low blue hills, an apron of light.

The water's not wide, though I can't
get o'er dark imperial Anatolia
where my language was made;
aconite, mallow, fennel at the root.

Visitors

Ivor Gurney

Is that Gurney at the door,
stepping in and out of the light, face down
out of the dark from the bowl of hills
and the impossible message of the stars?

From your submerged green county,
your fortresses of Birdlip and Slad;
sweet Ivor listen, hear your music,
long in the making, brief on the air.

Hear the sea about this house,
the winds lost in the mountains summer long;
from here we map the night and
walk in the light to the houses off the road.

Lee Harwood

On the sea of glass Spyridoula sings Thalassa Mavri
in the Cretan night at the end of your road,
we go under that wave in the war of fish and molluscs.

I name this ship The History of Lost People,
she has her champion aboard;
the cudgelled and heterodox for crew.

Imagine a speech without metaphor,
the transparent borders of new nations;
who knows what happens in that far countree?

Talk keeps our aerial republic afloat,
the benign network from Brighton out
Spyridoula singing Thalassa Mavri.

Mr Halsey's Triptych

Bright morning shines across
Mr Halsey's triptych and remotely
not everything is driven.

The gentle powdered light
on the worked surface of the picture
a garden for the airy medium.

Silver bright the unframed thought
let me see it close enough to read
for the aire you sing of generous pith.

*

Jack came by for the art event
Jack the lad of morning's spy sir
caught the green boy singing.

Leaping over the language we speak
disunion Jack with a cigar stuck in him
will not see a Halsey in the sky.

Will not see the worked service
of your debt handsomely paid
the padded waistcoat unbuttoned.

*

Alan your work has caught my clever girls
– this is what I want to do in art
– this is how I think I think.

I'm looking at the waking world
the march of emblems at my door
comes rattling by 3 by 3 by 3.

These ikons open a second front
an unknown country we might
with a racing chance inhabit.

The Harbour at Night

In Agios Dimitrios the faultline sounds,
the radio plays and the last car I know
the language of birds calling;
Pephnos rises, Malovos of the shadows appears
and the harbour is an amphitheatre of air.

Open to the west, the sea glitters hidden light,
the fishing boat passes where the Dioskouroi stand;
it is Helen longing for her brothers, already immortal;
the hunting owls above them live on darkness
dive into the roots of blood contending.

I listened at the edge of the anti-clockwise sea,
staring into the eyes of the serene empire
the outposts are closed, the captains all gone home,
with Taygetos, the barrier, at my back
sending down green terraces in waves.

The maqams of my brother's music
slide and return on the water, sing amanes at the sky,
and if the rocks follow along the shore to the south,
shatter and explode in the mouth of hell below Tainaron,
then the whole world goes down with them.

Away in the dark Leuktra is awake tonight,
free city of a walking kingdom;
Ino speaks in dreams in a garden above the sea
making a pathway of living things,
so that Pephnos rises and Malovos of the shadows appears.

Over the calm, clear shining water

Over the calm, clear shining water
with smiling face there came to them the longing
for a bench in a ship to scar the sea,
assaulting the divine.

I am a straight black line, black as the cypress,
tending my relations above the harbour;
soon the ground will open up for the last one,
and I will join them in this earthy gallery.

The radio voices, the cicada telecom, sweep over me,
they mean nothing, I am a black line from the sky;
my son went to the new world, the America
– there will always be men with ambition leaving.

What I don't do won't ever be done,
the shadow of the Far Away One falls on us all;
if my son in the west thinks differently
may the earth rest lightly on him.

I listen to the secret conversation of things,
the village chorus and sea-polished stone
in the light of the pomegranate and fig,
if the bones are white then he is free.

*

Behind Yorgos' gate the sea casts white words
filling our mouths, making us say whatever we think;
all summer long we roll and shout and fall,
go down as the body of water takes a deep breath
and the world comes crashing in wave by wave.

Washed up, abandoned on all fours, shining
in the attitudes of delight, despair, of knowing nothing,
we stand with all the creatures the dark earth feeds;
where transparent altars collapse drink cool air,
the submarine foothills and rivers say welcome.

Open your arms, let Pephnos go, those figs, that life at sea;
Helen's black ship is a shadow passing over you,
the sun, a golden hand trailing in the water,
signals come, follow to the further shore;
and in its wake you swoon and spit and fall.

*

When my brothers stood in the upper world
on that rock with their hands raised,
for all my life they looked like statues.

When my brothers stood in the upper world
they promised safe passage and saved the drowned,
there was no stealth in them, just brave boys.

So when my brothers … where are they now?
they wanted nothing of me then
nor in this divinity the other side of Kythira.

Between here and Crete the murex fails
in a deep blue vertigo nations collapse,
there's no end of feeling.

They say the earth trembles still
and I dazzle the armies of the plain,
they walk on insurgent fire at noon.

What means they have for mineral wealth,
but one day the molluscs disappear
and the purple to decorate an empire is gone.

When I rise up into your minds I see
a fault runs around the world,
my brothers walked on water in mercy.

*

We go out into the world in the name of the first wave
breaking over the bow as it dips: blessing; baptism; ambition:
against the countries making conspiracy in their islands.

Call for the ships of Kardamyli and the fifty towns,
the earth opening its little red mouth, set back in the mind,
covered by logistics and the secret invasion of the sea.

For one moment there's no sound on the water,
the roads closed, the electricity cut, and between two bodies
light picks its way down the mountain.

We follow the head of a bird, rising and falling eastward,
sail into the heart of rage and fix our hold upon the lands
as far as the circuit of the earth for the bright pathfinder to guide us.

Inland of the shadowed coast, in the kingdom of rivers,
locked in the contracts of the world below the world
sings the geology of great wealth, starry sex and the life of ease.

Those of us who crossed the border; our seed is not.
Those who sailed into fire; our ships and goods are fallen.
Those who turned back; we don't even say the name of the place.

*

At the slow colouration of the world
milky dawn transposes blue
and the acacia is a net of light
thrown to catch the great iconoclast.

The wall of mountain casts off shadow,
on the opposite arms of the harbour
the chapel and Christeas's tower
stand as blown powers benign.

Where he sets his foot
the music of many drums begins,
the sound's in Thalami I think
no more than girls playing.

Leukothia, steady my sight,
let me align the arms of the harbour
and fix the point in mid blue
where all nonsense is washed away.

In that telescopic ellipse
swim all the living things,
our quick lives coming and going
in the unpeopled cities of stone.

It is light, morning light
comes walking through the village,
out of the folds of the mountain
into the folds of the sea.

Roger Hilton's Sugar

Setting Out

I slip down the road under sea light falling
slam into the giant red women,
ripping green split on both sides
through electric spring wet with flame
to St Ives, the secret island, to find the Hilton.

I sailed a painted boat fit for a boy
against the whole white and crashing world
– darling Bo, thank God you were born,
when I was boy there were horses in the field
and I rode in a cart to cart me off in.

My parents alive, I'm holding on, no hands
as I drift off into the anaesthetised sky.
What's the river doing around the boundary?
I can see you both outside our house,
your faces looking up like white words.

On the secret island, in the middle sea,
two figures dance on the Cape of No Hope,
Hilton sets out, feet first, on the bed of last days,
– the fun is over, what else have I got?
Miraculous pictures leap from his hands.

The Language of Art Critics

My discontinuous line is sexual, intimate, savage,
your fantastic anatomy my vehicle;
this is what they say – beast, charming I'm sure,
show the whole world, why don't you?

As is your life, so is your line,
a fragment made abstract and broadcast;
the human sensation we die for;
my nudes and other animals dancing.

My horses, carts, boats and flowers
such earthly bodies in motion overlap,
run into one another the quick sensation
behind the big secret behind all thought.

Bow down you Greeks, you ghosts;
I am on the last run, with no feeling in my feet.

The Hilton Biography — A Selection

I am lying under a bus in St. Just
– who wants this fucking medal?
It's a curse on me for staleness,
I could use this gravel, textured to my face,
fairer far than palace walls.

I am drinking 300 bottles of life p.a.
and to hell with my perambulation to the pub,
where my nerve endings end I don't go,
in the dim light creeping under the beast's gate
these painted glyphs are mocking me.

I am writing a list of things for you to get,
so get them – the good paint (will gouache fade?)
that Italian bread from Soho, the garlic and good broccoli,
and a decent pen, one that fucking writes.
Forgive me, I am a shit. It is all my fault.

I am making these quick pictures
to keep my family when I am not,
a water soluble inheritance,
to clap their little hands in the breeze
when I am launched into nothing.

I am freezing in this sodding plane,
seven hours to Antibes, freezing for some sunshine,
for the little circus and the afternoon sea;
at last at last, they'll wheel me up and down
and I'll see the god come raging from the water.

The Hilton Catalogue — A Selection

Chaise Longue 1964
gouache, charcoal and coloured chalks.
A small naked woman
dives into the blue pool
chaise longue for you to sit upon,
the water is a naked woman
already for you to swim in.

*

Big Girl 1972
pencil and crayon.
From Big Girl Valley
massive curling breasts,
ohh on her little mouth,
secret dark heart
for you to swim in.

*

Sunbather 1974
gouache and pencil.
Antibes? Yellow woman
white breasts
lolling on the sea
of a yacht
her thighs harbour me
Ahoy Captain Rope.

*

Gouache, card, pastel on paper 1974.
She is looking at me

pink and red and blue,
my friend the snake
above her head.
Her nipple is red
by the rail for pots of flowers,
my Eden, my charmer
– open your mouth.

*

Gouache and charcoal on paper 1974.
White naked bird woman
behind the grassy bank
or sea meadow, populated
by small leggy horses
of orange yellow breed:
we are out of our
paddocks now by God.

*

Gouache, charcoal and pastel 1974.
Is the lizard king
in barbwire jungle
and all the birds of
Cornwall sing,
these buds and leaves
grow out of my body
like girls in Spring
we go down into
the fibrous earth
to return above ground.
If you see the King of Botallack
tell him that all the boys
are thinking of him.

*

Gouache and pastel on paper 1974.
All the exploding
flowers of the world
boomed in one mind,
we are shape colour
looky – how can you resist?
Oh my purple girl.

*

Gouache on paper 1973.
Two in the cart no
horse power pulling
little dog jumpy
rides over
the burning bush,
giddy up into
the dark country.

*

Gouache and charcoal on paper 1974.
Away on the racing green boat
my sea snakes below me
the waves lilt a jaunty angle.
I'm away boys out
into the big oblivion
alone with three clouds grey.
I will leave you the song
of the blue spotted snake
as I lean into the yawn
of the mighty sea calling.

*

Gouache and charcoal on paper 1974.
My red girl locked away from me,
the sex mountains her home
rise over our luxury bed,
our green firework forest
fizzing across the sky.
If I could ride the strong aeroplane,
propel me to her through
all the house descending,
my red girl steps forward to me.

*

Gouache and charcoal on paper 1974.
My name lost
underwritten
no code to read
lost down the lane boy.

*

Gouache and ink on paper 1974.
The room a forest
of shining transepts
around the big cock centrepiece.
Shy creatures peep
smooth branches wave
the organic dance.
Snap Snap Mr Cock
supine for sport
in a chamber of the forest.

*

Gouache on paper 1973.
Written across
an angelic field
of lights
– Fuck you
 Where's my
    Suger?
Here it is.

Radio Hilton

The radio that told me about the death of Roger Hilton
was a thousand mile frontier closed down
was nothing left worth looking at
was torture gardens and out of town shopping
was a ghost economy tuned to my heart
was an empty seabed
was a hop skip and jump out of my painting hands
was all the animals falling down
was the work of art itself.

The radio that told me
was an instrument of truth
was the rod and the staff
and the walk we took by the river.
Shall we bathe again in that blue lick
snaking through the valley of pictures
shall we bathe again
in the waterfall of miraculous bodies
in the valley of all the pictures?

Seeing Hilton

1
Nothing can replace the long, steady gaze,
face to face with the picture.

Swindon Art Gallery and Museum.
Well we'll be closed until 6 March,
for reorganisation, and then yes, I think,
our picture by Roger Hilton will be on show.

The Tate.
I went to the wrong branch,
freezing wind off the river.
No picture, just a postcard of Oi Yoi Yoi.

Bath Victoria Gallery.
Answer machine.
One picture. One question.
No answer.

Nothing can replace the long, steady gaze.

2
Through warm rain and dense traffic
down the southern slope, petrol war stalemate
thickens the Friday night call to air,
to arrive at the moment of seeing – mappa mundi.

1953, oil, neo-plastic work
flat colour from Mondrian daddy,
piling up the words my mind in stripes
of blue of white red white.

Tilting off the edge of England
I'm standing here in the gallery,
all proportion thrown overboard
I see you wave the flag of a new country.

It's 1953, one light floods the dark room
and outside the Atlantic dynamo firing.

3
My cover girl, middle name Matisse,
your anonymous face lifting out of nowhere
has me talking to the wall.

And what is the emotion doing outside?
Snow falling, oh the cold drift towards election
in the western world turning.

Where are you from? Passport? How did you get here?
Archetype, it says. Where's that then?
Floating up from The Levant? The Cyclades?

Head held up, left hand touching the sky
in the storm of stupid questions
the fantastic anatomy falls upon me.

A great passivity settles on the world,
beauty is not difficult, it's as easy as a new earth
rising into view your arms and legs harbour me.

4
Holding the day more firm in unbelief
the sky empties itself on the streets and fields;

I won't travel, snow falling on the frigid circuit,
abstract but suggestive of a figure, a giant.

The country shrinks, clamped down on itself
by the dirty rush to flatter the voting servants;
remote, rigid and slick,
the light thickens and could get arrested.

I won't walk in the capital today,
not even for one painting by Roger Hilton;
I won't emerge from underground near Westminster,
the air full of the sound of reason asleep.

Vision gathers under the frozen bridges,
the picture's far from clear, it's February 1954,
the vertical lines and square shapes
must give way to irregular, expressive forms.

I am only thinking of the journey I did not take.
I am only thinking of the nation that was not made.
I am thinking of the genius of Hilton's painting,
like a brand to stick in the eye of the state.

5
To Swindon on the chuffer train,
milky fog lies in the valleys
clearing slowly for Spring to rise.

I am looking for one picture,
the network firing messages around the cart
and the trees wanting to be green.

This is a ticketless journey,
November 1955, oil on canvas, 44x34;
I should have phoned ahead.

A voice from the store – I can't get it.
It's very black and white and big,
you should come back next year.

A tall Ben Nicholson saved me
like a window into elsewhere,
a composition in lit stone

Left my eyes unencumbered,
and the bowls by Lucie Rie
and almost Cretan pots made me thirsty.

But no Hilton, November 1955,
– I am back on very sober things,
austere to the point of extinction.

Sunk without trace in earth,
rough forms surround a yellow door
poised with calligraphic lines.

The network firing for Spring's revolt.

6
I've walked into this box of summer
and I'm here in the Glynn Vivian telling you,
coastal breath breathing in the circuits of the town
all along Wind Street to Botallack.

Two pictures, six paces and ten years apart,
from the organic forms of a new landscape in '64
you sailed off in two jolly brown boats
into your signal colour and fat red, blue, black.

Reinvent figuration, find something to paint about,
let the white thighed giant dream of heaven;
there's a red wheel to sail by and a red handbag
to keep my ambidextrous hands in.

Roger the green fields, I saw you in the river,
the thermal camera dance, body over body over body,
each imperfect fit, a facsimile of layered truth;
you were pouring water on the sorrows of the world.

The St. Ives Section

The flat screen television of the sea is on
this morning, I think the whole town is
launched at a tilt into the water.

The dead and the living unhoused
founder in the fizzing interference
of not knowing the picture, how composed.

With no recollection of the hovering sky
we're all on the seaslide, what remains is
to tidy up the mess with a few strokes.

*

The revised plan for the Hilton dwelling
will enlarge his lordship's domain;
first we must let in all the plants and animals,
invade the transparent menagerie passage.

But the keening boats and birds won't do it,
not even the limby women and snakes
with their cats and secret harbours;
he will have to jump out of his skin.

*

In the gallery of 18 pictures my delight,
on rough white board the black boat
in a black frame sails on a dark sea.

The figure in the water sees the mast like a cross,
shouts inside an ochre circle making an O,
afloat up to his neck, painted and abandoned.

My boat is framed by an arch or cave,
the bleak mouth edged in thin cerise
says everything about departure.

Away on the horizon, bisected by the mast,
it might be land, an island or promontory
low on the water, a peak made red by the sun.

*

the spiky tree of big fat amber blossoms
leans out into the harbour where two boats make ready

the sun is written over with the ideogram of a lost language
or a black cockerel, chest out, facing the day

leave now in the red boat, leave now in the black boat
on the first morning spread out under the tree of life

*

We're all on the seaslide to a new figuration,
last light at the window, across the moor awash
the sea, a thought of my left hand, my right hand;
red dog grin, charcoal corpse and woman akimbo
all ready and waiting in the cart together,
last light on the February walls, on nine pictures dancing.

From Botallack Out

1

Where Hilton wakes restored
in the small acrylic fields of
fabulous women and dancing horses;
Celtic meadows, nocturnal and compact,
tip over the edge of the world
to raise a rampart of dreams
out into the Atlantic morning,
a white line under the door
he walks towards grinning.

For the pleasures of boats on the sea,
of returned desire, of animal breathing,
of abstract animate forms entangled
pouring through the windows,
jump up red dog, jump up:
what else have you got to do?
Your master's scraps fly from the table,
run in the blood of the living,
splash over the loving face.

The tone too is arranged by plan,
plains and contours, the simple colours
of the people's of the sea singing,
who will not let me sleep
rocking the sea all night long;
they ooh and ahh my secret acrobatics
as I cartwheel on the canvas of despair;
at different depths the light changes
aqua, marine, ultra and the green gods.

2

Q1
Is the text of your painting perception itself, so that we see the work of the mind only in the act of painting?

A1
I thought when I was dead
I would not have to explain anything;
green branches shoot from my wrists
instruments of truth or nothing.
Horses caper at my back,
the tide of neuritis rises at night
cold and black licking at the gate:
text? text of what? paint?

Q2
Is it the layer of living things, through which other people and things are first given to us?

A2
Layer of living things, that's good,
up to my elbows in that, paint,
bloody neck more like, Christ,
cat milk spilt bastard fridge broken.
My love the radio's on the blink,
will she ever tune to me again?
The signal's not clear, do nothing,
that record with Caruso singing.
I'm shipped up, skin flaking off
float me away in bloody bedroom,
the hidden life made apparent
free as painting the air blue, red,
vitamin B injections useless
first person lost down the lane boy I.

Q3
Are you conscious of the body as the unperceived term in the centre towards which objects turn?

A3
No getting away from it is there,
especially when it rots raw umber,
nor pens that don't work, empty bottles,
Ronseal awash in the whisky ditch at 3.30 a.m.
fucking objects bite back all the time,
garlic, spinach, blue lake acrylic.
I saw the ghost body under the boat
at one with the waves, the fatal current
all my life, that face emerging:
it's all my fault, I am a shit.
The medicine's a vicious circle,
I sailed around the cirkle islands
swapped pretty boy warbling
for Lord of All Things Moist,
ivy wrapped my every limb afloat.
I bear the young tree sprouting
in my craft or sullen barque,
good dog Spot
              got through another night.

Q4
So, in the sense that all thought is thought about something…?

A4
Afterthought I am, I found something
to paint about
writing The Night Letters the
for enjoyment, only for
something to do between pictures,
my figures come breaking out

light will break for another
creation and haddock breakfast
from Botallack out, my figures
left on the table for your edification

3

We came in after a swim,
the rain didn't fall and the sky
rose again into depthless blue,
Taygetos refocused and the temperature
climbed the bronze terraces for summer.

Inside I set up my Hilton gallery,
ripped open an A4 cardboard envelope
stuck three colour printer copies on it
and propped it on the chair,
Oi Yoi Yoi, two boats in the harbour

A third, late gouache, half abstraction,
a brown eyed sun top left and
two blue figures dancing by the ochre band;
I think it's jungle music,
I think it's jig-a-jig time.

Sealight across the square lifts
at the window, the heavy perfume
of white stephanotis butters the air;
each picture is a revelation
surrounded by torn cardboard.

What they say is unbearable,
beauty burning through our veins;
we wrapped it up for years,

the life that isn't life, a proxy framework,
full of holes and useless.

Look: rip open the envelope,
they spill out, splash and shout,
women and gods and boats
go charging around the house,
– Oi Yoi Yoi, there's a fire.

It snakes under the skin,
sways Arcadia and lifts the tide,
sends birds with messages tree to tree
singing all the names of fire
from the back of Hilton's cart.

The Unpainted Hiltons

You see I am surrounded by these things
a medium like breathing under water,
the Royal Bokhara, the pictures on the wall
I wave as I float by with transparent hands.

My wife's sexy dress hanging there
taken off like a season transformed,
and the organic food jumps into my mouth
as your warm arm falls across me.

The light from the floor landscapes your sleep
and those would be cabbage roses descending,
like red kisses on your perfect cunt
around the dim margin he is on his knees.

Then the great secret settles on everything,
you're sleeping and I launch out into darkness;
ivy pours into the courtyard, I'm half drowned,
face emerging in Spring – Dionysus.

*

Even the island I speak from is painted by Hilton,
to the rhythm of dropped seeds into instant oleander
and open mouthed cats into swaying boughs;
the riot of ants know the plan
and blue drips from the mighty swimmer.

Interior darkness dissolves in the air
and perfect weather wraps us bodies;
hand in hand like nerve ending sex
my eyes have seen the glory
riding in on a big clam shell.

Let the breeze stir and sing,
lift the shirt off the girl with ample breasts
and cool the hairy god slumped in the breakers;
the two-master is trim, we're ready to leave,
the white circuit snaps and ignites.

The all-sea shines lit from below,
children's voices scud across the bay
quick ripples enskied in acrylic;
– will you wait for me there?
on the shore of the morning world.

*

I think of the fields at night,
the compact Celtic geometry
laid over with darkness
and the black sea rising.

The Gulf of Sleep invades my room,
waves rise with each breath
drowning thought under the door,
go down you beasts, you bastards.

In the compass of the sea
I am abandoned, absolute,
but let me keep the way
of talking to my children.

The lights on the other side
shine out clear and bright,
my boat is one word sent
in the language of my painted hands.

The shape of morning rises,
white ribbons of light
unravel across the sliding waves,
momentary chart of all the sea lanes of the world.

        *

If this window opens on the world of free running senses;
your filthy mind in the cart pulled by my bonny horse
– see she prances, treading the liquefied air
falling like amber on us sorry bodies,
so that our limbs are restored, magically proportioned,
and we lie and roll and walk in one another,
the anthropometric secret in our hands at last
as easy as talk floats out of the bedroom door
across the evening laid out in this land of good weather;
the game is up – and if the window doesn't etc the game is up:
we must settle for the living creatures we have about us,
and that would be the Hilton in this earthly paradise
awake in a sea of trees breathing underground,
ambidextrous, prolific and grinning.

        *

Melanie I want to say in plain words
how at night when you're sleeping
and I come to bed and you fold into me,
my hands resting on your breasts
drift into the lovely south of your belly.

I see in the dark, my hands painted your colour,
and it's too late or early and I'm awake
with work sliding down the chute
and there's no sound abroad, nothing;
only my mind full of you sleeping.

My love, stir and fold into me again,
turn over to me your naked self;
let me taste your swimming body,
catch you again in the great waterfall.
How on earth did I find you?

Out on the circuits of stupid chance,
along the burnt-out motorways of nowhere,
in public buildings dressed in a suit;
there you're saying – What did you dream about?
My mouth hanging open in a new world.

*

Yellow slabs of light rest between the houses
and the names of streets are lost this morning;
earth colours flatten out, it could be winter.
I'm in the pathless dark with the spooks
doing the low drift over the smoky roofs.

The whole thing shrinks to a few acrylic strokes,
congealed and pulsing momentary scribble
to make the world again,
what was barren adorned
what was fallow the green riot.

The cat saunters along the tower wall,
over the birdless branches
she carries the piled up sky on her back,
through a blue gap time is sliding away
and the Hilton sea shouts Roll Up Roll Up.

*

All night the sea broadcasts white rage,
the radio plays dumb, drowned in the pelting air,
and I launch the box on the bobbing waves
– inside my wife, my children, my home.

My hope is all enclosed in that thought,
there's nothing to be done in tearing space;
foxes and magpies on the roof sharpen their knives,
there's nothing personal about it, just their nature.

It's the ancient world calling, are you receiving me?
High in the wind an aria is sounding,
my mouth is empty, my hands are claws;
come back come back, my heart answers like a beacon.

It's the ancient world calling – over.
Her hair streams back like rain,
flying fish and plastic bottles dance in strings of light
and marble giants rise from their alluvial bed.

*

The sky over the mountains in layers
steps down to the surrounding sea;
black lines drawn over the surface
rope it in, let it go, abstract picture facing.

My eyes are open forever on this,
I see the boats coming and going,
time in their wake pours in and out
and the light tilts westward.

I keep watch on the waking world,
the morning call to air sounds

and the shortwave towers turn,
centre the static band of knowing.

Each grove, each bank and field
erects a column of bird song,
lifting a thousand notes into the air
rising and falling in apparent chaos.

The birds singing make the sun rise
and figures released emerge again;
the woman walking to the first house,
limbs proved in earth, kinetic.

Sing birds sing, tune up the day,
blow the wild flowers electric leaping
along the roads of Spring's republic
where she sets her foot this way.

*

Stick it in your pipe, said the Hilton
and the moment is expansive and English;
a potential life, a deep breath taken
rising from the 1950s, a fresh wind over the fields;
let me walk you around the animal town.

We are winning, so stick it in your pipe;
smell the sea in the air, we could live like this
unaccounted for in serious clothes,
the light in waves making the hidden form apparent
shapes the dark door in the burning wall.

So we escaped to Antibes, a new world,
and the work flowed in beats;
we ate the good bread in the white mornings,

saw the days sail by like painted boats
at a jaunty angle in a square of painted blue.

Each day was a gem in the anatomy of the sea,
each facet of the red flowers, the free woman,
the dog, the horse and the black scribble of my love;
and on that ripe, round occasion
Captain Bottle saw the truth and jumped ship.

And with my right hand and my left hand
I made the picture of it all.

Alexiares

My Journey to Euripides

Because I knew my Euripides I survived the Latomiae,
I was of the 4,000 of the quarries;
we saw the ships go down, the sea burning
and the passes of the fertile plain blocked.

Those who did not die were sold as slaves
– somewhere to the south? I don't know;
others, like me, a few, climbed out on poetry,
the Syracusans like poetry.

But they did not see, on my inner arm,
the tattooed ivy, immortal imprint
of the immigrant stranger, lord of many names,
they did not see I was of the god of all blossoming things.

In the pit I remembered the spring when I was a boy;
in my village we observed the rites,
the year I was chosen, both parents alive,
the procession of all of us made the round.

> We walked with the year, the season
> of trees alive and the rocks moving,
> rumours took on flesh in the mountains
> and at night on the water light sang.
>
> I remember Hermes gave me moly
> that I might resist her,
> white flower, black root
> that I might have her.

       We ran to the high meadows
       out of the arms of the leaping god,
       the wet earth his chamber
       spring tripping in our wake.

After I had recited my way out of the pit,
I went aboard a merchant ship across the Ionian;
I swam with the low life of small fishes and other fauna,
driven by brigandage and buggery mostly.

You can spend days staring at the surface of the sea,
the gulls wingtip acrobatics, feed me feed me,
the occasional blue fin and the confused bee
– staring in fact at the glossy reflection of nothing.

It has meaning in a lost language of sound
sliding across the water and familiar harbours;
smoke drifted over the ruined villages
and starving fishermen threw dog shit at us.

By slow stages and different ships I went south;
all along the Peloponnese the same story,
a war economy with the wheels coming off
and rumours of the big crisis to end the world.

A storm wrecked us into the Messenian Gulf,
we came into the first harbour still open;
Helen's brothers stood on the rock called Pephnos
and on the water I heard the songs for Leukothia.

The village was empty of people
and I knew they would be out in the fields
at the ceremony of return and uprising,
the greater journey of the earth.

We cooked the pots of all the seeds,
the white poppy, barley, pulse and lentils
but not for human food
nor for the strengthless heads of the dead.

But for the earth people, to take down with them
for the unimagined harvest,
carried to all our weddings
when the fields rise up and each root blossoms.

We don't eat abstractions,
we burn pigs, snakes and fir cones
in a blackened hole to make the earth part,
for the unimagined harvest.

I went south in the oven of summer
around the bare finger of land for Matapan,
those days the sea filled my mind
and Laconia filled my mouth.

The submarine cave into hell was crowded,
victims of a precept blown half way across the world;
poor souls – no ghost of mallow, asphodel or orchid
flowered in the burnt dust under their feet.

And further east I arrived at Trozen
to hear the white women singing all night,
love wanders in the high meadows
in every atom of the swollen sea.

I kept Euripides before me and made for Attica;
they said Athena was lost,
all argument over and the squares empty;
incarnate city of the mind left to slow rot and irrelevance.

I remembered Pericles's speeches,
their perfect syntax cut from marble
singing over our heads in the market place,
we repeat them even as we fall.

Those monuments of the air,
made from what is sweet and what is terrible,
drove us on to meet what came
– by then I'd had my fill of both.

Later, when Spartans planned to raze the lot,
with Euripides silent in final exile,
one voice rose to sing his words
and no hand was lifted against Athena.

Well, my soul was pastured there too;
unscorched by invasion, in the glories of knowledge,
my journey became a perfect map of itself
and I walked in two worlds with each step.

I had been north through the Vale of Tempi,
mountains piled up, wall upon wall of snow
polished by the sun, serrating the world,
the passes gone over to a sort of blindness.

Did everything turn to a whiteness in the end?
Even the turquoise sea in a white rage
lifted each wave into a booming nothing
and the levelled plain was not the floor of heaven.

I found him at the court in Macedon,
I was not the first to make the journey;
in the bowl of the mountains, at the end of reason
the great mind near empty.

He looked like bones collapsed, half blind,
fit for the dogs or whatever ceremony was there;
his breath like a bird passing
made one note in the frozen sky.

I am Alexiares of the Latomiae,
I stood where Athens overreached itself
and landed in a hole, 4,000 at my shoulder;
I stand opposed, above ground in the air.

I repeated each word, each strophe
lifting me out of the pit,
out of the dumb quarry into the light;
and the seas and islands echoed him.

> I am Dionysus, lord of many names,
> of the bull, the snake, the lion
> mixing all forms of life;
> I glide over the pit.

> The city is drowned in ivy,
> I will give you what you want
> and the streets and precincts catch light.
> Is it dawn rising, my fresh girl?

> I am Dionysus, I call in my own
> from the fields of Lydia and Phrygia;
> when the cup is empty, even to the shadow,
> I am manifest, the empire of confidence.

Odes of Alexiares

1
The thing is Imperator, you don't rage in the Capital
nor in the tents of the enemy but sip nectar with empurpled lips,
and your ministers dance around a mound of dirt
moulded in the likeness of Leo Strauss.

So thought stalks Babylon along unmade roads
and ignites a village of unknown women;
you can smell it seep into the circuit of mineral rivalry,
you can see it inflate a mighty god of swords.

The style of the project here is cinder block houses,
and with the order sent we have to finish the job;
misinterpretation razes another town on the bloody edge,
it flickers then evaporates in the western syntax.

The thing is Imperator, you open your mouth of lethal zero
and in another country the sky is sucked down a roaring tunnel.

2
'Accept our offer of a carpet of gold or we bury you
under a carpet of bombs.' And before the snows fall etc.

Negotiation whispers down the pipeline, Pax Americana,
pronounced regime change one bright morning.

Pronounced the Caspian region is the key,
the Bridas bid ended with the assassination of Masood.

Before the snows fall etc, one bright September morning etc.

3
I know that my speaking to you is as pointless as raising my hand to a hurricane; listening as if to speak words to the circling sky of full spectrum dominance. Call things what they are; you never swung out into theory neutral space but had them read 2.5 million pages, covering the trail to that day.

On that morning was the fire a thousand degrees short of what it takes to burn a steel framed building? Was the steel sold off to China and Korea as scrap before forensics got a look in? How quiet are the answers? As quiet as a flight for Saudis in a total flight ban? And the captain went a singing through the fields of bright flame, 'Go massive. Sweep it all up. Things related and not.'

4
I would have you study these Hazara war rugs,
though they are not easy to read the images speak,
handmade and stained with vegetable dyes.
The Taliban murdered the Hazara, village by village,
late converts to Islam, with good faces from the Mongols.

Can carpet design convey irony?
The bold colours and childlike shapes
of B52s, stinger missiles and tanks
in the style of first generation video games,
would make the rug fit a boy's bedroom.

Stick men jump from the towers,
first and second impact are marked;
the noses of the aeroplanes disintegrate
and at the foot of the scene
an aircraft carrier floats off, as if distracted.

Across the middle of the towers
a dove flies uniting the flags

of America and Afghanistan;
most of the words remain unreadable
– THE TEARURS WAR IN THE AMEIRCAN

Here, Imperator, you can see,
the sky sucked down a roaring tower
and the words remain unreadable;
the border of abstract flowers is carefully executed,
soft cream and sage green on a band of dull red.

Interview

Q. How did you get here?

At night from 36,000 feet fire
rages in the bowl of the mountains
a thunderstorm caught lightning
ignited again and again my god
I've heard the pine trees explode
on the smoking hills and cowered.

Q. What are you doing here?

When Roza Eskenazi sings
I fall under that wave.
How's it going Roza my child?
Amanes, I sing and spit and swoon.
She will strip your heart
cleaner than the sea.

Q. Do you want to leave?

Leave this screen of Tamarind and Eucalyptus
surrounding our aerial garden?
The limby green layer of living things
breathes on us painted out ghosts,
by morning the white frame made empty
and the day pauses in mountain air around us.

Alexiares in Exile

1

After the last journey I began another,
though not exactly Ithaka, despite Cavafy;
I opened my instructions in a different country,
sailing blind in the sea lanes of Morse code.

The sun strikes the tower, a massive gnomon;
time is nothing here, over and out
the land running south in blue layers,
the villagers call it a promontory of song.

It rises as a sort of Egypt of now and then,
a land bridge of animals and plants
for Martin Bernal to dance across
so that imports follow in strict measure.

An early naturalism, alive and immediate,
the African Blue Lily or Agapanthus,
your name in a burning circle on the ground:
work it out by next dispatch.

2

Again last night the sun died red into the sea,
this is hardly news I know but the sky caps the black
and my mind is elsewhere over the singing water;
engine of the world, ace of ambition, floored me.

Thalassa Mavri they sing, well they might – Greeks;
I am in exile between textual variants,

head down in darkness dancing out such poems
would make the emperor of goats weep.

Here I barely stick to the rim of the world,
a brown river and a thin wall against the hoards,
they come screaming off the frigid steppes;
it is a strange form of exegesis I suffer.

On the sea's bend sinister stands the bridgehead,
I hide behind the wall, holding a stick, shaking;
Athena – come, love me again, give me one more chance,
not this brightness pissed into a marsh under a black sky.

3

What am I doing here? How do I know?
I was sent out into this condition
with no secret gate east or west,
this is Tomis, Samos, London transit camp.

My body's made invisible to me,
a shape inside a shape of nothingness;
I float on my neighbour's language,
it leaves me undisturbed, untroubled.

They seem well disposed and incomprehensible;
the other morning they were up early,
before the sea had taken its colour
and went off singing in the woods.

Later, bread appeared on my window ledge,
it was cinnamon bread, I ate if for breakfast;
I am not speaking truth to power,
I watch the sparrows peck about the broken wall.

4

At night the sea piles up its sound,
no one will sail against this wall of water
and the mind falters, sliding off the wind
over the boats abandoned in the harbour.

Smoke thickens and songs by Xylouris go round,
– at one time all these songs were banned;
the little red tanks of the eager insurgents
arrive in waves, their eyes like heavenly spheres.

Will we survive the brilliant strategy?
security calculated in ships which sink;
they say the logos was constant in Athens,
all aliens thick-tongued barbarians: what nerve.

I held the idea of an island suspended
in the deep sea between three continents;
and this song can make you drunk,
just listen and you will be big time intoxicated.

5

When I walk through the streets of mud,
between the wooden palisades and nephos,
garish billboards cover the sky
sending the dumb dumb message mainstream.

I walk out of their dream, the war on abstract nouns,
and see we have fallen into the hands of thieves,
the barbarians who need barbarians
to make the bloody business spin.

After the blast I witnessed illumination;
the family photographs tattered but untouched,
poor souls they flew away at last
but nothing will replace the absence of your face.

A massive darkness sits on my shoulder,
I float in the broken signal of the shortwave;
all night the black sea spits out our first language
and the streets falter in earthy tracts.

6

I found co-ordinates to prehistoric creatures
lying frozen in rockpools, the first cuneiform;
a music like letters in polished scales
lifting up from the earth every spring.

I found the uncovered mosaic on the cape,
a ditch, a temple, a chapel and god
the model worked – but if the ground gives way
no bloody aroko of the Rebus tribe will save you.

Nor does the meaning of the sky vary
– trail of stars, boom: trail of stars, stop:
those who sent me don't see the indifference,
how perfect syntax dismantled Ilium.

And god the beautiful trees of the mountain
in banks and hills go rising up,
like promised countries around the world
the beautiful trees opened their arms.

7

Rain has released the smell of wild garlic
and splashed blue cyclamen across the path;
mosaic of light on the insect-laden air
bears the unfinished music of the small gods passing.

In darkness the outboard of the fishing boat
binds the edge of a black sea blanket
and marine white noise floods the frontiers of the world,
the work songs of the faithful at the final catch.

In these lost villages of the terraced mountains
the most complex ladders to the stars
were made by Ottoman musicians,
masters of the clarino, the sisters of amanes.

And all night I hear them shape from the air
the heavenly body of our starry queen,
they open a door in the endless sky
with Apollo's bees dancing attendance.

8

The sun strikes the tower, a massive gnomon,
time is nothing here, over and out;
on the collapsed ramparts of the golden west
they have lost the power of naming.

What am I doing here? I don't know.
My neighbours sing – the black wall of the far one
leans over us closely tonight – I would not surrender
one moment of happiness to explain this to you.

It looks like Apollo, the whole singing world,
laid out across the grey slab,
but there's no end of feeling in the sky
and the lights of home are like poured honey.

The wind is looking to blow the village flat
and the sea boils in a white rage at the harbour wall,
a child in a wedding dress over her jeans and trainers
flits from door to door like a bird.

From Alexiares's Separate Notebooks

Three village children walked into the courtyard last night,
they stood in a line singing and ringing triangles
– may St. Basil bless you, a long life on your house;
this was for new year's eve and a reward of sweets.

The boy Apollo, both parents alive, would lead the children
in our procession of the spring, they would strike the door and sing
– all time is blossoming, green stick, dry stick, young shoot sprout,
strike the door and anyone in the path of the risen year.

I heard triangles ringing across the whole country,
an Orthodox suite for a thousand manic bell towers;
may there be a long life for your house the air chimes,
teach us your alphabet St. Basil, the voices rising call.

*

At night on the corner of the post office
Hermes of the underworld takes flight,
his jet steam curls and sense of purpose
alights on the thin faced Albanian boys.

The 15 Euros a day labourers smoke and commune,
they ride in the back of early morning pickups
straight backed carrying a remittance economy,
experts at shaping stone for traditional houses.

Vagelis told us, in Albania, once ago it was ok,
I had a home by the sea, a big house;
the rich countries suck in the poor across the world,
15 Euros would be for something skilled, like tiling.

The boys saunter in this easy darkness
and the village kids play slow-mo football,
a balloon floating over the collective heads;
the whole scene swims in sweet air like honey.

*

Fat leaved ivy pours over the broken wall
down the sides of the Taygetos
splitting the rocks of the terraces.

I stuck my head inside the box of spring,
sweet song of flowers, frogs and birds
rising up from the green in one breath.

The day comes calling out of the blue,
on the salt pans and rockpools
the sea drops a whole synod of little gods.

*

What did Ovid do all day,
smell the harbour, count his syllables,
see the black sea light soak the wall
mapping the edge of utter darkness
and curse the frost on the face of Augustus?

I pile the white stones in the corners
for their click, the beautiful painted bodies
of the men and women who take their shapes
from the shapes of the olive groves, smoke rising
over the blue hills of the earth turning.

I follow Europa and her bull in the wet meadow,
they vanished in the spray zone's magnetic air

beaded with every singing world;
she holds on, mouth open, I don't know,
his smile lights up another country.

*

I've not written a word to you for weeks;
the Spring weather is gentle, the air like balm
has made my mind candid and I can't bear to be inside.

So I sleep and eat and fuck like a little god,
the sea shush shushing us land children
out along the shore running to the end of the world.

The village wakes to dog-barking dawn and
all the birds practise their scales in Greek,
I can feel the earth tilting into first light.

I dreamt the music of how the night comes
in the lemon groves and orange groves of the Argolid
and walked the rising hills to the village of lights

Towards a mask of gold, behind which there's no darkness,
only the dreaming air sweet as mountain honey;
here it comes, here comes the night, the Beautiful Door opening.

*

I have not told you enough about last night in the Albanian taverna
where the wine is deep and takes you down with it;
these boys in their red nylon jumpers and football shirts
– Sweden 1986, the poorest of the poor of Europe, Jesus
their ringtones and house building for English and Germans;
in this absurd channel of the world market a Chinese girl
walking from village to village, now goes table to table

not selling plastic toys and watches to displaced peasants;
you almost imagine a country they've left at home.

They are gentle in their manners under the American film,
under the presence of men like Alec Baldwin actors;
heavy on the common air the atomized cash circulates
around the table where Ovid stares, writing letters Roma/Amor,
save me Augustus from these fucking barbarians;
– next time you come and dance in Albania;
the big screen blonde in a blonde bikini in blonde America
snaps the boy's eyes like magnets to attention,
then they return to their beer and smoke and courtesies.

Ritsos tips his head to the glide and wail of the clarino,
his hands hold that face in the mountain village,
rearranging the white stones of his risen nation;
an archipelago of men and women reaches across the Aegean.
Look Ritsos, off in the corner, the wrecked sailor stands,
Ithaka the birthmark in the crook of his left arm;
he wants to write the final chapter, straight as an arrow;
and then we can scatter the bloody pages of the Kanun
in the mouth of the harbour to feed the silver fishes.

– And next time you dance the deep wine in Albania,
the clarino rising over any mountains and valleys we have to hand,
its slide and figuration describes what land this is Illyria lady
and I am letting the little iambs out into the fields;
we do a Kaba, Berati say, and then step it up Koftos for a wedding,
– I thought it was from Epirus, yes yes is all the same music;
I am letting the little riot, wave the flaming napkin, then step
over the border, see, the generations in my feet, step
the frontiers disappearing dance, and step step.

*

Beyond all of this with morning just risen
a rumour in the mountain villages,
the white horse runs from his shadow.

Nostrils sharp as fluted marble,
the vaporous sun streams from his flanks,
muscles flicker in one wave.

Pulse beating on the chambered earth,
the white horse in the high meadow
runs over terraces of light.

Ulysses in the Car

Melanie, I'm in the dark car staring, where are you?
and the keys? The sky unlocked pours lament
along the cold slot where I wait at the foaming gutter;
enough of this place, the great divide is real.

The house is full of darkness, the wine we poured
unfit for breathing or the brimming crowd;
my mother transparent before me could not stand
without my help, now rises in that company.

Melanie where are you? Are you driving home
between the low warehouses and shamefaced politics
plotted across our country? Are you cutting a smart V?

I see your face suspended in the great, dark rush,
faint interior lights daisy below your gaze, ignite
the bright metallic splash as you open the door.

*

From the Holiday Inn Athens
by the blue neon bridge
the ancient sites have been tested
with earthquake simulation.

The temple of Zeus withstood 6.5,
its size and design triumphant;
the theatre of Dionysus unmoved
as if speaking truth to power.

At night the city is a bowl of light
offered up by the Penticlean Hills,
from the dark altar of the orchestra
the world will hear you whisper.

*

Pinter in a wheelchair
performs *Krapp's Last Tape*
not even on his last legs,
it is beyond drama.

The act will stand unlike
the adventures of Wolfowitz and Rumsfeld,
the fantasies of Leo Strauss
burning in the desert.

Aeschylus wrote *The Persians*
from the viewpoint of a defeated enemy
after fighting the battle of Marathon:
imagination alive imagine.

*

The investigation remains live
into the mind its own place to make,
westbound eastbound darkness into darkness
the circle line around the world.
Shall I meet you there before work?

The knights of monotheism wear
white T shirts, dark jackets and baseball caps;
they are happy, euphoric, it is the calling
I make du'a, the people I am singing to
– she is my sister, he is my brother.

The knights of monotheism, their good deeds,
riding the circle line, their good deeds;
a virtue free of forensic analysis,
the belief in mythology as fact
comes roaring out of the tunnel.

The investigation is the glamour of his lordship,
the siege of Jerusalem, his sumptuous gifts
for the continuation of the campaign,
the [army] [made an] at[tack]
from the [tem]ple I went out again[st] abomination.

Britons and non-Britons, Christians, Muslims,
those of other religions and none,
– Shall I wait for you before work?
comes roaring out of the tunnel,
the investigation is the singing of the dead.

*

Daunted by the five hour drive
we paused at the door of the day,
then with morning sped to the west
across Attica, the Argolid and Arcadia.

From the Holiday Inn Athens
we know the way forward,
by the villages that defeated Sparta
and the roadside shrines of lives saved.

The sky opens over the secret valleys,
the tractor towns and their satellites;
on the other side of the blue dome
a girl's voice, high and driven, sings.

*

Outside rain rains in this room
with only Pritchard for company,
vegetation luxuriates from the earth
[approximately 37 lines destroyed]

The poem speaks of endless war.

I seized the Lebanon entire
and cleaned my weapons in the deep sea;
you liberators will not have sweets and flowers,
there will be none: my name is mighty.

The people I sing to are dead.

You will hear my music in Mesopotamia,
beards and banjos, the Baptist sentiment
for fools to mouth in the public square,
see the river gods turning their backs.

I cut down stonepine, cypress, many nations,
the air thick with fragrant dust
settles on my men like a blessing,
like tributes of gold, boxwood and rich garments.

The Pax Augusta does not stand here
between the great green and the towns of mud,
Rome is far off, even the idea remote,
zealots gone west wiring faith.

For you caught on the border
the local palette will run to blood,
the markets fluctuate like genocide:
the people I am singing to are dead.

*

Lyric voices crowd the sea to sing his mind away,
from the secret meadow and heap of poet's bones
you see a life continue day by day on that green shore,
as if in the tradition of the music of the drowned.

What reason did for Spicer is locked in a box and sunk,
subject to 28 lbs psi, full fathom five approximately;
Coleridge is down there too, the surge in his veins
recalls the contours of the earthquake zone around Kythira.

How soft was the air when you wrote the music of the drowned?
Is that you girl leaping from the edge of the world
into a massively blue and absolute idiom,
hair spread like a dark net to catch the little poets?

Each point in the trajectory confounds impact,
the intervals are harmonised to make us leave.

*

Each green field my god the waves of grass
flooding over the hills break your heart
to the first of the houses we're all awash
and you came in like the genius of the rolling tide.

The telephone wires radiate from the pole
holding the sky aloft a thousand messages of
are you there can I speak the weather here is
the accident of us falling together into.

The conspiracy of your shape, your colour
touch me the substance of you I want to
have eat and fuck in that gold jacket
silk with the little clear buttons like rain.

There's a name for the work on the big loom
you tell me as you walk on this side in the shining air.

The Artemision Tunnel

Between the Mountains of Artemis and Lyrkio
crossing from the Argolid to Arcadia – switch on your lights –
we drive into the black tunnel, the eye of day closed.

Artemis, lady of all the animals and living things,
lead us into darkness, lead us under the mountain of your shrine.
Can we even breathe down here? We are in your hands.

If the earth drips off roots threaded through our eyes,
lady of the wild things, light-carrying Artemis,
our theme is order and the springs of Inachos rise with you.

On higher ground, surrounded by the hall of trees,
the sacrifice is without distinction, all living things
– oxen, goats and ending with small birds, thrown into the pyre.

Flocks of quail crowd the sky, as thought flies without shadow,
red hem at the knee, date palm, stag and bee, we see all of this;
against the city of unjust men she tries her bow.

The Alphios marks the boundary where her genius attends,
and after the fire in the artificial forest
I see my own family in a bright circle restored.

My parents, my children and the familiar dead stand again
at the stations of the road, westward from her hands
we climb the high, watered meadows around Asea.

The sky is empty above this temenos of orchard and arable land;
there's a garage, a collapsed house and an abandoned speed trap,
and we stand again in the great common field.

*

Another day pours down light in waves
and the sea settles a blue question around us;
one end of the earth at our feet, the other falls away
beyond the aerial terraces stepping into the sky.

The English newspapers have gone from the shop
and the village retreats into itself for the season.
With no other island to find, what if our bodies fit?
suspended here, not even waiting, what black ship?

Where is the map of anxieties, the darkness chartered?
Apart from all that grows, nothing rises and falls;
the idea that the idea that – O Xenophanes, genius poet,
what have we done since you spoke?

There's no proposition written on the wide air
but the waves breathing whiteness into the world.

*

When the Spartans came over the mountain
and made us their slaves,
self-appointed lords of the way it is
with their global credit, pipelines
and smart weapons in phalanx,
our irrelevance came to an end.

The hills at a certain hour turned mauve
and these men emerged in our fields
as if out of nowhere, clouds around their thighs,
their mouths barking – Helot – Barbarian – Outdweller;
they made Leuctra into an arms dump
and the Crypteia proved themselves at night.

We had invented six languages in the dust,
mastered the olive, grape and grain
and tied the knots in an epic poetry;
on discs of light dropped by the gods
we walked the broken path of the sea
and still knew the songs the birds sang.

Your picture of the world can be undone,
stations off the air, iron ore shipped out;
the sky as blue, the terraces of the sea rise and fall
enough to break your heart each morning;
we no longer walked the ground,
the earth a shadow for another's empire.

*

Nameless on the water, nobody steps ashore,
she sees that other life unravelling on the threshold.

It could be the picture of a man returning,
if not on the loom then in the air of all her thought;
his deep red running on the blue sea stripe,
the cleverness in her hands binding their bodies together.

Birds dyed and sewn, fish of spun wool,
a bull dancing in a field of flowers,
a border of black ships turning;
to forget the liquid beauty of linen was like death.

Carded on her thigh or the fitted onos,
terracotta shell of her absence held her;
the slow television of her longing held her
and could not be unpicked for the whole world.

*

After the final mountains we roll down to the sea
south from Kalamata around Taygetos on the Aeriopoli road,
and this is meant to be the literal poem of that journey,
one of a series joining seven songs in transit
as if your whole life comes in on the glimmering tide.

The road turns in a certain way and you see everything,
along this coast where gods and babies are washed ashore
out of the sky into the doorways of abandoned villages;
you can pull up and buy oranges, potatoes, honey
from the last ones alive in unpopulated places.

In the meadows and olive groves myth takes root,
paths in the hills lead there, if you can crawl and scramble;
the snake renews itself and polyphonous birds call,
strophe by strophe in the month of fair sailing
the world takes off to a single tone breaking underground.

The road turns in a certain way – miss it and you die;
ceremonies lift the earth people, gibbering at the edge,
and the voice from the well asks – what do you want?
The route is lined with bright and useless answers,
as if anything could keep us from the great descent.

Where the land ends Helen's brothers look out for us,
striding over the contours of the sea, they say;
as candid waves explode on harbour walls
a girl from Kythira rises, from the epicentre,
to leave us drenched and shining in shock.

*

If we walk by Christeas's tower above the harbour
to the Greek and Latin sea at the centre of the world,

swim in the bowl of waters cool and deep,
not even the dead will call over the white signals.

There's another life radiant on the dark tide
and we're released into it, limb by limb.

I was awake thinking of two bodies asleep,
side by side in that unvisited country;
I set my thoughts to your breathing
and we went bobbing out into the gulf.

I think I dreamt it at the courtyard gate
and saw the painted waves supporting us,
out past the automatic lighthouse at Matapan
along the magnetic sea lanes for Ithaka.

*

Eroding even the walls of Neriton
the subterranean fresh water stream
rises in the harbour or further out;
I dreamt I swam into its frozen heart.

How strange it looks to wake up on this beach
without speaking the word for stranger;
it's because I am thinking of you in that house,
wearing the dress with the splash of red roses.

I'm thinking what it is to sleep with you,
of the delight that settles on me in your shape,
and how I taste the first language in my mouth
articulate in your hands through which I move.

Until morning light rolls out into the gulf
and the backward turning sea beats time.

Coda

If one day
you hear singing
from the street
it's the colour
the thickness
of her hair
a waterfall
a blessing
the song said
the light when
I was the king
of the ocean
my kingdom ran
around the world
you reigned there
by my side
before even
Orpheus was
sounding don't
turn away
listen before
I died the
song was.

Hotel Shadow

'These centuries of the decline of ancient philosophy
 Almost forgotten'
                              —John Hall

From Where Song Comes *or* Keeping the Empire in Order

From Where Song Comes

Descended from tribes of the Tarim Valley,
lost in town, open-mouthed at the end of
someone else's tether, heads back, arms up,
offering music for money – some hope.

Eyes flicker like English trees in the park,
picture a scheme planted for self-improvement
or maps where the houses and circuits will be,
bloody generations scouring the veins.

A chorus of phonemes, not even ghosts,
we stand disjoint, signatures broken
drilling holes in work, family, the whole lot;
those first words cling like a jacket of smoke.

'Woman', 'arm', 'speak', 'weep', 'hit', 'stone'
differing in fundamental forms, thick with roots,
sound unintelligible, shut out – you were shouting
I didn't understand, doors banging in the street.

If we sing our belonging and away,
listen to the neighbour's rising call;
the song's never the same twice,
if we sing belonging and away.

*

There was a moment, perhaps as polyphonic flocks rose from the dark edge of the forest at dawn, an impelling code fills the sky, a code that previously didn't exist when things were themselves.

The village empties, even the dogs leave. This could be in east Sumatra, the Saami steppes, anywhere unrecorded. The hunter-gatherers stand like stone on the green path which has just become unfamiliar. Terror.

A conspiracy foisted on them from the wet earth itself had them invent the seasons. They take their place in the telekinetic supply chains and the plough sings it, the long slow lines in classical tropes of ridge and furrow.

*

Key terms were dropped along the route
polished and ardent, the sun boiling lowered
into the dreamed sea of lyric voices.

Out of the secret meadow and heap of poet's bones
as if in the tradition of the music of the drowned,
they step forward to sing, we know their names.

In the earthquake zones, they speak lightly,
elaborate buried contours and the lost harmonics of
the green shore, the risen mountain, the first house.

How soft was the air when you laid word by word,
is that you girl leaping from the world's edge
hair spread like a dark net to catch the little poets?

In that massively blue and absolute idiom
another life surges after impact, out there
mid-ocean waves, banks of weeds, dark harbour.

*

The words remain part of a composite unit. They may even ignite a fire in the theatre of the fields and sky as framework of the ritual. Some groups did not attain intelligible song but prayed repeatedly. Such as: 'Spear spear strike home,' or 'Father father give me game to kill.'

We can be certain that choral song followed, everyone in the group singing one thought. Archaic survivals are a different matter, waiting in

the shadows by the rude door, at the ragged limit of the worked land,
buried, and belonging to others unnamed.

And then that moment arrives, the world tilts and everything is
changed. They dug shallow trenches in various scandalous patterns and
filled them with honey and other animal products. He said – the words
come of themselves, shoot up of themselves, a song.

*

According to our notions Orpheus has returned from
Egypt melancholic and is teaching weasels to dance;
chant the empty road, the muddy field,
chant Spring cocked in the buried dead
and the dubious benefits of the last revolution.

The behaviour of animals and men is hardly distinct,
the finer points of conduct lost in darkness;
from the garden and the secrets of the house
syllables as emotive sounds take shape,
drowned in the ground plan of abandoned towns.

On the shores of the glittering, frozen sea
they suffer a savage and wretchedly poor life;
feed on wild plants, wear skins, sleep on the ground,
we're at the end of the known world
everything beyond is in the realm of fable.

*

What the world needs now is a theory of song,
a thesis on the ballad to free the words in our mouths;
there will be songs for dancing round, songs for sleep,
a song for helping a person across a river.

From the licensed street corner, a version of a version
from another country rings out many voices in one,
songs for masked dancers, performed for the girls
songs of the laws of the school, kneeling on the ground.

Let it unruin many a poor boy, standing next to the gap
an oasis or total knowledge maxed in the echo chamber,
and work songs for Spring, for weeding, planting and rain,
a song of gifts of beer, for wife takers and wife givers.

Boys dancing with reed pipes, girls with drums,
the other time we enter now is everything.

Sing Campion Song

Today the trees are massive and the air in limbo
makes me think of those working hard to keep me in sunglasses,
to keep me in song, – it's worth it to send me gliding along the streets,
through the flushed and coloured map of unending desire.

Thomas Campion is my neighbour, he lives on the top floor,
he breathes the pure countertenor ozone from the tower of song;
though the civic society wanted him out, he's not coming down,
he tells them to drop it and sings louder every night.

But imagine a common purpose in breathing the next breath
and the blossom bursts so candid, like love unfolding,
like a river of untethered clouds naming a new country,
to make us unsay each hectic word in the artless plan.

*

Sing Campion song eyes closed
this ayre is not recorded on a mailbase
leaning onto the edge of darkness
step out where comfort is she will.

*

Campion's perfect iambics oh
what can we do what can
equal the lute river melody
of English poetry beginning.

*

Their boat sailed up the Thames
wood oud Italian loot to her

making fowre parts in counterpoint
that they might move stone by sound.

> *

My Campion is singing
in the mountain grove
3 for 2 and petrol rush
the wanton country made.

*

If we talk like this I don't know that I get it,
impasto Sam in the Darent valley, the boys at leapfrog,
error message 208 sings in the forest of night
and the precipitation trailing westward peters out.

At some point for the locals it must tilt,
and where shall we find our colours then?
The forgotten use of realgar, the decline of arsenic,
will you make me a white to match this radiance?

After the abandonment found on lyric stairways
the theory of craft labour took hold in Cambridge,
the Sunni triangle of old learning and money;
London das kapital of foreign occupation.

If songs make us free, we already have them all,
called conflict of interest in the history of the English jig.

> *

White van man morning
paths in the sky announce
Campion Restoration
a cure for pain antique.

*

Flicker of Solanum trails clouds
as if by one voyce to an INSTRUMENT
the robin's erratic flightpath tells you
there is ever one fresh spring.

*

At the back of the house the green
shaft releases a day from
the box of song all around us
from holes in the lid the light beams.

*

Campion in two three and
foure parts radio nowhere
glory intermittent fills the air
burning down the house.

*

They say he can explain music, that's the way,
whisper in our bones ape heartbeat, I like it,
guarding the gate at night against
running around the poorer quarters
or the sea's endless sifting of the land
so that our children might sing in the vetch and lettuce.

They say he can explain the ship that left us here,
dark imprint at the western edge, disappeared,
to rise as factories plotted across the fields,
a history of betrayal, a history of anything other than
– this is what I do now and the rest will fit,

coasting the unknown world at first light
my girls laughing in the empty chambers of air,
a herring gull cry linotypes the sea.

*

Tuned to the moving spheres
Apollo made village music visible
dot dash radar narrates the sky
our migrant route unearthed.

*

There's a face in the garden
a ghost in the house   forensic trace
of the lost songs of Astraea
a red oh on her ripe mouth.

*

Winter on the stave rattles
the window winter on the stave
shakes the rowan sheds light
raising the house acoustic.

*

O Campion swallow your fate
unlock the logic table submit
dark ravisher the chiefe beginner
may well be soong.

*

```
C    A    M    P    I    O    N
A    S    T    R    A    E    A
M    U    S    I    C    K    E
P    U    R    S    U    E    S
I    A    M    B    I    C    S
O    R    D    A    I    N    E
N    A    T    I    O    N    S
```

Outside

This may well be what's called outside.
Are you going outside? From outside you can see
the massive walls built to guard the capital,
the capital and its monopolistic discourse;
various birds fly into it, their brains, dunk dunk,
another brace, a bag of feathers hits the deck.

We set out over snowfields in glacial air,
there's music sounding underground
magnetism conspires in black soil furrows,
the rise and fall of it, as if all our lives we're leaving
and the place was not even here a generation ago,
now there's no telling, the telegram stations unimaginable.

It's not that you're some traveller in a strange land,
it's not that you'll log the days after occupation;
but your tracks inscribe a name not yours
and the sound hangs in the chambered air
– what invention it took to shape one song,
and how the children's voices flood the trees.

Reading *The Cantos*

1

Fell asleep in the courtyard reading *The Cantos*
after swimming rolled on white waves and ankle stones,
Malatesta and the Magnificent, the bloody mechanics.

After the dazzling verse and magnetic names
I remembered two hours sat before the girl Aphrodite,
the intermittent light and the crowd parting occasionally.

Her hair lifts, she dreams the name of a new world,
the sea surrounds us on all sides and the light
comes and goes over her meadows and pathways.

What does Pound find to admire in Sigismundo and the Medici?
Hands grasping the rods of power, banking and patronage,
polishing the azure air for the faces of Tuscan gods?

I woke up in cherry season, ate the cherries ripe and wet,
the sea breathing in the olive groves, clouds rising from the hills,
to see ants hoist crumbs to a depthless sky.

*

The wind cases the house all night
rolls away to reveal the harbour washed
the sea lanes rise and fall.

How grand to propound the big idea;
interest rates as rented money
made all art go rotten after 1527.

A species of modernist ambition
to synthesise the culture's cache,
a gesture, anti-Semitic and parochial.

The wind cases the house at night
to reveal the coastline hung out to dry,
Europe and the Faithful heard on the air.

Chanting of dumb beasts sanctioned
their reasoning is shallow
they speak to popular prejudice.

Small birds drill the sky in an agony
of Spring it is it is it is the force of them,
they sing song a theology of awake.

The merchants of the Morea carried
the sprouting branch and sharp mind
where she sets her foot to the sea.

What nerve they had to outstare
Methoni and Koroni, eyes of
the serene empire's trade routes.

Platsa, above us on the mountain, traded
directly with Venice on donkeys, down
the kalderimi to the harbour of the world.

*

And then in Canto XLIX his genius
speaks in stillness, imperial power is
what it is to us rushing particles ignite.

The little owl glides to its shadow
high on the wall of the broken tower
above the middle sea that makes us.

The widow walks across the square
she is not long a widow, she is a black line
carrying roadside flowers to her neighbour.

Turning the dynamo Cadmus turned
Euratos rises on the running wave
Europa of wide open eyes steps ashore.

Everywhere
         scattered song
the host
      a fishing boat draws the west skyline.

2

In Pisa at night the wind rattles the gate of the cage and fingers a poet's bones.

In Pisa at night he dreamt hypostasis, he dreamt he understood the poor and sided with monsters.

In Pisa at night the modernist preference for antiquity over the present was stuffed and hung upside down from a lamppost.

In Pisa at night hell in a black wave rolled off the Tuscan hills drowning the terraces of Dioce – learn to fear your own stupidity, the wind rising in your face barking bad economics.

In Pisa at night our beautiful singer broken, his mouth removed, his thinking fills the death cell.

*

Last night with a half moon risen
we watched the fires across the gulf
reduced to five points of yellow light
Koroni burning, the sea dark and still.

A silver jackal started from the undergrowth
quick paws running in the dust
and we felt the weight of him
sounding on the hollow ground.

*

In the stacked heat of noon
the sparrows will only come down
in the narrow shade of the bent tree
to bathe in the dust bowl stubble.

Later the wind circles the square
making a conference of the trees
the eucalyptus to the olive to the pine
sounding notes one to another Aeolian.

*

Moon, cloud, tower – here Christeas's tower stands against the sea
to protect the harbour from pirates and other crude usurers or, where,
after robbing their neighbours, the Christeas hid, and they're here still.

Morritt in 1795 speaks of the splendid generosity of the Captain,
a picnic set out in the long hall of entertainment and on the green
around the tower, a hundred guests enjoy the hospitality of the Boss.

Pound is out there, battering on history, raging in the square,
the fluty music of various birds on various wires indifferent;
Musso, Confucius, Odysseus swap places in his empty mouth.

Pound's out there, gone ape in the Broken Anthill Book of Reference;
let them run through the groves at night over smashed marble,
let their music saunter from a distant village on the scaled air.

You could sit still in a village abandoned under waves of summer,
just look at things – people and animals and trees tell you everything;
moon over cloud over tower and the owls making sweet kills.

Know that if you sail south from here the first island you find is Kythira:
Come Aphrodite, our lady of honey and liquefied limbs,
Come seafoam girl, come out to us on calm water and in storm.

*

Peter, an unexpected mildness came over me this late afternoon at Yannis's taverna. The sea rolled in and out, I drank a Mythos and half recognized Márta Sebestyén singing a version of *Deep Forest*.

This was after a night of shortwave rant, belief burning in every language of the world like a tight band around the neck. You hear it coming through, 'the low percentage of reason which seems to operate in human affairs.' It makes uncertainty a gift. And tonight on Radio Rome…

*

Rain fell this afternoon, mid-August rain, rare,
afterwards the earth came up smelling spicy
at the bedroom window, rain for the Panagiya.

We make a party for God's mother,
lights strung across the harbour, ribbons of light
and tonight pork and rice and beer.

Also for the fishing men Christeas,
amplified music late into the soft night
with fireworks, flares and guns.

Boats tied up:
>Alexandra
>Veloz
>Maria
>Alexandros
>Argonautis
>There's no boat called Coded History.

>*

Vatic recital of bank rates does not
make for the revealed truth of history;
this ideogram means overbearing insistence
about a pile of broken sticks
does not make a tree.

There is no argument.

No boat called Coded History floats.

The temple is not for sale,
let the old man at the gate rest
you can pay when you leave;
the grass sways, his mind swings
asleep awake fitful magpie.

This green pot has outdone
your arrogance out of it
from 3,000 years ago a smell
orange blossom honey
and the freedom of doubt.

>*

(drafts and fragments)

The slight Mediterranean tide paints
the rocks a pale margin between worlds

kids squealing dive-bomb off the harbour wall
there's a snake in the water trough to bite your feet

and the waves lazy flop reaches afternoon
translating blue green water and light

Ezra Pound is rolling rocks down the mountain
at the edge of the European mind, rubble, empires of rubble

the empty house where the sky spreads
stands in the dry river bed abandoned

saved by foxes and cicadas
                                      their parliament.

From the Hen-Roost

'War, one war after another, men start 'em who couldn't put up a good hen-roost.'

1

Black ships drawn up for ten years
to get an exquisite woman, to get at all the women.

To master trade routes, grain supplies, pipelines of wealth
burning lights of acquisition scored on the map.

Make a poem of it; a bayful of weapons in the sun
a poem; the fertile plain a killing ground unrolled

Runs in every direction – delight in slaughter found
the great host fell upon Asia's meadowland and marshes.

2

Karl Twitcher out in the field geologises
no water or gold found but thought
there might be oil out here, let's talk.

Philby bows to the father of his new nation
lips wet from Zamzam, sets about God's work
the American concession secured.

Osama sits on the banks of the River Gash,
wives safely stowed in Khartoum,
sings – ain't gonna study war no more.

At the crossroads of Nejd the Word rose up
from the Buner Mountains, the King of the West,
farming abandoned to wire the faith.

Osama dreams of smart women, burning towers
of Qutb by the waters of Manhattan
of an old bitch gone in the teeth.

Every grain of sand becomes a gem,
and Lord – Israel's tents do shine so bright,
Aramco on the tribal mat, afloat in the Gulf.

3

We had thought them easy meat
for jackals, leopards, wolves
but now ... across the moat on high ground
Trojans reaping.

It came down hard on us
what if we pull out, wait off shore?
the rampart breached, Europe stranded
by the ships, politicians at the old business.

They go licking up the paid, fat words
in a greased circuit of ignorance;
gods in bliss in Houston and Riyadh
granted the power of massacre.

My brothers dropped in to the sleep
of bronze, their accents mapping
the poor cities of an indifferent country,
as they leaked into the ground.

4

Breathing long alcohol afternoons he might tell me about the war, thick layers of it. The stories thick as beer and rum breath and I still don't know the truth, the final version. He volunteered himself out of the Free State and poverty to cross the Irish Sea, the gulf of sad song misery, for the spitshine British Army. Out of what? I don't know.

He was shipped out to India and off to fight in Burma with the forgotten 14th. He went on about the filth, the child prostitutes, just girls waiting in alleyways with men shouting the prices. Bored, they would set traps for kites, tie bread with string and allow the birds to swoop down, swallow the bread and fly off, then yank them out of the sky and kill them.

They were half buried in jungle tracks, tunnels of festering vegetation without names, and the stacked humidity just makes you rot – and then, Jesus, the bloody insects at you, at you, all the time – and on top of that the Jap bastards trying to fucking shoot you for free.

And if men like him had not gone to it?

I don't know what they made of their fear; dark bird hovering there for years, just out of vision, ready to slide off the air, dive and tear and shred; one of Chadwick's beasts would do, sharp eyed, clawed. Armitage could identify the model; outline its shape, as it ghosts in and out of the mind for decades.

5

And Thatcher's nasty little war
and Blair's nasty rented wars,
at some point they believe
then retire to revelation on the Red Sea.

We hear their voices like ghosts on the air,
the false tone burning, smeared on a nation.

May their houses be drowned in black dust.
May their words be as waves of dead locusts.
May their fake empire be struck dumb.
And may the names of the dead be made real to them.

6

The bay empties itself, the deep sea ships sail away
Homer doesn't cover this, if he did I would rewrite it.

The boy looked out to sea, it was empty, he was astonished
– nothing on the radar, just static, just radiation ghosts.

Peace like a white vision, bees murmur in the marram,
and light paints the surface of the whole world.

Somewhere, ships low on the water, take cover,
their discrete weaponry a design feature.

Somewhere, rewritten – speedboats take a punt at the Cole,
Odysseus already dreams of Ithaka pitching under his feet.

And the elemental gods flatten the rampart
as if nothing ever happened here.

A Thesis on the Ballad

Barbara Allen

Are you singing from that other place unbearable
though you would not have the girl
look away in Scarlet Town with her killer beauty.

From that room when I was young
I saw the light lie low under a sky of blue hills
after the houses where I walked but was blind.

I think this song may be locked in the brain
even at death, it sounds out as cells close
– Oh Barbara Allen what have you done to me.

An Expanse of Water

The water is wide I can't get o'er
possessed at every stroke the great
aching distance between us
across which I would row, swim or ski.

If the waves break in common measure
fish in the sea you know how I feel
when she walked to the water lay down
and spoke her underwater words to me.

The Truth

'The Seven Sisters was a true song. It happened back yonder in Mutton Hollow. I was there myself. Somebody got killed over the girl. I was there soon after it happened.'

Psychopaths

Edward and Lord Randall want nothing from you
your part is to fall into the ditch of absent motive
evil and misery exist: you cannot rhyme them out.

Edward and Lord Randall want nothing from you
the greenwood mulch is stuffed rich with corpses
my love lies unalone beneath the sweet birdy trees.

Edward, Lord Randall and the Demon Lover
run in the blood at the singing edge of the world
and you will never win those shining hills again.

Class War and Sex War

We shall all be made to pay one day
lying on the snowy bed of silk
to fiddle music in the wood unceasing.

Red and grinning Little Musgrave returns
arm in arm with Lamkin, a blood-dark night
away boys away to Ireland and the Hebrides.

To the roots of narrative in rock, ice and fire
before the saga of riches crashed
where the mind might lodge at zero.

Out of a shining sea of its own telling
we shall all be made to pay one day
hear the dogs bark and the footfall at the door.

And So

If anyone should ask you
do you know who wrote this song?
It was I and I sing it all day long.

It came from the dark dark earth
and all those lives of beasts and men
go doubling in the wood at night.

Those figures still unstill
ford the black river rolling
and the vocal bird calls – here here here.

Learning to Play the Harp

The lost poems of W.S. Graham written
as a boy in Govan and in all of his life,
the shipyard night shift listens still
to John McCormack on Radio Éire sing
The Harp That Once at closedown.

Silent now, night tenor of silence
shed on the dark waters of the Clyde,
as if words might launch the boy across
the black river, another world, no more
at closedown and dawn, they're gone, as the smoke.

*

Have you ever heard anything as sweet as that?
though Sydney's radio was not bought at Spicer's shop.

And that would be my dad around the house somewhere
singing the same song, he drones in and out of the tune.

It was all taken from us you know, by the English, the war
of loss and burnt letters, the despised and disappearing past.

His voice steps in and out of the tune, up the stairs
making still the house, the garden in deeper silence.

Fixing the boy in place counting down he sees
the grain in the black wooden chair deepen.

The anti-Orpheus, darkness spilling from his hands,
pity the man in the alcohol box: you can do nothing.

*

Of course it was the morning
up early for apprenticeship
when the radio played the harp
before the train to Glasgow.

My good mistake at first light
to sing the song I didn't know,
the boy dreamt the night before
the poem unwritten in the shipyard.

Andrew – your term, migrating
over the border and awa' for
Scotland and the Duncan generation,
the savage survival flightpath.

Turning back on itself, the past
a brown river running through town,
invisible the dead crowd the banks
made quiet under a ribbon of mist.

I remembered walking home
in the early hours thinking of her,
her mouth made me dumb
– will you come across the water to me.

The moon sat on the top of a hedge
at the end of her dad's garden,
half the night we lay there
her face in victory in a square of light.

Of course that was the morning
walking by the closed shops,
the river is green not brown
and above the weir it widens.

It speaks and slips its rhythm,
and I launch the One Hope off the map
from the mud and flattened reeds,
the sky wheeling and released.

News of Aristomenes

'…and the gods would be kinder to them because they were defending their own and not committing a first injustice.'

– Yanni, what do you know about Aristomenes?
– Hmm, not too much … we could Google it.

1

I am Aristomenes of Andania and I will tell you everything,
what I did and did not do, how I invented the moment of decisive action,
the birth of fear which clears a field of men, Messenia of Laconians
– that was the history of the second rebellion.

What in the world would make me leave my village?
The buzz of bees, my olives fattening like black jewels,
the wagtail patrolling my patch in familiar light,
though the wind plays naughty in the Stenyklaros Valley.

It's true I refused the title of king, I accepted Captain,
I keep close to the men and their leaders, keep them even closer to me;
I can spot the traitors and be magnanimous, for others to deal with
and roll them in a ditch for pigs to snout out and feast on.

It's also true I ran once, from those bastard godly twins,
that doubling of them, against one mortality, defeats me;
I ran, I lost my shield, they may have been in a tree, or hovering
in my mind all along, in an empty sky, dread undid me.

They hail me three times Hekatomphonia – well, so it is then,
I am spattered in their red words up to my elbows;
a fox at the chickens makes feathers fly, and a little blood travels far
– of course a fox can slink out of the mouth of hell and look smart.

It's true I stole into their capital and laid tribute to Athena,
I danced into their heart, the brazen chamber, how flashy, how dazzling;
I laced their gruel with panic that morning, the streets trembled:
war's in the mind, I invaded theirs, my mouth's a weapon.

The stories of my charmed escape from capture are all true,
the stories of my escape from death are all from my mouth.

Think, no man returns from below ground. Have you talked to him?
Shared a drink? Held his hand and felt its warmth? No, I think not.

Yes I did consult the oracles, sources of power I plugged into;
the making of a secondary meaning has a single edge: action.
The dark contract, unseen, unspoken, of the earth, I know what I want,
you know the names of my victories and they will not be forgotten.

As for the mysteries, like a snake even nonsense bites, mock as you might;
the matter of my birth is secret, what I buried on Mount Ithome is not,
who knows what happens if you sleep in the narcotic shade of the fig?
the old goddess may rise a girl, trees thicken, the stream run fresh.

From the beginning there have always been stories about me,
I uphold the oracles of Lykos and I will recover Messenia;
my watchers are out on the hills and I'm ready.
I am Aristomenes of Andania and I will tell you everything.

2

In the bar opposite the Blue Café
from the heart of mechanical song
why not why not why not take time out,
this is what comes of beating pretty on a log.

There's a kiosk and a prize grab cabinet,
you can win a pink dolphin, a bear, a gold watch,
you can see the sea through a glass cube, the sea dancing,
where we parade sunlit after the earthquake.

Off Navarinou the Ottoman fleet goes down,
Gregory Peck steps up – don't argue with fire power,
in town three pyramidal wedding dresses in a row
prepare to go ballistic, lick of smoke whispers 3 2 1.

Finally on Shoe Street, the oral tradition is fixed,
SOUTH EMPIRE rises a line of fortified cities,
a realignment of the world, we have photographic proof,
ends in a fault running down Aristomenes.

*

According to Herodotus Aristagoras said to the Spartans – the Messenians have no gold or silver, or anything worth fighting for. So why should you bother fighting them? Go get the Persians. The Spartans did not listen and Aristomenes stepped forward.

*

We stayed two nights in the Hakos Hotel, Kalamata. It's on the seafront, scene of the allied rout in World War 2. As the Nazis bombed and strafed the crowded beaches the sea ran red with the blood of British and Commonwealth troops. They headed down into the Mani for evacuation to Crete. In the small harbours the dilapidated ships were bombed repeatedly and, although not hit, collapsed from the vibrations in the water.

We watched a film in the Hakos Hotel. Bruce Willis set out to rescue some good Africans from some bad Africans. There was talk of mineral rivalry. In fact Bruce's mission was to helicopter out a white doctor, she was French but with American citizenship. Bloodied Bruce, heroic maverick, went against orders; he wasn't meant to save non-Americans at all. The advert break on Greek TV is long and I was able to go down five floors, buy beer at the kiosk and return before Bruce resumed bleeding and rescuing liberally.

*

To test the endurance of the oral tradition and the life of myth I was thinking what to ask in Andania, where Aristomenes may have been born perhaps 2,600 years ago. 'Messene: A Dream Come True' by

Eva Maria Leng and Waltraud Sperlich speaks of the Messenians as a people seeking and dreaming a homeland, drawing parallels to migrant workers in contemporary Europe. It espouses romance, destiny and ecology with the unsuppressed mood music of the great homecoming. I think it must be written for idiots, tipped that way. The 3D postcard of Delphi is more useful. The picture has a fine corrugated surface, like a mechanical sea in regulated waves. Tilt it one way the ruin of the site is seen, then at another angle the theatre is restored and time dismissed; an illusion printed in ridges. Remember Pausanias – 'These are the stories; believe one or another according to which side you want to be on.'

*

In Messene the stone base for a bronze statue was discovered built into the wall of the apse of the basilica. The inscription is
      ΑΡΙΣΤΟΜΕΝΗΣ
By the 4th century A.D. the city was abandoned, ruined by the collapse of Rome, earthquakes and barbarian raids.

*

And then a morning so fresh
like a massive wet diamond
suspended above the white sea
with the tatty mimosa blowing and
the container ships stuck on the water
we went off around Taygetos
tottering and twisting in the air.

*

Mount Ithome folds itself around Messene,
layered blue hills, undulant olive trees white and green
roll out beyond sight to the plain and Spartan wall;
the city a natural amphitheatre, Hippodamian and mighty.

In founding Messene, above all they sought Aristomenes,
invoked and asked to return and dwell with them;
hillside rubble and scrub, bare earthworks, postholes,
roots turned over, the light invades every mote.

All the birds of Mavrommati sing and gentle rain rains down,
music falling in a green chamber for the river god of Pamisos;
from good red soil, over buried pillars, anenomies, hyacinths, daisies,
Oh Artemis on a bed of vetch most purple.

Later Melanie said – that flower we saw everywhere
that was mallow, sort of mauve, just everywhere;
and above all, at this point in the poem, I wanted to tell you
exactly what was there, unintoxicated, in April, recovering.

3

The best of it was our night raiding with the Fox,
blood released runs like black soup in that pitch;
with his rage on him he was a sight to behold
but once you looked there was no unseeing then.

It was a sort of sacrifice gone wrong, like butchery
the soft plopping of purple organs, knotty innards
by way of knife and spike onto our innocent soil,
eviscerate steam rising like a shitty ghost.

Hekatomphonia means we always counted the dead,
if you don't count the dead the dead don't count,
like in the kingdom of the two rivers, remote slaughter
remains on the eye and a terrible blindness is born.

We would slip out of Ithome into the arms of darkness
and everything smelt good, the fields in perfumed waves;

we were like kids rolling around a herb garden,
rags wrapped around our blades for silence ungleaming.

They would stand in dumb rows at a stockade – ripe for slitting,
or we'd catch a troop in a narrow pass and open the last gate for them.

*

He certainly did steal into Sparta one night, disguised,
right into the temple of Athena, bronze chamber, keeper of the city,
and laid his shield in tribute, as if from another world;
as intended, terror fell on the Laconians, like a knife to the bone.

He came trotting back after the mischief that morning and told us;
he had a charming tongue and could undo ropes and women with it,
you might ask Archidameia about this, devotee of Demeter etc,
she released him, covered her tracks and off he went like a boy in Spring.

You could also ask that farmer's daughter, she dreamt of him
and he turns up captive to a gang of Cretan archers, and again
the woman sets him free, and off he went driving out Laconians;
we wrecked their markets and made riot, whole areas abandoned.

He was chief kidnapper, cattle raider, three times Hekatomphonia,
we sang that streets would be named after him, in Pherae say;
he knew the meaning of action like a distinct language,
he was the tin-sheet Andanian mystery boy and, as it goes, our saviour.

When it was all up he did the right thing by us, our captain;
we went into dread exile, some place – Zancle, Sicily – to the west.

*

They would have us kill for words but you can take the story
as you see fit; whether the fool floated down borne by an eagle

or his shield let him bounce like a little lamb is unimportant;
the point is he returned and killed lots of Laconians.

They say there was something strange about him from birth,
he was favoured, his mother slept with a god in the likeness of a snake;
well that's pretty special – no wonder there were stories about him,
they talk and talk and he did all those things.

If he walked into town everyone downed tools, ribbons and flowers
    would fly,
the women would start singing impromptu, raising the dust and the rest;
he fought at all those places, Boar's Grave, Great Trench and led us out
    of siege,
we weren't serfs then, backs bent in the fields for another's tragedy.

That winter snow sat on the mountains all around us, a white bowl;
the river beds flooded and froze and old ones died by thin fires,
shadows of clouds like bunched black fists fell on the hills again and again;
he led us out of siege, in a spear shaped column we tore through
    Laconians.

I know another thing too – at the end of defeat he went to Rhodes;
he was old, he thought of Sardis, of Ekbatana, and died.

4

Aristomenes hunted Laconians on the plain and high mountain.
Aristomenes went into Sparta at night, left Spartan spoil in Sparta's heart.
Aristomenes laid his shield in the bronze house temple for Athena.
Aristomenes went into Argos and Arcadia, allies and exiles returned.
Aristomenes charmed Demeter's priestesses and escaped to Ithome.
Aristomenes believed in the execution of memorable action and
    terrorising Laconians.
Aristomenes fought at the Boar's Grave at the Great Trench and escaped.

Aristomenes and his 300 stole corn, cattle and wine and drove the
    enemy out.

*

When the Spartans came over the mountain
and made us their slaves,
self appointed lords of the way it is
with their global credit, pipelines
and smart weapons in phalanx,
our irrelevance came to an end.

The hills at a certain hour turned mauve
and these men emerged in our fields
as if out of nowhere, clouds around their thighs,
their mouths barking – Helot – Barbarian – Outdweller;
they made Leuctra into an arms dump
and the crypteia proved themselves at night.

We had invented six languages in the dust,
mastered the olive, grape and grain
and tied the knots in an epic poetry;
on discs of light dropped by the gods
we walked the broken path of the sea
and still knew the songs the birds sang.

Your picture of the world can be undone,
stations off the air, iron ore shipped out;
the sky as blue, the terraces of the sea rise and fall
enough to break your heart each morning;
we no longer walked the ground,
the earth a shadow for another's empire.

*

Aristomenes has been thrown into deep Keadas and left for dead.
Aristomenes has floated to the floor of the chasm on an eagle's spread
    wings.
Aristomenes glides in the bronze light of the eagle on his shield.
Aristomenes has drawn his cloak over his head and is waiting to die.
Aristomenes has woken up to see a vixen nosing at corpses.
Aristomenes has followed the vixen out of the shadows step by step.
Aristomenes has been dragged by the clever one to the light and to Eira.
Aristomenes went down into death and came back after three days to Eira.

5

Aristomenes buried [the thing?] on Mount Ithome
[   ] what   [it . . . .] was   [was]

Andanian   [   ]
[unknown] tin sheet – mystery   stamp[ed]

brazen chamber, bronze jar and [inside]
beaten to fineness [there was] a scroll

rescue [   ] old woman, you see
inscribed   goddess   the Great [one]

from her [hands]   instructions
[after death]   how   [to live]

*

(To do the right thing even in defeat
Aristomenes buried the thing on Mount Ithome,
defeat as inevitable as the wild fig
bending to the stream or an oracular pun.)

*

Cities buried, walls gone under meadows
olive groves over sanctuaries

they talk and talk
and the mountain grows

Meligala – on the upper or northern Messenian plain
– honeymilk

In Pig Valley, thick with trees, dark all day
– a sanctuary of Artemis

the names: marrow in the white bones.

*

Aristomenes buried the thing on Mount Ithome
Epaminondas dug it up after centuries
drew a circle on the ground, drew in streets and walls.

*

Messenians absent for 300 years

did not change their customs
nor lose their Dorian dialect

rain-broken, thunder-broken
the white bones.

*

And they went to Zancle, Sicily
the west darkening, the record dim

        short is the way
        and our Lady golden
        long is the way
        and our Lady golden

the Greeks there sing songs of the xenitia
of living away, to the north, to the factories

from 800 BC in Salento, Calabria and Sicily
Doric still spoken from a 6,000 word lexicon

Doric spoken valley to valley
villagers untouched by writing

        Oh my beautiful Morea
        I will not see you again
        I have my father my mother my brother
        all buried in the earth here
        I will not see you again

Old woman climbing steps
    the Great One   a girl
from her hands the song
    our Lady golden.

*

In Andania the tattered banners proclaim
the perpetual season teased by the wind, a dog,
it could be new year – may you have many years.

The dog tears another strip and it could be
Easter for the god risen indeed
or No Day for victorious defeat.

Time sits by the road smoking
the bus is late and there's no post,
Aristomenes sits by the road breaking empires.

6

I sit in the shade of this fig tree
and wait and watch in the still air

washed from the backward turning sea
blue mountains fade in the haze

moment by moment the many words for light
rise, enough to hide a whole country

she laid the path over rock over water
everything I did she held in her hands

they will return from there
eyes gone dark with seeing

nearby a woodpigeon calls and
small birds sing in a chamber of sound

chirrup nations of chaos chirrup
a message draining the secret meadows

but slowly through the afternoon
the bronze bowl of silence fills

over there they are building
after fire and earthquake and war

tap tapping away for hope
shaping stone time will pock.

*

The fact white hot and near silent
in the squares and streets of Eira,
burning like a chamber of fire or forge
for making swords, proving men.

At the heart of it Sparta,
can only make itself in other lands
can only enslave, stamping Sparta
on strangers' faces in rows.

At the heart of it system collapse,
weapons technique, hidden deals,
the abduction of women and
cattle raiding dreamed night-long.

Fire makes a mirage of walls and towers
the sea sounding in a tunnel of
turning air, those voices high in the Taygetos
fall upon us to map the risen world.

*

With morning coming over the roof
shadow falls on shadow to disappear,
something has driven the world into this
dark pilot of the course taken.

Self-appointed arbiters squeak by rote
 – if it is fragmented, inchoate, so it must be written:

baleful Anacreon, get out of it,
go learn the song again.

Light steps over the roof, shadow on shadow,
war reports shake the air, wave after wave
piling up women and children in mounds;
this is what we do, only the names change.

We didn't stop from raising Messenia
lest Spartans took exception;
we hit hard, employed art, watched the hills
waited their approach – and for what?

The tangle of branches on the wall
a language, trace its slow progress;
the cicadas' dry music its signature,
day advances, all meaning's changed.

*

What I do is sit under the fig tree and wait
at the point of death everything comes to life,
time stops and then whips, on the crumbling edge
of Keadas, birds wheeling below.

It might be a gentle wind lifts your sleeve
fresh as my love's breath, the light shows through
each fibrous thread, like wings extended
and their hands on your shoulders push.

The unimaginable darkness breaks out then,
in the pine trees bending and scattered rocks
whiteness pushing up through scrub,
rats, jackals, birds and frogs swoon to earth in a rush.

As in battle, it breaks out, blood leaking
from a young face, close up, the black hair soaked,
it all snaps shut, silence, and then the roar exalting,
a town goes up in smoke, a gleaming pile of spoil.

I sit, I wait, they keep the noise down around me,
dust falls in dark rooms, the sea nearby translates time;
smiling physicians appear through the curtains,
I expect a song and dance routine of sorts.

*

She sings in the morning in and out of the kitchen
as birds sing because the sun rises
saying I was awake late last night,
her mouth opening and closing in yellow light.

I've returned several times from where there is no singing,
from Keadas, from Trophonius and at Leuctra, to Spartan frenzy;
they will call me exegete of the katabasis, or some such,
and each time there was never a girl singing like this one.

You have to go there and strike a dark bargain,
lie down, hold barley cakes mixed with honey,
go feet first into a mouth in the earth and shoot away
as if caught in a river, a river of blackness covers your head.

The return is difficult and never the same route as the descent,
I scratched a few words in seeds and blood on the passing rock;
she laces the air with her singing, there's a lucky boy in the village
and bees drift through clouds of flour as she claps and claps.

Coda

Even before Lycurgus launched Year Zero
and exported familial sadism as empire
everything unfolds in the high meadows
of the Hellenic subduction zone, its music
travelling westward at 3.5 mm per year.

Leonidas' palace is a casino of vanilla and gold,
the taxis of Sparta are red with white roofs
and snow shines its April message from Taygetos,
against the wall of that wall the sea a bloody memory
of Aristomenes sword dancing on the other side.

The language of action has dropped us here,
the forces of Anatolia, Africa and Eurasia
converge, grind and slide under our feet,
if the roaring speaks another poetry
a head lifts up pouring roots and red soil.

The Family Carnival

Apokriatika

Driving across to the Mani this February we broke the journey in Corinth. Slept the night in a stone cold room in the Hotel Shadow and ate at the taverna used by the villagers for a night out. We thought nothing of the children dressed in Pierrot costumes and Disney. Later I thought I saw a goat-faced man outside the door in pitch darkness wearing a white veil, I thought his friend was wearing a Dolly Parton-style wig.

Next morning we drove on and saw big red and green kites on sale everywhere. Men standing and talking at the *kafeneio* were dressed in ball gowns and wigs. Well, village life we thought, you make your own entertainment. We found out the next day it was carnival – Apokriatika, the last weekend before Clean Monday of only fish and vegetables, but for now Pre-Lenten celebrations held sway. I remembered the carnival songs; cocks and cunts dancing around fruit trees, young boys being taken in hand by aunty at the mill and black straw faced devils chasing through the streets.

*

From the Hotel Shadow on the edge of spring
under the lit rock of Acro Corinth
flash of white wing on the black window,
figures waiting by the door to the world.

Surrounded by the sweep of orange groves
painted booths line the sacred way,
women on their knees whispering Aphrodite
stirring a dark perfume in the deep green leaves.

From Hotel Shadow on the edge of spring
the utilitarian stables of Euro business
fall away to the gulf of crowded boats,
transporting televisions, cars and kitchens.

The lower world cracks apart on successive days
and we open casks, cups and pots in turn,
I think this is before the church, for Dionysus – yes yes,
Dionysus in flight from winter making us mad.

*

The earth cracks in season
and memory set aside rises
by generation, vivid, unchanged.

I think he died in great pain,
drinking aftershave – Old Spice
and boot polish – on parade.

Are such themes found in folk song?
I don't know. Who is singing?
It's just the nature of the alcoholic.

But I am fifty now and still
I can barely tell you,
here's the last line, I made it.

*

February is the month of the dead
the month of purification.

The wine god in his garlands
flirts and slips and stumbles.

The earth parting for the eager dead
they come from another country to have their fill.

We are not who we seem
we don't sing what you think.

*

They lived in a village in another country
my mother would pick out its tunes,
hymns by ear, forgive our foolish ways
– Well someone should, and laugh like a girl.

Lead kindly light between the wars,
her father built a business, fruit and veg to market,
all gone in the fatal crash on early morning ice
and the children taken in by relatives.

And before him the journeyman tailor,
a tall, dark man from Slad the narrow valley
and Tightmouth, his wife from Bisley,
an even meaner place if possible.

I know them only by her stories
and she's been dead more than twenty years,
they set out across Hardy's fields,
their rough old songs beating in the heart.

*

And dancing uncle is pregnant with a balloon,
he leads his son the satyr with lopsided breasts,
and his daughter, Happiness, skips in circles laughing;
tomorrow is Clean Monday for vegetables and fish.

No – your feet like this, two two, one one, you lead
for Anthesteria, the days of risen ghosts about the city,

let me daub the doors with pitch and chew the buckthorn clean.
Souls – you've had your dish of grain and seeds – now go, now go.

Plastic trumpets and party poppers announce
you can beat Mr Death with a squeaky hammer,
hit him hard and run around the busy tables;
uncle gives birth to a goat, here's the skin to wrap you up in.

A Season Below Ground

Melanie this is the motorway we always drove
then and now the fields and towns at rest
falling away in darkness on both sides.

To the west a circuit of lights around a distant hill
rising as if beyond the sea sounds the history
of families made quiet under a spreading sky

Or in that house they might have outlived youth
before all their choirs went under the waves,
face down in the wet garden when time stopped.

It was always this road, up and down the country,
always the blinding cartography in endless parallel
missing the point of where we go.

I think this interior light travels with us,
your face looking forward as the music wanders
the dark enfolding road we leave behind.

*

Arrhythmic mouth opens and wordless speaks
electric buttons random firing, circuit shot
down amongst the dead men, out behind
the dark and dirty, crowded door – Anacreon.

It's about the size of a man flat on the ground,
hidden in the garden, and hardly seals a vacuum now;
we need trees here for the birds to perform from
and there should be consideration of the robin.

Chipping at the window, augorous, aggressive and bonny,
will you do your wings down bury me in mulch
song and dance backward routine to rain black streets?

Take the fires of hell on your breast for us,
slice up winter into strips of transparent sky,
catch light-bearing breath on the sounding screen.

*

When I wrote *The Red and Yellow Book*
events interrupted the writing dream,
a marriage, the mighty book, a death;
a series made indiscrete, bloody and personal.

In that line my own relations gone like smoke,
across the white fields as if from nowhere
my girls turned into young women
like beautiful possibilities in the world.

Hands move over piano keys, a song lifts
and we're undone in that moment,
the music runs on, green days spinning,
there's no standing aside and we're speechless.

Somewhere around here all the imagery is abandoned,
stubborn, it litters the ground, and I see you step around it.

Hearing Mishearing Doug Oliver

1 The Owners' Enclosure

Though some raiders will die, we could surround this place,
block the exits, take the rooftops and scope the winner on the plinth,
the lizard faced millionaire in duck-shit-green tweeds and pointy shoes.

Imagine the panic, the crowd as plural arrows convulsed and streaming;
he's in securities, he's in transport and this man combs the jumps:
we could call it *Killing the Rich at Play*, set that one dangling by a trope.

PR demands we don't harm the horses, the beautiful horses;
feel the thunder, see their bellies and legs full stretch over fences,
hear that gliding moment like a line cast out in an arc on still water.

Another problem: the Hussars are here in ceremonial costume and tall hats,
with their comrades away in Helmand, they're on big black fuck-off
      chargers;
if you imagine a troop of them advancing, at Peterloo say, history will
      falter.

That disenfranchisement will rise in your children's hearts like death;
so although some raiders will die, we have the taking of this place,
reduced here to transparent terms and moral confidence – off you go.

2 The Vaccination Queue

I queued at the surgery for the flu vaccination. I was with the old, saw our ageing and I got it. We trailed out of the building and accepted our parts as extras in a British comedy. A queue is an opportunity to be orderly, anxious and complain in the service of humour.

– Look it says here, if you are breast-feeding or trying to become pregnant, tell the nurse.

– Well, I think you're safe then Edie.
– This is like the army. They didn't keep the needles sharp, just jabbed 'em in you and off you go to Timbuktu.
Most of the women shouted at most of the men.
– He can't hear me. Stand there, just wait. You're a bit deaf aren't you.

Many were the respectable poor, who no longer exist in any political discourse. They wear cheap clothes; the men in pressed grey trousers and thin brown slip-ons; the women in sensible three quarter length coats and shapeless slacks. You queue up because it's free – and they have paid all their lives. So they act sniffy, like a posh hat on humility. I'm at home with them and try to be helpful.

I remembered my mother talked about the doctor visiting. He arrived on a horse.
– He was so tall up there, he'd shout down at you all of your personal business, everybody heard. He was a kind old soul though.
A doctor making house visits on a horse? Have I made this up or read it in the sort of novel I don't read?

One winter my dad came off his bike, cracked his head, staggered home delirious and collapsed through the door. She tried to lift him up, saw the blood, shrieked and dropped him smack down on the flagstones. Later, the doctor, discretely dismounted, asked if she'd tried to kill him – I'd understand Mrs Corcoran but all the same, best not.

I suppose the accident of him not dying on this occasion, and the succession of generations, drops me in this queue. It helps me stand here and shuffle forward. I imagine every one of us standing here must be informed by such events – like a bright axis of personal identity intersecting the queue unseen and unheard. Our queue, snaking back through history via Beveridge, the Empire and beyond, is of course the English class system as vernacular drama. You know your place and how to behave, thank you. Nobody waiting for the vaccination pushed; one man faking confusion, cheated. The general disapproval unspoken hung in the air we all breathed.

3 The Harbour Open to all of the World

The pinman hero, half in half out of the water,
stretches ardent across the mouth of the harbour;
he's keeping the harbour open to the whole world,
if you could only believe he'd hold that posture.

Red faced expats walk and talk their foreign languages
and Albanian builders dance over the roof tiles;
a generation ago children walked down the mountain
and took the boat to school in Kardamyli.

There's evidence here of Neolithic settlement,
 – did they paddle out in boats of stone, logs and leaves?
their art of carved bone dynamic and literal,
their rituals drove the seasons in their course.

Helen's brothers stood on that island there,
calming the waters as she fled with an astonished Paris;
after Actium Antony chased Cleopatra this way,
at last they spoke, then did sup and lie together.

The fishermen Christeas in the Argonautis putter out,
their outboard weaving sleep on the black water;
cast far like a string of pearls by merchants of the Morea
trade routes pour into the lap of the Serene Empire.

Out there subterranean streams emerge on the surface,
cold and still, a fresh water ellipse like a glassy eye
reducing the waves to a flickering circle;
becalmed we float in the origin of all our telling.

Looking back, the forgotten harbour stays open,
the whole world rolling in and out of its arms.

Byron's Karagiozis

This lake and town of Byron's escape
appears as fresh as a boy's face;
milord's playthings arrayed across the plain,
the shoreline stepping in and out of the ever living past.

The Pasha scans the mountain paths for rebels
rising to the blue of Ottoman heaven,
saunters along the landing strip of the unaligned
– my palace, my lands of blood, my lord – welcome.

We dropped out of thin air over the Pindus,
a door opened became a flood of light;
landing gear scarring the face reflected
the water full of boats and sacked women.

This the first Albanian song of Lordy Viron,
the second a lamentation of unrequited love;
the clarinos sob sob, the real men howl
– ah your pink ears, their coral portal and lightshine.

*

Scene 1

Enter Spiridion Foresti, British Consul, dancing with the Governor of Malta, cloaked in smiles – 'We can send young Byron to traverse the province, let him bind the Pasha by his vices to our cause, and just think how well it will be received – an Albanian front against Napoleon.'

'Does the young lord have to know? Reputation says he's of the same kind, he can be our Karagiozis, with a big fat cock to catch the devil.' A paper boat bobs across the screen, the Spider, British warship, flags flying, and off goes Byron to Prevesa, dumb little thing in a puppet show.

*

The music is different village to village,
in my village Konitsa, it is lighter, other places
sadder – like the stone we build black or white,
the stone is just for that village, the right stone.

But the songs, most songs, all over about the same,
being away, not home, songs of away, to say exile,
as they play for you, you know Saturday, off work,
the longing of Albania or another Greece or Germania.

*

Eleftheria showed us the painted Ottoman door
taken from the dump, under the blackened surface
a blue green meadow of flowers and birds interwoven
flooding a lattice of apricots and pinks.

Idealised peony or rose, an eternal spring at the centre
the habitation of songbirds, rescued from the tip,
 – we keep it here, not in our rooms, so all can see
and the colours of the house are taken from it.

*

From the capital of the East
two experimental cantos,
the minarets of Tepelene like meteorites
 – who now shall lead the scattered children forth?

Journey made difficult by Ramadan and rain
nine hours lost in the storm at Zitza,
we lit fires, fired guns to find the party;
Byron, cloaked to his eyes, under a rock, content.

Remembered lowering coast and the name – Missolonghi,
dark mind on darker waters held silent;
Wahhabi's rebel brood, their pious spoil
a path of blood running to the west.

At Ioanina the houses and domes
glitter through gardens of lemon and orange trees,
the lake spreads itself from the cypress grove
making a track into a land of no fixed boundaries.

*

Scene 2

At the Karagiozis staged for Ramadan, Hobhouse and Byron agog;
on the other side of the art of the theatre of shadows
Captain Leake unloads guns and ammunition,
Ali Pasha enters, raises his eyebrows and pats the ordnance.

Byron skips on in Albanian finery, begins a letter – My Dear Mother,
he reveals to the audience an enormous penis strung from his neck;
straining, he soliloquises and beats the beast, rolling across the floor,
admiring his guest's performance, eyes alight, the Pasha approaches.

*

The stone villages rise and fall
as if abandoned on rolling Zagori,
we saw photographs of children
on the walls of all the tavernas.

Formal, dressed in white
for a festival in the platea,
rows and rows of children
from fifty years ago.

*

You must be quiet crossing the bridge,
stop the music, dismount and step softly.

Don't let the one sacrificed below
catch us at our wedding in this upper world.

If she hears the music she'll join the party,
the bridge collapse and we'll never cross over.

*

Scene 3

A large room paved with marble, a fountain playing at the centre, men lounge and suck sherbet; then to a rough fanfare painted boys in spinning circles sing 'Oh your curling hair and small ears.' – Ali, ornate craft borne aloft by many hands, responds profundo, 'You must think of me as a father, a father, a father.'

As the tide of seduction rises with pretty animals, sweetmeats and aerial Ali, the devil descends and affixes the monster penis to the image of every future lover, mistress, wife and sister of the alarmed poet: Byron darkens and grits his teeth, smoke from his burnt journals obscures the scene.

*

Streets dark all day, damp
tip tap from the dance school,
houses slumped in glutinous air
nothing for it but drown in the lake.

I am sick of vice, tried all its varieties,
it's time to leave off wine and carnal company

and betake myself to politics and decorum;
— a vast mountain that little word.

Then from the bazaar a wedding party dances,
her hat of gold coins, her face painted red and white,
the men singing — Erotica Erotica, a sweet song for ladies
echoes off the whole world, the girl in coins glinting.

Looking at you what language is left?

The passes we travelled have left a river running in my heart.

The dragomen were silent crossing the bridges.

In that small bay Antony lost the world.

*

The Albanian girls circle the square
on bikes borrowed from the Ingalish,
— thank you, thank you, we bring back,
silver spokes turning spindly legs push.

They circle under the tower's long shadow
and the day darkens for time to stop,
the mountains come falling down falling down
and the world walks away on terraced light.

*

Scene 4

On this side of the art of the theatre of shadows
Ali Pasha is beheaded by his Ottoman masters in 1822,

the blue and white flags of a new nation flood the land
and Byron, poster boy in exile, would lead the children forth.

*

By morning we woke in the bowl of mountains,
snowbound peaks shining up the sky chemicals
of the big fat day on its feet and shouting.

The clarino rising wails – what word, what root will break
the rock wolves in rounds, heads back sing, pelts spark
black Zagori night unveils the first light of another country.

Epicurus Is My Neighbour

He was the son of economic migrants,
the borders had holes in then, the bosses forgetful;
there were compensations on Samos – and fish.

He recruited his brothers as his first adherents,
and seeking undisturbedness he travelled widely:
Samos; Athens; Colophon; Mytilene and Lampsacus.

A car lights the dark road running,
we thought of the towns out there, subtle objects
in motion – the infinite as absence of collision.

Epicurus walked out on nonsense and uncaring gods,
let it come to us by this light, he sat in his garden,
written on carbonised papyrus, chipped in stone.

*

We're walking by the sea Melanie,
the sea's full of stories, wavering and drunk,
the olive trees whirl and stars like spilt milk.

The light slides over the water once only,
below it's dark, all the way down unthinkable,
– so don't think about it then, you'd say.

Let's walk to the house, it's after the next turn,
the air fit medium for the colour shift of night.

*

Epicurus stands at the door of the sea,
he fixes his mouth in place, seafoam

forms an outline like fuzzy television,
the trick is to read it as a poem.

I'm not making this up, Epicurus
waits for the fat snow to fall,
to calculate the disposition of the flakes
the dance of sensory data around the world.

*

Another night in, storm rocking the lamp
the red wine I think, roast potatoes, onion,
readings from Lucretius and a slight moon;
the sky falling away like a dreaming face,
a girl's face looking out to sea, eyes open.

We drove down through swirling fog,
Langada, Thalames, the mountain made invisible,
the roads in Sparta like black rivers run,
a Spring tide of black glass splintering
the roots and names of big gods and little gods.

With morning up early for Clean Monday
the kites sail high as white on blue,
a white word disintegrating the whole sky
keeps us fed, makes us free, let's me sit here
and stare at the green gate to the sea.

*

I saw a completeness	but would not step
it made sense I was	away please not yet
a boy and it was death	then my girls then
I saw their faces	two women looking down

but would not step	I saw a completeness
away please not yet	it made sense I was
then my girls then	a boy and it was death
two women looking down	I saw their faces

*

Herodotus before you run me down in Athens
let me give you a summary of my system.
Ataraxia: I've stretched it on a banner across the street
          ATARAXIA
for all to pass under and gaze upon in wonder.

There's no point in using words that make no sense,
that are unattached to the world; we know it, everyday
we know it, that's apparent despite the same old business;
look at the boundless sky – and my banner,
look at boundlessness at every turn, bodies and void.

*

The wind blows and the house stands,
the roof holds and I see us lie under it;
I see the garden thrashing all night and
the village launch itself into deep water,
the wind rolling off the sea explodes thought.

In mountain clamour the high meadows
blown white and bare detonate particles at swim
against our silver window, a lexicon
smashed and scattered uncoded bright beads
remaking the swept world by morning.

Mountains rise in the empty box of the sky,
the fresh green smell of sap fills the air

and if there's talk around here, it won't trouble
the stealthy ships of an unknown country
rounding the headland in silence.

*

A body of fine particles
dispersed
               furthermore

the birds in the bare tree
the birds in the green leafy

furthermore
the mode of investigation counts

attend to the visible
a bound or outer limit set

a single account is the business of those
who wish to perform marvels for the rabble

Thales invented water – Epicurus ease
he danced with Lucretius.

Madeleine's Letter to Bunting

Day 1

The year goes out in a high wind,
sunlight steps across the floor in stripes
and various animals come around for food.

The sea charges petrol blue and lucid,
the whole garden dancing at night
unparades me cat and black sleep owl.

I can see the red hibiscus in darkness,
I read your poem Letter to Bunting,
the start of the dream, in amazement.

Day 2

Sun lights the end of the year
the wind has dropped to nothing
Benazir Bhutto has been shot.

We dug experimental holes around the house,
broke a spade and hoe on buried rock
planted songlines, a lemon tree and shrubs.

Sixty Kenyans incinerated in a church
I climbed into the eucalyptus, swinging
through the world like a bug on a blade of grass.

The sea all around on three sides glows,
I grasped the springy boughs in my useless arms
I smelt good and hung on against sense.

This tree has such a colour,
is it blonde cinnamon, and the etymology?
– she might sweep me up if I fall.

At your age I thought I had a plan,
I did not, or it was the wrong plan;
it was not to be fifty and exhausted up a tree.

Speaking the only three words I have
to the local children bemused,
arms numb – Eucalyptus, if I fall, save me.

Day 3

Took the tallest branches out,
hit the supply cable on the way down,
same sun, same sea and dizzying view.

Face covered in scented sawdust
dancing the ladder tiptoe around the trunk,
no power, no light, no heating, no food.

Five cats and a dog came to be fed,
smoke drifted into the empty harbour
a bowl of smoke from the olive harvest.

Raked out the weeds and undergrowth
around the new shrubs, found a snakeskin;
how the roots take I don't know.

Anchored to rocks, strong white fingers
cling to the underground life,
only the radio news is fatal.

Later, after eating in Agios Nicholaos,
a fishing boat dressed in Christmas lights
would look good out on the water.

Day 4

High wind roaring all night,
read until 3 a.m. – woke to broken sun,
the whole village in its morning dance.

The sea turned a metallic grey
white riders outward bound,
a sound like understanding just born.

My lemon tree looks bonny in the breeze,
we walked over terraces, olive trees
flickering green and white, to see neighbours.

Dionysus has been sighted
all along this coast, the rocks speak
the rivers run his name.

Away cold brother of white thought,
what season sits on your back
over mountains covered in Spring.

She went away one night, left
the children whispering at the door,
her eyes empty, her mind leaping.

And at that, the bright green shoots
pierced our feet and hands to tap tap,
Dionysus rising answers – I want to.

Day 5

Madeleine, my unabashed girl, I'm saying this to you,
because of your poem – Letter to Bunting;
you already have the trick of writing from the body,
of not explaining that you are you and not you in the poem
but trust to the shape and weight of words as you go;
there's no passport for the journey you might take,
just breathing each beat, a young woman breathing
says – snake I want to be bit a little.

Day 6

Has the making of a halcyon day,
the kingfisher safe front holds
what blue the sea has taken on,
as barely tidal music surrounds us;
we sat and played starecat with the dogs,
the sunlight dreams an early spring
like the first morning of a new life.

Last night we went to the harbour at midnight,
fireworks explode, children singing St Basil
to bless the houses of the living;
the priest and the policeman danced together
and the old year tipped into the new,
quick fire shooting across black water
binding the time to set us free.

We could launch the ship of lights
out into the Neolithic darkness,
learn the many conditions of the sea
and sail south around Cape Matapan;
a risen world in that first moment lifts

the candid islands of lyric and rock and sky
from the Aegean heart of all our making.

Day 7

Between etymon and Eucharist
gum tree, I am stuck up a,
to get a text from you on Eurostar.

Saw the fire damage around Paradesia,
hills folded in ash, hills shadowing hills,
miles of it like burnt black hair.

At 30,000 feet out of my tree I
smack into an endless England,
the tendentious politics of a small island.

Beneficial in destroying the miasma
of malarias districts, I swing
wrapped around the trunk.

On the Xenophone Label

Propositions 1

On the Xenophone label
crackling late at night
from the outpost barbarians in the hills
at the beginning as one.

*

That these fossils prove
the earth was once sea
my eye on the substance
the whole world one god.

*

What men think they know
is no more than the impulse
of frogs gathered around a puddle
singing late into the Spring night.

*

From Syracuse Dear Parmenides
the sun is new every day
the sea has covered the land bridge
and the clouds ignite by motion.

*

The limits of human knowledge
do not excuse inquiry
you are not off the hook
the rim of the world burning.

*

The roots of the earth
and the unharvested sea
are above Tartarus the fool knows
set forth from Colophon unmapped.

*

Religion makes men hungry
they sing pray parade up and down
then crowd the taverna their shiny faces
take eat take eat the whole world.

*

In this airy space unconfined
I was not Homer's boy
I was not a mouth for hire
amber set fast about my buzzing words.

*

In the chapters of sweetness
yellow honey gods made figs
made all things clear
iambic frogs meteors first principles.

*

Empirical root holds true
thus I in rhapsody
at the edge of the dark sea
saw the town of men wake to light.

*

Not plague nor Harpagus
but mumbo jumbo mytho Pytho
brings down the city
bang bang you thought wrong.

*

And with my own eyes
silver jackal black snake
green lizard spring I saw
all things with my own eyes.

*

At first I heard the name
Xenophanes of Colophon
middle up middle down
the music of reason Xenophanes.

A Biography of Xenophanes

Son of Dexus or Dexinos or Orthomenes
against Homer
against Hesiod
against Pythagoras
outlived his sons
defender of the city.

Gadfly of Ionia, Sicily, Italy
gadfly against false wisdom
inquired into meteors, eclipses
fishes whirlwinds religion
the shape and location of the Earth
the substance of all existing things.

Inquirer into moderation of conduct .

Greetings 1

Parmenides my friend when
did we last speak how
are you and the horses and
your straight purpose I
am variously employed
in the many Greek lands
to make a living away
from home observed fact
came to call this morning
a warm wind of ignition
stirred the endless sea was
once land and my mind turned
to you in the market place
fresh melons that day off
the boat their liquid knock
as they collide caused an
argument atoms at war the
language of thirst exploded
one combatant quoted your
sharp mind like a knife
melons rolling everywhere
thuk thuk percussion subtle
as honey in sunlight a riot
you recall that day when
unmediated Harpagus
drove us westward the tide
the counter tide turns how
long do you think what is it
in such abandonment my
whole life strung out on wires
rigged the journeys made
lucid sea lanes of the
objective case a marvel

of song imagine song spun
around the earth even as
this letter beats its path
to you there's lightning
out on the waves revelation
along a long tunnel of
sound flooded the harbour
physis a chamber of noise
to knock me down the world
abides no less I saw one
moment the burning map
fire walking on water
they say that once sap
from pine bacchants of
pine in the air around the
house the voice and clatter
of gods they say
a voice in the resinous
body of night of earth
articulated a thesis
rising in a sort of song.

Biography 2

Only poetry can do this
from an island invaded
by the world   only poetry
to the west Greek earthed.

Xenophanes came here
his eyes open he walked
through the valley of temples
followed by twenty dogs.

Thought sharp at first light
reverence   scepticism
opened his eyes on an island
of white marble Aegean.

The cypress the mimosa
the fluted columns rose
from the same impulse
Xenophanes first saw this.

Propositions 2

Number magic is as useful as
a dog barking in the early hours
there's nothing to steal here
only sanctimonious cant.

*

Men's heads   melons
inside secret wet flesh
thinking: thuk thuk?
judged by action – who can say?

*

Let's talk of the old days in
Colophon when the hexameters
ignited first thoughts and we stood
together in the innocent air.

*

Saw a kingfisher flash
green fire low on the water
in the still air of the harbour
nothing of earth about it.

*

Black is their new purple
they crowd the market conjure
an empire of denial magazine hair
oh but I am not interested in this passing world etc etc.

*

The usefulness of fruit
as analogous to men
may be limited however
melons are less dense.

*

The old women sit out
in the slow evening talk
eat they might sing float
away over the dark mountains.

*

Up in the western market early for
weapons systems a new dawn
effaces an ethical consideration
holy script written in blood – yours.

*

The sea beaten out silver
surrounds the children's dark heads
bobbing in family groups
their likeness – another message.

*

Whispered in schools sung from towers
at dawn by rote in the blood
repeated in the houses of power
dog barking sanctimonious cant.

*

To think with darkness abroad
the whole world but one constant
oh my drowned friends all
lost in the bloody roots of reason.

*

The local bees here are black
heavy hanging in the yasmina
even the little white stars come
spinning down to earth from the earth.

*

post-Eleatic clean out of memory
1 earth 2 water 3 sun 4 return
= the moist ground of we who come into being
Gaia 1 2 3 4 ends up Gaia.

Biography 3

The idea shone like static in his mind
as bright as 92 summers in the Greek lands
as morning rolled out to claim its origin
and the seas and rivers exhaled the balmy night.

Watching the shadows run to ground
he thought of the visible, the uncontained,
reason fighting upstream on an ordinary day
as a boy where he stood in the land first lost.

Orchards of cherry trees, silver traced in white rock,
there is one source – constant and the same –
the conflict of interest is real enough,
their mouths big and slack with wealth.

What age were you when the Mede came,
when the sea invaded the land and left its mark?
Image of seaweed, a fish in the quarries at Syracuse,
a bay-leaf print deep in Parian marble.

Greetings 2

Parmenides the Eleatic sun
has hammered my brain shut
beaten flat the mountains and sea
to an oily picture of nothing
in a white hot squint I saw
the village idiot bring the news
he held up a letter and showed
all of us pointing at the black
headlines given the way it goes
he's the best messenger we have
look it says cynical butchers
revenge comes to roost blah the
blah bosses emblazon power on
shiny coins like miniature shields
hoarded in darkness their
commerce but war by another
name the world will end because
of a, b or c or any combination
of private armies skulk in the hills
eyeing up the port for a, b or c
the night barely dissolved at dawn
the tradesman arrive singing
the dogs barking loop the loop
dive under the donkeys kick up
biting the tassels choral yelps
you want these onions this pot
you sure want this cure make her
love you all night everything moving
against everything and the children
chase the dogs the mothers scream
from the yards the men shout
what is going on how can I
pray for a rent cut with all this

fucking noise it is a perfect model
of the One morning stark
the idiot can explain the lot
my brain as I've said is shut
the work comes and goes
the Big Idea holds true
I tote it about the dusty circuit
slip and slide drink the lord's wine
eat at his fatfaced table you want
this thought this lesson on human
understanding everything knocks
against everything the mighty hymn
of substance thuk thuk you know
the verb in Homer designates
the reaching of the water up to
Tantalus' chin and the action
of the waves warding off snowflakes
we're up against it   the world
of land and sea that lies all
about us   there   that's it   picture
me   mouth open   just above
the rising tide of matter   talking.

Biography 4

After what should be talked about
had been talked about, the men were quiet,
at rest, fed and lounging.

The girl sang into the still night,
Xenophanes was not old then, the years fell away,
the experience complete in itself.

She stood amongst them in their woven garlands,
looking ahead, unabashed and beautiful
– there was no philosophy for it.

It would take 2000 years
for this moment to be understood,
no-one spoke, the distance held.

O mediatrix clemens, O Beatrice,
a girl floating to the shore
steps through the door into light.

The End of It All

Plato's thought police and their like would not have it:
for espousing that the heavenly bodies are not gods
bent on doing only what is best Xenophanes would get
five years solitary and for its repetition – the chop.

How gentle is the exploration of the limits of human knowledge;
from inside such inquiry, a faint ghost in an empty land, we hear
a transparent whisper of almost nothing through another's history,
we're not even there and the imperial circus of claimants presses.

Exiled to the roadhouse circuit – stubborn, sceptical, unassigned,
Xenophanes saw one night the cold stars in a presentive sky,
heard the dogs barking tuneful nonsense village to village
and entered the network of the brimming world.

Propositions 3

The invention of coinage
and Lydian luxury   retail
gone to hell in a handcart
prepared the ground for invasion.

*

When I turned around
the garden's green shade
a thin green snake
whipped across my feet.

*

At night two villages away
 – who calculated the intervals? –
of perfect quarter tones the east
calling home in the blood.

*

The heat that summer
killed the cicadas stone-dead
power trembling on the air
the mirage of harbour defences.

*

My children in another land
my days are dust   stop
going around the Greek cities
to follow the money stop.

*

Anthropomorphic fallacy
eucalyptus bee dust sky
blue sky another house *agathon*
sing up little sparrow sing up.

*

The new wine of Elea is sharp
but softens the gathering night
as the memory of small fires
makes the sun rise every day.

*

The branches the limbs
of the celebrants surround my house
against divination fact finding
made me partisan of the One.

*

My hands deep in the logic
of our present language
a spring candid and common
others will come to unearth.

*

The honey-sweet wine
returns us to the earth
first light stumbling block
of the lower town in glory.

*

Champion of infinite logic
captain of the steady state
all things are one in Catana
running to the edge of knowing.

*

During eruption and earthquake
they believe priests wrapped in smoke
take the clamorous crowd as teacher
lest the ground open and mean nothing.

*

In the light of either 'into' or
'in' or 'to' earth (or the earth)
taken as head to foot
exact as human knowledge.

Sea Table

Words Through a Hole Where Once There Was a Chimpanzee's Face

Going Down

Then I was falling and blind
and an angry man was roaring
in my face   and it was me.

*The descent beckons
            as the ascent beckoned.
                    Memory is a kind
of accomplishment,*

Oh Dr Williams you clever man
your words came to me in hell
to feed the insubstantial dead.

That's right over to me, come on Bill
it's alright, come on darling
I won't let you go.

Shall I roll you over in the clover?
we're nearly there now,
I won't let you go.

Melanie how on earth
did you carry us through that night?
I saw you walk the black river returning.

Book 11

And when I was down there
this was in my mind
even though I was not.

The unnumbered dead
the blurred and breathless dead
brides and young men and old men.

Massing for blood honey-sweet
the nations of the dead and you
sifting through my hands – a shadow.

*

Lee has sent me a book – *The Wonder Book of Wonders*. On the cover a deep sea diver in a weighted suit sets to work with an acetylene torch, as fish swim by and submarine plants waver. There's an accompanying note, 'I found it in a second-hand bookshop in Harlech and immediately fell in love with the amazing cover. It's in fairly good condition, except on page 88 someone has cut out the face of the chimpanzee. Hmm.'

*

              wet season
                   most for
      animals earth
                  Herr Forelegs

*

I think I grew up in fear
my dad's alcoholic behaviour

unpredictable and cruel,
you never knew which way it would fall;
– well, it sharpened the wits
but wore out the heart.

    *

And indeed the male chimpanzee
makes a family nest in a tree
and sleeps under the shelter on guard
he dreams of words through a hole.

    *

In the darkening room Pat
– How come you make me talk Pat?
– I don't know, I really don't,
  it just happens that way.

*

I was blind and suffered some short term memory loss because that area of the brain was hit by the blood clot. I was unconscious, then raving and had to be told what happened because I've no memory of it.

It's a trauma for the brain to handle, I know how it feels. I can see fine, with some colour confusion – bright reds and pinks drain to bronze – but with greater clarity, oddly, though the world is busy, intricate surfaces invading my eyes. Unexpected harsh sounds hurt and I see the noise.

Apparently I vomited copiously and kept shouting – help me, help me. I kicked out at the equipment around the bed. – You kicked out like a horse in a box. Apparently I would only do what Melanie said.

I shouted – Tell that fucking man to stop fucking shouting. There was only me shouting, perfect. I babbled random numbers.

I saw faces floating over faces unseeing. Held out a hand to you, touching your nose and mouth, and said – This is your face isn't it? 4 a.m.

*

Brian emailed. – If you're well enough for me to make the journey. I will try to ensure my face doesn't assume a default setting of concern, although my face has but two default settings. You don't want to see the other one.

*

I like to think of Lee sitting at the window of his flat in Brighton, marine light making shallows of the high ceiling. He turns to page 88 in mild surprise at the absence of the chimpanzee's face. – oh.

*

Herr Forelegs waits at the door
a lurking confident bastard
his shirt of bloody platelets
his heart like a fist – bastard.

*

The greatest risk of another stroke is during the four weeks following the first. Two weeks to go. The ABCD2 model also suggests the odds are with me. Cold cold prose, clear as day. Come on you anticoagulants – take these chains from my heart and set me free.

Sentenced to Wonder

An open air church in California.
The marvel of bird migration.
A lifting magnet empties a truck-load of iron scrap.
The Vatican is a wonderful city in itself.
Air is practically a non-conductor of electricity.
A temple of the Doric order in the heart of civilisation.
The helmet and chin strap are composed entirely of bees.
Pompeii was a sort of Roman Brighton.
The victor ends by tearing her opponent in pieces and eating most of
    the body.
Many keen brains are at work on the problem.

*

A man in a weighted diving suit,
acetylene torch in hand makes wrecks fit to float.

The air's pumped in and she rises,
barnacled guns and Kitchener dancing a jig.

But see she floats grey and mighty,
big as a town, ready for salvage.

*

John Coltrane bends time
Bach straightens it out again;
stay with me boys
be at my side, my left and my right.

*

A recording of *The Text of Shelley's Death*.
Alan adds a note, – it might seem an odd gift,
but no, it's perfect.
To be avoided:
– romantic sailors
– romantic sailor poets
– death bed confessions
– sea bed confessions
– boats.

*

Ian's voice recognised
a back bearing shared
small town boys foot it
a blink in the world.

Herr Forelegs made his smell,
– Do you really mean to keep fighting this?
On the other side of seeing
in the crowded darkness, you belong to me.

I can wrinkle the world in front of your eyes
make the familiar unfamiliar,
spit you out like gristle
like a knuckle bone, like nothing.

September out this morning
taxied to the blood test
September at ease the sun risen
the town gets to work its logos.

*

Peter – just walked in to hear this
fell down a mountain, it was nothing really;
let's have no more from the fibrillation department,
it has pestered you quite enough.

*

John's voice on the phone
returned from Finland
the lakes and the land and the lakes
the breaded fish for delight.

*

philip called from the
dark and stormy moor
philip called a climate
of fathers to do me good

*

Herr Forelegs called
leaning in at the window,
– just checking on progress,
with eyes for inner darkness: the shit.

*

Geraldine emailed
Oh Mr. Headache
you poor little poppet
get proper better soon.

*

Andrew called, his voice
his restorative conversation,
here is your vision returned
you must come and see us.

                *

Goldberg skips decorous sprightly
along the neural tracks,
down the digital wood dark and deep
light walks through the trees.

**He stared at death.
Death stared straight back.**

These trees look designed,
them birds is on fire
in loops and swirls the sky ablaze.

A radar script inscribed,
What does it say? What does it say?
The word as non-conductor of electricity.

MRI shows the riot here and here,
let it rip Elijah, roll us in your boat;
phosphor trails a migrant route.

*

And then later, after I returned, you told me,
when you were sitting there by the bed
and talking to me and talking to me.

You opened my eye, my left eye, carefully
fingers opening the lid and there was nothing,
nothing there, just a milky absence.

*

Melanie what were you thinking
when I was lying there blind?
Did you fear I could leave you so easily
or return a shade with nothing to say?

I didn't see any of this from above, from the ceiling,
but I would see you leaning over me, your dark hair,
your eyes stare down burning
like the first night we spent ourselves on each other.

Rain-soaked fields at rest in darkness,
owls and foxes rooting out fresh words;
hidden music sounding from the earth
at each risen station another world.

I would always want to touch you again,
to know what you are wearing, touch your face;
there's no shape for me out there if not you,
our days like turning light open in our hands.

*

katabasis song plays backwards

up from earth, random numbers

dry grass close unfocused

this last word last katabasis

And Coming Back

1

Three women walk down the street
red coat, black coat, something else coat
because it's Saturday in England in winter
their cortex clip-clop echoes all along.

I think their memories match what they see,
I think they draw their colours from the literal,
the bare tree photographed by grainy sunlight
as they walk into town without a folded map.

From the aerials of the assembled cars
there's no network of messages circling,
no lament rising up from the shiny river,
but on its surface everything's about to go.

And if it was today the sky failed, the year
turned a bed of darkness and more darkness,
under it all the learning of the world waited,
all the learning of the world, packed and ready.

2

Red pulse beating black along the line
like an arrow meaning I'll be there
to meet you and read the book of the living
and see the moon float on the dark river.

The chapter of coming forth by day;
the chapter of giving a man a mouth.

The chapter of giving a man a memory,
of not walking upside down in the underworld.

To see the full moon suspended over us,
an unknown yellow world, its practices
lettering the sky for delight of the mind,
to set free the heart lighter than a feather.

The chapter of the raising of the body,
of making the eyes to see, the ears to hear,
setting forth the head, of giving it its powers,
coming forth from yesterday, coming forth by day.

3

To walk away from all of that
and to say I know you, I know your names;
the mind making its own patterns
along a low horizon of muted light.

I think I taught that girl, worked with that man
but no, only in Apophenia, not in the world;
and then to walk away from the buried life,
the trees designed and the light contrived.

I know you, I know your names,
dark ones at the door, sharp ones at the gate,
shadow swallower, eaters of the thinking meat;
my legs hurt, tell me I'm coming through.

From here you turn left, then right at the lights,
the cars pass in a dance, a sports ground there
and here are the shops and the banks of the day,
as almost remembered on the other side.

4

Imagine these poems of the ordinary ascent,
blinking sightless at the cardinal points;
to make a series of journeys above ground,
to know the names holding up the sky.

Here the banks of lights, houses, circuitry
descending to the river as if stepping down,
and in the air above the idea of a river
the satellites call and the trees darken thought.

A man in a red t-shirt suspended above
in a square of yellow light conducts
the dancing mind in the field of offerings,
the hidden city assumes its shape and returns.

Let me follow my heart at its season of fire and night,
and in the days of seeing let me see;
a field of flags, a flight of birds,
the waters of the world in flood.

5 Eight Things About the Arctic

At 71 degrees north darkness crowds over the rim and from November to January the sun rises only in your mind.

We're off the ghost of Finnmark; to distinguish mountain from cloud from sea at this lassitude is unlikely.

In Honnigsvåg the faces of tourists rip and fly over the white hill above the town removed by the wind and set free.

Think of the miners of Kirkenes stepping down into a cold mouth as the price of nickel rises around the world; somewhat ferromagnetic, Old Nick underground takes a high polish.

The weather machine cranks out its orders where time zones meet at the crossroads; bury it and move on through fields of ice, forests of seeing.

Broken plate ice, one slab snow smooth decorated by the claws of a bird, pitter-pat Mr Snipe.

Arctic convoys and U-boat shadows resurface; once there was a country called the Soviet Union of Uncle Joe.

If you pass the Lyngen Alps at night under a round, full moon the whole world is a dark photograph.

6

If I were looking for the source of chill in my bones
I might find it in Kirkenes harbour on the Northern Cape;
the abandoned Russian trawlers, a crane, white walkways,
leave me here where nothing moves.

We see the assembled gear and hidden lives,
lit from far below, silent and ready to play;
the King of the Arctic has quit to find the start of it all,
vacating a snow covered office chair on the dock.

And if I were looking for that cold cold answer,
in the last brilliant compartment of the sun,
the church bell would ring out its contours on the air
compressing the water to picture a polar sky.

Rolling out the sound condenses over ice,
sea smoke trails the boat, twists of light letter the air,
a language holding low around the edges of the world,
empty and endless for the mind to lodge at zero.

7 Another Eight Things about the Arctic

Ploughing into a headwind through the Barents Sea has turned this boat capricious.

Today Nansen you will study the sea running flush under the transparent shelves of vision.

The Sami say you should be quiet and not sing of the northern lights, be quiet and watch or they will come and kill you – but you can whistle them down to Earth.

You – pathfinder genius, limbs and head full of souls, lead us out on the thin skin of the unthought world, step by step to the oracles of snow; beat it out, beat it out and we'll follow.

Meteorite deposits called Satan fell to Earth to be buried here and rot your bones boys.

A cathedral sky breathing white and green waves and arcs; an electric pelt stroked by Chagall.

The King of the Arctic, his furs and people about him, has gone looking for the source of the chill in his bones.

Ptarmigan, snipe, seal – picture me dark night food; reindeer trot faster faster, sing it magical.

8

I saw Glenn Gould drag a piano to the North Pole
to find the perfection of number, the last of the land;
after the magnetic function of the Goldberg principle
and the hexagonal abundance of whiteness dancing.

And in the name of rhythmic continuity
and the abstract necessity of those structures,
I've taken my time to say these things to you;
the contrapuntal requires such deliberateness.

Looking back he saw the line of footprints
and knew another person not himself made them,
from this side of that other life survived
small red pools of light dotted the high latitudes.

Through the harvest of smoking ice, under a blue dome,
Glenn Gould took 32 steps northward into vision;
took fox sweep, dog bark, sparrow cheep
and the sun returning transcribed a new score.

9

With my ear pressed hard against the door
of the Thomaskirche I heard music,
voices through the locked door, a cantata
on the other side, deep in dark wood rising.

Picture in there a contrapuntal interior
of reformed air, stone and light flying,
for the architect of sound at play
up into the roof's incline of 63 degrees.

Dear Goldberg, do play me one of my variations;
da rump pa dump pa de is all we can say,
this music written for connoisseurs
for the refreshment of their spirits.

Da rump pa dump pa de, said the great transcriber;
the horizontal wind rolls up the European plain,
smacks the spire from the past into the future
to release a little aria dancing over Saxony.

10

Blue hills of Argos like distant smoke
drift into Arcadia and the fertile valley;
white on white, after such blindness
we sat in the courtyard of a Greek spring.

We sat in a box of no sides, the air moving,
to read *The Book of Things* by İlhan Berk,
saw the resinous pine tree – pefki
rise over the rooftop to net the names of the sky.

The mountain is a thing Taygetos,
the rusted showerhead speaks water,
the eucalyptus soft blond bow I cut,
the sea a question answered.

George, this might be a way to talk:
stones, ambergris, a fat bee awake;
against history the morning dance
and Souad Massi opens her mouth to sing.

11

I walked to the harbour for seeing
Yorgos made his boat ready,
a girl swam far out, way beyond the island
and the light filtered the rain with a message.

Facing death, love waits there in the deep,
as the lights burn out and the wires melt
the one word to bring to that moment,
the one thing to hold onto at the dark door.

Here in the month of fair sailing a soft wind
sifts the garden world of agalika and lavender,
two women talk in the afternoon, stop and talk;
listen to the rhythm underground, hands buried.

The air's a chamber of bird song and rain,
everything caught in the great rush of Spring;
that we're here at all in the dancing trees,
standing on the green entangled ground.

12

All night the storm stamped and blew,
wind offshore flattening the sea
running fast, suppressed and lethal
every leaf, stone and tile stands discrete.

The sky strums the wires all morning,
wear gloves for scorpions and snakes;
– Do you hear the singing underground?
No, only the white roots whisper.

I've had no news in weeks, nothing;
Leonidas, Augustus advance their sharp shuffle
but you'd best be ready for Alexander's sister,
How fares my brother? Oh he thrives, he thrives.

Yesterday a girl atop a white bull
went swimming past, Europa, the fool.
What sort of prospect is that?
Oh his sweet breath, his low moan.

13

Telemetry, telekinesis, Telemachus, holy shit.
Tell me another one, I thought him dead but he's back;
I thought him white bones cast on black sand,
his grin from the photo I inherit – and a world of trouble.

What zinger popped this one out, what fat mouth?
Radio Troy in the Greek Administration Zone:
father son reunion spells big trouble in Ithaka;
I might as well talk to the waves for sense.

But he's back, ready for action, ready for blood;
he sees himself in me, I'm far from fighting I said,
but then my heart fills – and this is the hard thing,
I've longed for him all my life.

He smells of smoke, drops into deep sea silence,
eyes wide, controls his face at sudden sounds.
What does it take to hollow out a man?
Black bones on white sand, his voyage, my voyage.

14

Of course he's come back, I knew he would;
they do go on the quality, like it matters:
pigs I understand – them I don't get at all,
but this one, not just crafty, he invented it.

They say the sea spat him out, he tasted tough,
spat him out in a river for a good wash.
They say a lot of things, there's a world of saying
and he's the best, it just tickles off his tongue.

He knows which side his mattress is buttered,
always has, my lord, that's why I like him.
I know I stink very bad, and I'm old but true,
it makes me young to look at him, like a boy.

I wonder if they'll sing their duet tonight,
banging her up against that bloody tree thing?
He'll get to it after the killing business,
a sort of cleaning up of screaming and smoke.

15

I didn't think he would ever return,
our lives apart unravelling, blue thread
floating on the air, a lost word gone pelagic,
but he's here, substantial, salty, like before.

His blank Trojan stare tells the story,
burning towers, lamentation turned to art;
I feared he was become no man nowhere,
and now it makes me hungry to look at him.

I was to be the woman surrounded by men,
the pack of them, soft, lascivious, grinning;
the light went out of me when he sailed off,
I poured my heart into a hole in the air.

Every night I talked and talked to an absence,
I've drawn him back, on and on I've said,
to the rise and fall of the sea – I won't have this,
come back, you must come back and speak to me.

16

Large as life Ithaka rolling under my feet,
I never thought I would get back here;
the sea never stops moving, the land now and then;
but here I am, I hold my nerve, I make it happen.

If there's an account to be given, no problem,
I'll say what I did and did not do – straight;
ships drawn up, burning towers, a woman,
if there's a pattern to this it's only visible now.

So that night I lay to sleep on the threshold,
thought of the undoing of these men, awoke
to the grinding of barley, knowledge in my bones,
the house flooded with light and the voices I know.

They stare like I've returned from the dead – well.
I look at my wife and it makes me hungry.
Dogs, see what you'll never have, never taste.
Sweet slaughter of limbs, wetness and her belly.

A Short History of Song Set to Music and Abandoned

Totteling State

I want a Wyatt I want a Wyatt
a Wyatt of my own, a whisper
in the bones Poetic, she sets foot
on the green path laughing.

Wyatt wanted a ticket
for the Petrarch sweet talk class,
he sang secrets stolen in Italie
for Inglish poetry beginning.

Planted country matters
smack in the fat porch of Henry's ear,
left Puttenham counting syllables,
for with such craft he was not caught.

Wyatt was pre-lute, short on honey,
slipped a knife into the padded heart,
a jest a jest or politic ploy;
this is the song of Thomas Wyatt

To sing the Psalms in Inglish
to dazzle sweet spiky Anne
to make a template fine
red and ripe his revolution unfinished.

*

The Hard Heart Consort to play a sackbut riot, rip it up and start again, softened only by recorders and bagpipes as night descends on the river of song.

Thomas Campion

Aswim at the source of the Thames
airy Campion cut his lute,
swanning to the capital, head high
for the season of learning song.

Each syllable slips downstream,
bound in sound free floating
for the abundance of invention
on the sunlight river gleaming.

Now winter nights enlarge
and I've given the day to Campion,
played chess across the chordophone
living in a song, Amaryllis let's say.

Kelvin, how can you live in a song?
My head's hidden in the sound box,
I think with my fingers, the words just come
and glide where Campion cut his lute.

*

The music: sing I Care Not For These Ladies but not necessarily in the countertenor voice.

For the Defence

'…everyday language is a forgotten and therefore used-up poem, from which there hardly resounds a call any longer.'
Martin Heidegger

1

Good reder, the workes of diuers others
Italians and so, the Latine complete, well
so can we, our tong is able to make
Britaine's gayn in that kynde a device.

Of harts Spring love fruite to rage
small hony, much aloes and gall,
the earle of Surrey and depewitted Wyatt
doe proue Englishe eloquence.

From grene yeares stalkying the chamber
to delight the minde, speake now
abundance in the eares of the unlearned
and feed them from your hand.

Good reder for my defence these Psalmes
these Songs and Sonettes singing plain.

2

To move stony and beastly people
and walk in Apollo's garden
where poetry may be found
and the wheel of Spring turned.

To send an apology from Arcadia
where rivers run and birds acquire their names
you must clap your hands over terraced walls
and drive off the black and green snakes.

To measure how Alexander or Darius
strove to be cock of this world's dunghill
dance the antistrophe unabashed
against their trifling trumpet victory.

At every turn contend abhorrence of the lyric
and let the blind old crowder sing.

3

Lyrick poets
ballad pleasure
to be sung
with the voice
reach for your
harpe your lute
your citheron
seek fauor
of faire ladies
and bemoan
their estate
that would be
Puttenham
in their place.

4

Protestant, iambic and triumphant
Spenser sank the Spanish armada,
dropped his classical anchor deep
and the waves came rolling bright.

So when Spenser sank the armada
his ninth line detonated the sea,
set men flying in the magnificent air
the bloody waves came rolling bright.

He planted empire's seed in Munster,
the rebel Tyrone dug it up again
despite the reign of Englishe words,
sweet earth's all turned to aesthetics.

What does it matter now? Everything and nothing.
A genius of acoustics, lived his life on a rising tide.

A Thesis on the Uses of the Voice

The vulnerability of the human voice
Handel said, Oh Cleopatra, that we perish
and it's a fucking shame.

A woman stands there in a red dress
her mouth moving beyond technique,
the vulnerability, few parts of the body

Can match it for beauty unmeasured,
a blessing pours forth out of nowhere.
And then, what to do with the face?

In the pauses of song, what to do with the mouth?
This can go on for days, there's no singing in darkness,
no life above life: work the means at hand to the end.

*

That the voice can turn brightness outward
despite all defeat, his voice was as the tuned spheres.
You might give me some music,
a shower of gold or a hail of pearls.

This is it, this is it, sang Neneh Cherry,
some sounds some burdens can release
answered Tjinder Singh – those sweet birds
launched from the stave into endless blue.

Shakespeare didn't know Neneh Cherry,
he knew Cleopatra, in duet and then solo,
he gave her the best poetry, her breath iambic;
she was Greek, learnt Egyptian of necessity.

He words me girls, he words me,
this chop-logic lawyer, this boy emperor;
Octavian was never known to sing,
he owned the world instead.

*

Orpheus was special from the start
neither village boy nor hired mouth
he made the language sound
across the wires of the world.

Small green meadow green
covered in April flowers
beside the track on Taygetos
speaks his one word to the sky.

Make nothing of this
but a platform of earth
dressed in one-time electricity
of camomile, iris and vetch.

Orpheus remember what is done
make nothing of it but
a credible and miraculous green
sing out the song simultaneous.

*

In this fashion the glitter of her language
washed up on the shore lacing the rocks
white silver then gold turning a song
entered the Indo-European core
bright bright a river running of many names.

Sing or else, Cleopatra said – beck, hop, luffed.

Sing or else, Cleopatra said, so he sang,
the intricate arrangement of larynx and tongue
the pressed vulnerability of a living voice
to lead us from the flat opera of the soundbox,
she looked into his face, it was the whole world.

*

Tweet tweet the echo chamber air and turn the handle on a million bird pianola. Blow through the papery holes, phpp, phpp splendid, the whole world comes rolling in, the intervals of splendour. Far off let a chainsaw rip it up to warm next winter with resin and sceptical fire. Campion, Keats and Baby Jack to form a queue, humming and a-plucking on a lyre.

Richmond Fontaine at St. Bonaventure's

If you're there when Willy Vlautin sings
I fucked up again standing at the mic,
a piano slowly steps through the way of it
he sings and *I barely know where I am.*

I think this is not a performance,
in the darkness of the club we're made still,
the piano steps through it, *just lost in this world;*
all distance is closed by a man singing.

Willy Vlautin lives in Portland, Oregon,
my friend knows his hairdresser there;
this song is taken from Thirteen Cities,
I recommend this music as a life saver.

You might like to research the origin of the band's name,
in such ways you can travel great distances and not perish.

*

*(The song is 'Lost in This World' from Thirteen Cities
by Richmond Fontaine on El Cortez Records.)*

Thomas Hardy

Thomas Hardy steamed up on a motorbike,
English poetry tucked in his knapsack;
he dismounted and stopped writing the novel,
fool poets thought he rode an iron horse.

He'd not come for the conference on the death of lyric,
but chasing a mortal song and sweet fiddle tune
out in the field for the licence deracination grants;
look away, it's unbearable, and if you don't, unbearable.

Hardy could have strangled most poets with one hand;
he left behind narrative in the service of the rural poor
and stacked boxes of shaped stones, as a mason would,
crafted from injustice and the resistant heart of stone.

*

In 1887 Hardy walked a trail of singing dust,
viewed the graves of Shelley and Keats
and the skylark burials of Leghorn,
went away and wrote his poems of pilgrimage.

The muse spoke clearly to him that Spring;
she said – You made me up, I'm projected from thee.
Time was a fiction, past and present made one;
music said so, the flashing central sea said so.

That scene in the cemetery stayed with him,
his fellow countrymen loitering on his shoulder;
Genoese semaphore, the anatomy of light
and all the mortal birds of Rome agreed.

Ivor Gurney

'If only this fear would leave me I could dream of Crickley Hill.'
      De Profundis

Tracing Gurney on bright tracks I saw England,
the Iron Age ramparts, GCHQ's inverted mosque,
what's left of Rome, a badger sett, the parish bounds;
dark waves of sound interrogate the coded sky,
Arabic strung up in loops like splattered pearls
binding lives in the secret wood mute and veiled.

Field-song of trefoil
field-song of flood
of stars in the ash tree
sing out Cold Slad sing out.

For nightshift duty lie me down on limestone grasses,
let earth and rooks rise in the blood a mighty tide,
from blue Septembered hills free the mind at last
away from trenches, berms and roadside elevations;
over the land made safe for darkness and all the boys
he sees a civilisation of lovely knowledge fit for song.

Field-song of trefoil
field-song of flood
of stars in the ash tree
sing out Cold Slad sing out.

Tracing Gurney on bright tracks I saw England,
the iron age ramparts, GCHQ's inverted mosque,
what's left of Rome, a badger sett, the parish bounds:
he marches off under moonlight, arms thrashing
through ridge and furrow like an inland sea,
speaks green syntax of Hawthorn, May and Willow.

Field-song of trefoil
field-song of flood
of stars in the ash tree
sing out Cold Slad sing out.

*

Arrange Georgian huff puff backed by a muted brass band; the Hardy, Housman, Thomas choir in the tradition of denial harmonises, playing anger management assurance to the sound of settled England of never was faintly faintly never was, let glimmering Butterworth well up, let Asian Dub Foundation rip helter skelter into Fortress Europe and end with voice crackle of 'all the birds of Oxfordshire and Gloucestershire' filling the air with space and everything swallowed by the wind in the beech wood.

Housman and Graham

I was walking the granite peninsula
beside the Housman Graham starlit fences.

They sped by in a motor car on a jaunt,
heads inclined, dipped in dial light, eyes bright.

There was only one thing they could talk about;
how to construct the bare line without fuss,

A gleaming gantry to scale the darkness,
to see a compact landscape close around their feet.

The old car shot by, Graham retuning the radio,
half-heard song like a river running filled the lane.

*

*The music: at the foot of the stairs, with someone clumping
about above, descends from the top of the house in a clear tenor,
a heartbroken ballad from over the border.*

Experimental Poetry

Experimental poetry exists in the speech of the people
on the tongue of a first lacustrine morning
talking aloud of all that matters and then ceasing.

That experimental poetry has never changed is an archaeological fact,
its faultline running back to prehistory vents wafty abstractions;
if you set out by laying the plan of a ballad anticipate trouble.

Experimental poetry is an unsound source of income and leads to the workhouse,
it is to be found everywhere and is for the good of others assembled;
better walk the Valley of Stones and expect your friend to remain sober.

Experimental poetry wants a mad mother and a vagrant sitting on a bench,
wants them speaking their language adapted to the purposes of poetic pleasure,
living with the birds and trees and the hidden pulse in the life of things.

Experimental poetry is written in the terms of a conversation no-one pursues,
its secret gaudiness snagged on a thorn shapes the dumb wind in a remote spot;
experimental poetry exists in the speech of the people.

The Romantic Tradition

Keats is out there chasing another vocal bird,
skimming leaves, mulch and the circuit of odes;
he trudges the dirty river burning his lungs and
rests on the green altar where everything's ritual.

The green altar stands for the Great Romantic Tradition,
covered in the fingerprints of eager boys and girls.

Fat magnet, capstan, favourite haunt and project
for the tuberculin, addicted and immune deficient,
for every demon daunted MacSweeney made free
by sad song misery sweetly rendered in Birdland.

The green altar stands etc

Lift the trap door in the grove at the last turn of the lane,
drop down through zero, under railways, canals, history;
the music plays backwards, the roots make Neolithic faces,
those people from the village step up together as one.

The green altar stands for the Great Romantic Tradition,
covered in the fingerprints of eager boys and girls.

*

Play it forward Jah Wobble style
unearth the muddy subterranean mix
add that chorus from Tosca the sound of
revolutionaries at the gates of the lovers' city
to strokes on the big guitar swoon ah
then break
blow a soprano sax through a megaphone

*full throat from Shelley and the Many
flaunting heaven slam car doors on the edge
of night   the sinister tunes of Morrismen rising
their occult gestures in a bonehead chorus
Shelley jingle jangles lost childhood diminuendo.*

That Poetry Best Not Written

1 Beware the poetic voice which wants to be your friend and any poet who makes the same claim on your attention.

2 The poetry best not written is artful prose rather than poetry with little regard to the ear or other formal considerations. Most of it could be set down as prose and you wouldn't know from listening to it.

3 Instead of an awareness of what poetry requires to be written there is a foregrounding of cleverly worked images with a self-caressing cuteness.

4 The imagery developed in this sort of structure is a type of luxury item making unfulfilled promises about itself; it's circumscribed by the logic of the snap, photographic moment of the given stripped down plot, undeveloped situations and figures – the imagery only serves that purpose, it's rendered safely bound up in that formal chain.

5 The structure normally reaches a predictable conclusion telling the reader something meaningful, sad, amusing, or tragic about the human condition; it pretends to have reached this conclusion as a discovery.

6 So, this digestible hybrid of formica lyric lite produces anaemic prose cum limping poetry and is delivered in a strangely flat, modulated manner which aspires to a sort of ordinariness – I'm like you underneath, believe me. (See 1)

7 I think I read it to see if I've missed something but its mighty emptiness, oddly, just induces claustrophobia.

*

*There is no music for this, only
the noise of dust, reduction and deafness;
play it backwards, it's all the same,
some dull fudgy bass fingered by an idiot.*

All the Poets

All the poets were in one room talking and not talking,
I was asleep trying to join one note of bird song to another;
it was impossible, it was that sort of thinking made obvious
and the blank days were far apart, months apart and gaping.

– Well, that's just fine, the over voice said to the assembled,
some people like to go out dancing, others like us we gotta work;
fine, it reminds me of the one literature and decades of expansion:
nothing makes poetry happen, and all the poets said me me me.

I heard the reshuffling of the nations on hidden cards,
it was murderous, the markets going ding-dong on the border
and the embossed names gouging trends across mineral lands;
this part isn't complex, just a form of repetition to dull the wits.

Nothing makes poetry happen, not manifesto, drones or regret;
but for all the faithful ploughing of the hexameter field,
for all that learning made to serve a clotted tongue,
poetry's already there, beating the bounds of our rushing days.

Ghost House

There's a ghost in my house
the ghost of your memory poetry
or what I misremember each day
and over which I walk.

R Dean Taylor sang this to me
when I was a boy seeing the future,
I danced that Tamla riff iambic
smack off a sprung floor.

Afterthought will nominate
ghosts unevoked but present
as if the house is big enough
to admit the clamorous crowd.

There's a ghost in my house
poets whisper in the walls
the sad troupe at last a choir
in my house raising one voice.

*

*Repeat the ghostly big guitar riff, 1, 2, 3, 4,
all the way through.*

Elizabeth Bishop

Elizabeth Bishop leapt from the tender at Santos
danced across the snappy waves on sprightly toes
and swam the muddy tracks to Vigia.

In Petrópolis one night she listened to the ticking rain,
the wealth of insects eating through the walls;
rain come rain on my effulgent, flowing garden, come.

She collected animals and cared for them,
a big fish, an armadillo, a crab and various humans;
she had the sharp eye hungry for the brimming world.

Magnetic north, the taste of iron faded far away;
she found how the green country answered her,
a hummingbird in foliage offering precise dictation.

*

The music is to arrive from the future, to be played with cold hands, a lost samba dark and buried, drunk and discordant with insistent insect accompaniment in the manner of a heart-broken love song.

The Senior Choir

After the glory found on lyric stairways
a theory of craft labour took hold in Cambridge,
the Sunni triangle of old learning and new money
made London capital of foreign occupation,
though Milton would refine the franchise.

At some point for the locals it all tilts
relaxing into their novels and morality,
at one time choirs on the street saved the poor;
if songs set us free, we already have them all,
called conflict of interest in the history of the jig.

*

Tap out a muted canon on the White Stones *of Jeremy Prynne, every moment, every note counts; the climate is entirely musical. Each city emits a loyal note, play it for all you are worth, at each station the music accumulates as you go forward. The tempo is to be anthropometric, expansive and exact; brass crescendo to clear the sinuses and eyes. Make the cadence rain down, without thinking about it; strike the final chord to reveal a fresh place.*

When I First Got Geraldine

It was a reading in Sheffield
                         the song
swooping and running on
compassion to lift up a child
a witness   against unkindness
against the pompous and powerful
and the other works of men.

And Geraldine was singing
the small parts of words
to get under their skin
before the scheme took hold
and I got it – just, *bloody hell
you what,* all the rubbish
wiped off the words for kindness.

Another time she was on a ferry
with Kylie and Kylie had the hiccoughs
and was a murderer or murderee,
the poor little thing, and the M.V. Kindness
takes us all to the other side
with Geraldine and Alan, Kylie and Nick;
across the River Tagus in the Spring.

*

The Kylie Minogue Nick Cave duet Where The Wild Roses Grow is on the cd Murder Ballads *but we were singing all together Happy Birthday To You late into the steely night for the dancing trees in the garden and the taxis coming and going.*

Peter Riley

I think the way to read poetry

Bars of light fell on the page
and delight returned,
out of those black shapes life poured
the spars of meaning, struts and arcs.

Screw up your brows and peer at the words

In the ordinary commerce of our speech
syntax breathing its first immaculate,
somewhere from the back of my head
I don't know what I'm saying, it's allowed.

In front of your face one by one

Here now this book of Peter's and his reading,
little book in this various world
make your way with truths unfurled,
with night-time voice of house and quiet.

Believe everything you hear for as long as you can

I think the poetry landed me here,
a line drawn out to the origin of song
placed an invisible lute in my hands,
knotted my fingers in the sounding strings.

*

*And the music – play any song sung by Grigore Leșe, sung quietly
at night from a neighbour's house.*

Let's have the Roger, Sydney

This is a song about Roger Hilton
reading the *Four Quartets* to Sydney Graham,
which he did rather well,
the Atlantic knocking the cottage all over the moor.

And both men and Rose flew up to God
armed with the Eliot, a few drawings and a bottle,
three faces like full stops staring out of the porthole
see the Earth far below and unfamiliar.

Ah well, we never thought to stand before you,
said the three of them. I know that, said the moth,
nothing's changed by your trip, you won't remember,
just get on with your work, that's all you have to do.

This is a song about the space poetry makes
in the mighty works of Hilton and Graham;
Eliot was never better read for entertainment
and time can be held as a watch from a friend.

*

Begin with Britten's sea interlude Dawn
played on massed kazoos then crash it
shanty in the yellow tone and manner
of pub warmth flooding cold night pavements.
Make a great fluttering in the godly air
for men and women to sing the yeasty blues
fade into the theme tune of Fireball XL5
my heart would be a fireball Plato said.

Little Song Don't Fade Away

From where song comes
she walks asway on light
running shapely down the street
at the next turn whether the lyric
voices a new awareness of self or
the needs and rituals of a community
from the autonomic nervy system.

She comes on tippy-toes pushing up the
drums back brain ape heartbeat mix
the whole field a net of lights tracing
the question of poor Keats and others
sitting on a sparrow's wing
riding cheery into endless night is perhaps
only known to us in song if at all.

*

Sound the Anakrousis then direct a tinkling
of musical frost and running feet at dawn
to make the world new, then sound the Katastrophe.

Sappho

Sappho hit the water and rowed across the Aegean,
popped out like a cork at the pillars of Hercules;
at this distance each stroke a trochaic ripple
joined word to word on the manuscript of the sea.

The gritty sand of Lesbos scours the hands,
shoulders ache, head thickens, sight fails;
bite your tongue, recall the springs of Aphrodite,
pull Sappho, pull over the liquid lexicon.

Her voice entered the western lyric
on the gleaming tide of the capital
like honey in the ear to soothe then madden;
honey, then gall, stroke by stroke said Sappho.

*

*Play the lyre low on the water mixolydian mode with
tympanon for pace, on and on, to be heard even at
this distance.*

A Nightingale Improvises

Last night from the hollow between here
and the first hill climbing towards the mountain,
a nightingale poured out its plural song.

Rising like a quotation out of darkness,
out of the dense plot of trees for tender
the glittering sea as backwash and a bass frog.

The manifold song lifted out of nowhere,
the middle register recitative, the ornamental trill,
slow liquid slide notes and the unimaginable difference.

We walk our shadows along the white road,
the night is singing, out of nowhere, the sound
the night is singing, everything is given away.

Glenn Gould and Everything

1

Along Commercial Street at homing time
he plays Byrd's Sixth Pavan and Galliard,
we're so inland my eyes change colour
from playing the piano since Year Zero.

At night the dead knock on the words,
place the fingers of your right hand
over the left to free the object in mind,
that ghost singing behind the music.

There are those voices which travel
on time by train from Berlin to Leipzig,
three birds at distance aligned.

That the world may be an orderly pleasure
the chart's littered with its symbols,
everything from one thing for delight.

*

Along Commercial Street at homing time,
the air sits a certain way in November light;
at the dance school door she said to her daughter
– Oh well you've remembered that then?

– Yes I did, it would be good, don't you think?
and the words hover as if on the air eternal;
above the grey circuit of the tilting world,
raise my flag here, unfurled with the turning leaves.

The music clattered down the stairs and out the door,
she released her mother's hand and stepped up to tap.

*

He plays Byrd's Sixth Pavan and Galliard
and the winter trees seem to move accordingly,
spare transparent leaves of unremembered green
propose a season of satellites and backlit thought.

There's nothing to see here, just the earth turning
through an interval sustained, though I think I hear
the king shall reign for ever and ever, sense soon
returns and Byrd's bass-line like the world breathing.

Sunlight steps up from the floor at the window
and I see everything come in and begin again.

  *

We're so inland I think my eyes change colour
sea shanties go unrecorded in the local cults,
only the sky whispers maritime, cathedral blue
for the circling beasts over fields of mud.

After a low in the South West approaches
the country shrinks and the money migrates,
you can imagine the spineless tribe in charge,
telling lies about the poor and their care.

The weather is not a sign of the human condition
but attention to it is one way to let everything in.

  *

From Year Zero to play the piano
he sat on the chair his father made,
eyes level with the keys suspended
his hands like birds descending.

> Guerrero's technique and the folding chair
> hovering 14 inches off the ground, no brakes;
> his hands rise and fall and run thinking
> to climb the black and white ladder of sound.

> *

At night the dead knock on the words,
they come in from the street and line up
with their black mouths open, they tap tap,
on the empty heart of the poetry of the world.

The struts and curves wear and break, case obscured
the breath leaks out of them across the table.

A dark inheritance, that tap tap, then nothing,
a voice about the house barely heard
the other side of the wall, at the next door,
all purpose fails in the senseless dust it stirs.

> *

> Glenn place the fingers of your right hand
> over the fingers of the left, good, now, tap tap.
> Can you feel the exact pressure required?
> Tap tap: that clarity calibrates the singing world.

> *

He sets out to work with object in mind,
the shadow ace in layers, slight at this hour;
one sound answers another in calm geometry
and the landscape's there, with or without us.

At this point Apollo takes flight again
and the idea of music invades the world.

It says what we think we have we don't have;
the thought of a voice singing behind the door
discloses at last the shape of it all,
before we spoke against the wordless surface.

    *

    Is that ghost singing behind the music?
    A faint responder in the great profusion,
    from Lake Simcoe across the whole world
    humming the safe passage in deep ocean.

    Subject to the advance of a cerebral embolism
    cell by cell the brain closes, a raging fire
    he knew and let go of knowing in one move,
    walked across the room and opened the door.

    The sky pours backwards in bloody darkness,
    the living medium of all that music gone;
    and if the hand is part of the mind
    it rose up and stopped and he let go.

    *

There are those voices which travel
along the airways above the street,
one to another making the marvel
out of the slow evolution of speech.

Who placed these words in my mouth?
What shall we eat when we get home?

Turn around three times, hold steady
and tune the truth to everything.

Open the door, a second door of light
lies on the steps we climb to the lit world.

    *

    By train from Berlin to Leipzig on time
    sky and flat fields, the first green of Spring,
    there must be a name for this exact colour
    a stand of birch surrounds the shining water.

    Through Südkreuz and Wittenberg
    listening to Glenn Gould turn the crank
    of Herr Bach's magical banjo;
    how would he have travelled here?

    Wig flapping birdlike on a horse,
    aboard a coach or roaring in a sidecar?
    The horse runs and the heart will not stop,
    the music pours out miraculous.

    *

Three birds at distance aligned
lifting in a south west sky
examine the quality of experience,
then two, then the light running.

Layered vision in place where late
the low grey curtain falls.

Contrapunctus the faithless choir,
sparrows blackbirds risk their arm,

flit the garden as the weather beats out
bare hymns for us men and women.

*

    That the world may be an orderly pleasure
    rendered so by the architect of sound
    even the spaces and intervals charged.

    Singing the Goldberg to the waking birds
    Herr Bach and Glenn take their morning walk
    arm in arm around the Thomaskirche.

    In the moment of human invention
    a language immaculate and unambiguous
    fills the innocent streets of Leipzig.

*

The chart's littered with symbols,
an asset floated here, a sell-out there;
expect a low front from the west,
starry signs for a prince views a food bank.

There once was a mythology of weather
but meteorology ruined it,
let brute cause out of the bag of the sky
and we had to be taught humility again.

Schematic rain rains on the just and unjust alike
distributed unevenly, an unkind music in the air.

*

30th Street Studio Manhattan
Dear Mr Gould Dear Mr Davis
deep in the wood panel
resonance under a kind of
blue and Goldberg sky.

The child plays one note only
leans in to listen diminuendo
away from home a dark wood
the world a closing silence
and again one note, listen.

'Producing everything from one thing.'
In the heart of knowing, not knowing,
architectonic passing sound we are
music in the mind compresent;
everything from one thing, for delight.

2

Published for the Leipzig Christmas fair 1741
aria and diverse variations for the harpsichord
with two manuals, for forty Louis d'or,
from nowhere or Count Keyserlink's pocket.

An arrangement of sound held in the air
speaks the idea of a rational world, one voice
not one voice in that sort of dance, the mind
like music moving makes another space.

To walk by an elaborate colonnade
without resolution or climax, each step
substantiating a ground bass, each step
as if from nowhere on earth accomplished.

These pieces of a soft and lively character
symmetry in every part as if just found;
listen, here's someone cultivating good art
Bonae Artis Cultorem Habeas.

    *

Bonae Artis Cultorem Habeas
arranged in variation 9 his signature sounds,
chromatic bar embedded in the fabric
B natural intones the secret art made known.

And yet for all this talk of counterpoint,
the mind as singing thing at first light,
what does it say as we walk off into the woods
knowing the thread runs out or will one day snap?

Count the knots as they slip through the fingers,
descending into the Thüringer Wald at night,
darker still the indifferent birds and beech stands
for the fables lost on hidden paths and buried.

Here in music coming and gone
caught in this scene and devices,
a voice says – do the work you must
by the means at hand to the end.

3

Up in the high room on the sprung floor
from their mothers' thin-lipped aspiration,
the young girls circle and dance – whump whump.

They walk long-legged in the street, through the door,
two boys slope by grinning, – ha, the old dance school,
delectation whets their eyes – whump whump.

Up there in the sky, dance girls dance, for all you're worth,
teeter on the starry blueprint above the town's design;
the piano threads a silver trail for you to set your foot – whump.

    *

    What little music they allow me here
    like dry bread crumbles granular,
    confined to nothing neurones firing blank
    just imagine the reverse, the opposite nowhere
    of the opening of Partita number 4
    so that absence ascends the empty air.

    Only background radiation wrapped in itself,
    imagine the arrowed shadow of blackbirds.
    What rooks? Execrable spelt Stravinsky?
    Darting over the canopy of lit trees
    What sycamores? Anyway that's it,
    shooting across the boundary of the world.

    *

Cathedral clouds coming in
we might fall from the land's end,

sky spinning the sea around
the compact fields telemetry.

Foxes running the dark fold,
the old dog-fox stares straight back
the cubs darting like sparks
on the edge of vision in falling light.

*

Hello, it's ok, ah, I was thinking
out of the Arctic night of radio waves,
What time? Does it matter? The earth turns
whiteness, you know about what I said.

To travel north, sun down for one season
and return to the latecomers, their stories,
spliced and reglued voices elide a climate,
at sea, a south west wind smack in the face.

If you return after long absence
you smell heather from the cape.

*

Walk across town and back content
to see the green plastic Buddha
a model of an inter-city train
a varnished guitar with no strings,
my eyes filming November sun.

I knew then the meaning of airflow,
circuits of action, oxygen absorption,
though the day was dark and down

all of us walking the ballad
de terre vint, enterre tourne.

    *

    Leaving the black hut I hear
    the ice lake crack and chime,
    the wind in the snow-heavy trees
    answers in A-major I think.

    What sort of trees? White shapes on white shapes.
    Countless phrases dance glissando in the clearing.

    I know it's impossible but remember
    my mouth's stopped, my hands still
    the doors frozen shut, a solid wall
    the mind full of whiteness sounding.

    *

One morning you catch the rot of leaves,
the layered problems of the poor, a lost estate
left hanging between the stripped trees;
nothing on earth recommends it.

Vaporised on the breath after the work's gone
the mineral stain leaches out for years,
walking in the shadow of the splashed negative,
there's only a memory of the colour of her hair.

There's only the self-effacing ideology,
down the narrow street the sky doesn't peel back
the walls close in like iron syntax,
half-heard that near music boxed as not for us.

    *

    I pored over maps of the region
    Great Bear lake and Great Slave,
    far north possessed of magnetic powers
    one true note rolling underground
    a wave synaesthesic and undiminished

    Rises from bergs, sea, the blue and white land,
    the voice a shape in air at these latitudes,
    a halo of high altitude ice crystals
    a mineral order acquiring a value unearthed
    and the ghost talking low on the water.

    *

Another day floating off on the big white bed
sky turns white and an unidentified bird sings,
monochromatic his analgesic song
rising to fall and spill from the edge of thought.

No other music joins, even words slip
send the whole enterprise on the tilt.

And here should be – one day at my window all alone
I saw the truth revealed but no, asleep what, 500 years?
The blue roofs at the back of town run on, bright
stepping stones, the sound of distant traffic enough.

    *

    I didn't like the piano, on the other side of it here,
    my tactalia of the harpsichord in flight;
    I remember attack and release, air flowing backwards,
    my sense of the horizontal line rather than the vertical.

How can I tell you? I can trace the dark coast,
adrift but caught in a series of acoustical events
inside the sound of another human voice;
how close the mute restraint surrounding me.

And further along the passage, the mind
a garden emptying itself of song;
the dunnock, the nuthatch, the sparrow,
no attention can equal: all gone all gone.

*

Early morning ice cracks across the park,
we're privileged to wear dark coats and boots
to go shopping in the free market for essentials.

This is an allegorical picture called recovery,
a return to conditions that led here in the first place
and the one language won't do for the other.

There are facts and events or opinions and remarks,
weigh the portion of each presented, stamp on the ice;
it's not my opinion that the sky is blue and unbound.

The bare trees around the park look brown near black,
they won't turn green yet, so you see through the branches,
see the shiny cars zip along the roads in town.

*

I drove through New York in blinkers,
left a horse in a field of light ecstatic
capering tiptoe, bounding the scales of day;
try variation 1, try leaping the fence,
a rhythmic continuity as if just born.

    I nailed my 32 theses to the church door
    of the 30th street studio – tap tap done;
    I remember the sarabande and street songs
    ghosting the Goldberg in darkness,
    an X-ray of the score and my hands thinking.

    *

The miraculous music of the living
pours out of one mind to another to another
into the ears of how the mind is made,
wearing Bach's face, Glenn Gould's.

The unaccompanied singer fresh off the boat;
stepping through the world without metaphor
the miraculous music dances thought tip-toe,
the song escaping us all in or out of time.

    *

    As a boy he defended the fish of Lake Simcoe
    roaring along the shore, the fishermen shouting.

    After cold war tours to amaze the Muscovites,
    recitals in Tel Aviv and Jerusalem of early Israel.

    With all Bach recorded to begin a variation
    on the Goldberg Variations, to make it new.

    Enough, it's enough, hands up, step back to the lake,
    he's rattling the old Chickering serenading the birds.

    *

Up in the high room poised on the sprung floor
you shoot across the boundary of the world,
stand on the edge of vision in falling light
smell the heather out at sea from the cape.

The ballad of *de terre vint enterre tourne;*
the mind full of whiteness takes soundings,
half-heard that near music boxed as not for us.

The ghost goes talking low on the water,
stepping-stones, the call of distant traffic enough
no attention can equal, all gone all gone;
see the shiny cars zip along the roads in town,

An X-ray of the score and my hands thinking
the song escapes us all in or out of time,
rattling the old Chickering, serenading the birds.

Sea Table

1

From this wooden ramp
the total blue spectrum
lifts the sky westward,
the wave cache ascatter

Shaping the Neolithic deal
and Mycenaean rethink,
my table at the window
sets off into the gulf.

John Gould owned this table,
then David and Linda;
he drilled eloquent into the past
we all crowd around it.

One leg tilts, a saucepan ring
embellished in soft pine,
cast off into white particles
launched from the slipway.

*

Change came hand to hand
along new exchange routes
dreaming a map of desire
goods and beliefs unwrapped.

Copper tin gold silver
amber marble lapis lazuli
oils perfumes wines we want
trained horses and wives.

Change came across the sea
on a boat, men with different hair
their words on the water
their eyes sea-green asking.

How do I get over the shape
of your mouth its upward
promise eyes wide around
the words into which I fall?

*

Orion rises over my gate
rests his right foot on the tower
there's movement in the sea tonight
but no fireflies flicker in the harbour
no thoughts ignite the world.

Only the lit graves of Easter
keep the dead with us don't
let them go into the falling darkness
that's your own life you see memory
a stream of cold air in the riverbed.

*

Renegade, excommunicant
Platonist, revolutionary,
inventor of the Renaissance
beloved of the Medici.

Gemistos / Plethon
opens his pagan box,
draws up to my table
and looks at the sea.

Here's the point Gemistos:
to set things right in their kind
is not a trick, secret law or CDO;
the end is different.

He walked the shore scheming
saw heretics flung in the glassy sea,
arms and legs broken – swim, swim;
true faith gasped at every breath.

From the lookout point,
the plain rolls out to Sparta
the future at his back westward,
further even than Rome.

The ocean of thy goodness,
thy boundless mercy to man;
the flow of ideas turns
and is fatal, yes we have no.

*

Recordings of the sea from
several locations in Messenia,
from behind the tower
in bright April swimming.

In the harbour at night
wind and waves funnel music
the dark sea
working on its language.

Shingle channels in from the left
echoes an orderly sentence,

though the bay, the stones chorus
sounds submerged boustrophedon.

And a bird a finch I think
above the path back from the sea
lyric rising and falling
Spring visiting the world.

On wings of digital mimesis
the god of the air releases
modulated below the red zone
his new ancient song with a bullet.

*

Mystras might rise and fall
the Ottoman tide turn but shit
my foot is riddled with something.

The fingers on my right hand
white and cold at the tips but
still there's an argument to make.

And another winter comes sluicing
through the Monemvasia gate to wash
away Aristotle and repaint the gods.

All night I dreamt I heard the sea,
the voice of the sea
in the blue morning made visible.

What is the light doing to the layered
slopes of the mountain and the cypress
climbing out of the dark folds?

Something without name
calls – Byzantium Byzantium
by morning visible for miles on miles.

Plethon meaning plenty, abundant
a furnace lit in Anatolia, Plethon pitched
between Sparta and a piss-yellow dawn.

Malatesta retrieved his bones
carted off to adorn Rimini and
invent the west's Renaissance.

Ships sink and without trade – nothing;
without the border guards' songs – nothing:
calculate the fallout of the Fourth Crusade.

    *

A poor man runs by the table,
his hand takes the food, the light
shines through him, oracular.

The throne of dread necessity
occupied, the voice of fire speaks
in every square where reason lost.

Antiquities taken to order, clay figures
lamps, vases, a Mycenaean seal ring
a horse long-legged spare and free.

The running man loose limbed
running the force field bronze,
the light shines through him.

Boss, help me boss   iPad
see is good   stolen good
not Mafia look in the box.

Look I give you both help me
my family both €250 for my family
look I give you you take home.

In Monistraki, the desperate
a man in a suit of Ikea bags
woven blue underwater shuffle.

The running man flickers by
the newly immiserated
in procession under the Parthenon.

                *

Radio Byblos on air
sang the Anne Carson summer
Big Money fails to buy
alphabet soup for the poor.

The starting point is
ordinary language and this
a claim from Gemistos
yes we have no bananas.

The water is deep
and we can drown
by repute it's crowded
all us men and women.

So all that summer
my neighbours were

the hummingbird moth
and the carpenter bee.

Boats out of the water
the empty harbour receives
bougainvillea wedding
and everything that is.

Swirling through Taygetos
light's gone behind the sky
we cut the eucalyptus, the pine
tuned the wind for winter.

Last square of sunlight
warmed my feet, a day
won from the season
the sea loading its gun.

So all that summer
my neighbours were
the hummingbird moth
and the carpenter bee.

*

Then set said table to breakers
four legs up, rigged a sail, held on,
paddled like mad, farewell
Koroni, Methoni, golden Venice.

There were days of no wind,
bands of darker blue proved false;
days under a magnifying glass
held every sound where it began.

Set course for the Cape
a periplus of the mouth of hell,
What dance is that? Against time
wave after wave, into the Aegean.

White engine of thought
brought to the table;
of marble, of obsidian
the first figures stand.

2

We found twenty signs on the way
though our boat was lost mounting that wave
and below us a ghost boat unmanned,
the water coiled black an episode in our mouths.

The terms, a wall of water running, slick clauses
of something we barely saw through;
we sang from boat to boat in darkness
– Are you there in the deep? Are you there?

We found twenty stones the way we went
by the way a language, not a language,
baked clay or composite, stubborn, gouged,
scratched out on the deck, chip chipped.

So we set an approximate course,
surrounded by the material principle
wave on wave for explanation;
in sight of land with people like us but not.

The stones speak where fathers hide;
at first after the wars, then from their children,
all the fathers in that sad place underground
where the sea sounds zero zero zero.

*

To rescue the drowning is hard;
some with arms raised, others O mouth shout
– How many of us can you hold in mind?
and some swim the graphite sea.

I don't remember the town I left,
only the sun filling the pocket of garden;
I remember that girl, her hair, full of light,
and walking all night to see her again.

A formal rhythm marks white blue white
assumes forward motion, the mind conspires,
each wave different but the same sea running,
all thought held in that furious pause.

There are no ladders under the sea's surface
though speculation wants it so, no step is taken;
though hexameters roll on, not a line will save you,
the dead drift like thoughts cast back in the mind.

There was an island where fresh water ran
my love would call from that greeny shore,
she filled my hands and lifted my heart
but she sang in underwater words to me.

*

We'd drawn up the ships and were waiting,
pitched the goods and talked our business;
had an easy sailing of it to these Greeks,
a tidy harbour, tucked away, wealthy.

Days went and the wind turned favourable;
a crowd of women and girls came down
sauntering in the shade of the stern,
they spoke their words, looked and touched.

Dib-dabbed their feet in wet pebbles like jewels.
What do you want? Look what we've got here.

Dib-dabbing splashes, legs rising and falling;
then everything cracked apart in a single rush.

Everyone saw it in the same white moment;
some of them weighed next to nothing,
a half sack of corn slung over the shoulder
or a live goat kid say, hardly kicking at all.

Waves yielded, opening and closing like oil,
our transit of V and the plural ocean – stop;
that was our entertainment each night,
like dragging a fingertip through spilt oil.

*

I learnt their language letter by letter
reading the names of their boats;
Captain Adonis, Maria Sunday, Lifeboat:
the sea's glossary made me its drudge.

I also learnt to play the zither and the harp
to fancy up silence for common show,
I took up shop keeping and soft clothes;
I walked away from that, it had no flavour.

When rumours of Harpagus or another
closed like arms of a press, like jaws,
I ran to the west on the great slide of the sea
scarring the waves to find the unknown.

Voices of the village square remained,
an echo chamber Spring, of voices overlaid;
as the light enters a shuttered room
the first stories of the old – you remember when…

That island there, the soft blue curve of shore,
looks close, looks reachable and inviting,
but even with a good wind it's a hard days sail
and we don't know what trade they want.

*

And there I listened to the sea
the waves like grease in a pot
slip and slide from the spent storm
no bearing true, no surface sure.

The sea is a different place,
we tie and untie its chords all night;
what we know doesn't count
a song of the mind not in the mouth.

Do you think for all your artful calling
it will unlock itself and let you live there?
Just one day? See that block of basalt black?
Think of darkness, original night unyielding.

And we came to their empire afraid
made our way ashore to hidden villages;
it all began in a house underground,
inside a mound of dirt, a pile of bones.

Like a song in the mouth but not of the mind,
we saw signs that looked like pictures
snakes, birds of prey, four-legged animals
insects, abstract symbols, flat red stones.

*

Whether this was a plan of their harbour
or the altar of the unknown woman I don't know;
in the village there was no evidence of luxury,
they lived off shellfish, dolphin flesh, a little grain;
it was a centre displaced, lost to the new kings.

So we landed there, crunched up the white beach,
there was no business, the obsidian rush redundant,
there were no answers in the high places,
just the archipelago displayed like the first chart;
dawn drew her fingers across the face of heaven.

They had piles of figures in house and grave,
mostly female, their meaning forgotten,
their purpose for living or dead we never knew
but see how the tiny beauty fits in your hand
her limbs and breasts and tender V.

It was a warm still day, the air lucid at rest,
all thought suspended, not even the sea sounding;
there was no saying if you saw or touched it,
a substance drew you out and made you hungry,
it looked like the whole world laid out before us.

*

Setting out, the boat's heavy, low,
pots of oil, wine, furs and wax;
take the safe passage, nothing flash;
unloading our goods and stories
we ride off higher, just born.

These pots we use for ballast
empty of the good oil, the wine,
they go mad for them out there

those barbarians of the far west,
pretty up their houses, unbelievable.

So we Greeks went down to our ships,
not that abducting women meant much,
no more than any other plunder –
honeyed wine, shiny trinkets, decent meat;
we went down to our ships meaning business.

At first you see the sea lanes, the promise,
remember the markets, their special deals,
the girls and their ways; then it's battle lines,
then spar wreckage littering the shore,
Darius or another rewriting the terms.

*

Then without warning we came to
the god/morphine morphine/god moment;
the golden sun falling into those arms
the world turned music in every part.

And she, little Miss Poppyhead, took us
a-sing-songing to the hidden places,
the watered groves and coves the locals know,
the high meadows and the lookout point.

We came off the sea in rags, standing there,
a mighty thing at rest breathing in our faces
held us in silence, the sun leaning down,
in red wavelength red with water for bones.

She gave us honey that blonde, her bearing,
alert, inclined, I think herbs are involved

and bees on the hillside disputing their labour;
she gave us honey and spoke the dark word.

We left under a sky of layered pink,
might as well say we made up the dithyramb
saddled a dolphin like buckos
and rode around the mouth of hell.

*

When the world came crashing in
there was an eclipse, a day of flying fish,
the earth breathing, a night of vision
making the harbour a bowl of light,
then black ships to the end of seeing.

There was a Phocaea we always leave,
always a Massalia of arrival;
along the red routes for the next ore,
shaping a script like a lethal poetry,
finger tips white, then blood returning.

When news of Marathon reached Darius
he knew fury – he sent out messages
for ships and supplies to towns and cities;
he turned Asia upside down
to be shot of these Greeks.

So when the world came crashing in
we set our minds on a darker course,
saw empty spaces around the table
a lookout bird became a white rock
the light rippling red on the water.

*

Into the cave mouth, a wet hole in the earth
where it all goes, the end in darkness bidden;
not at the sea gates in blue light running,
not even a ghost of the bow wave whisper;
the sleeping stone cast and never retrieved.

We suffered the vision of closest things
the whole world washing around us;
thalassocray drowned to support bees,
to house the pretty sea slug, the lichen spirals,
the crab waiting to loosen your sinews.

A fouled hull scours the soft flesh
the face, the genitals and suchlike,
the water's red but no memory lingers,
your dangling feet, dancing dancing,
below an unfixed blue ellipse closes.

No number. No glyph. No account.
Virgin Face. Bright Voice. White One.
Undone by half human song, made mad,
driven down into a ditch of no season.
Virgin Face. Bright Voice. White One.

3

My neighbour's music sounds across the square,
the song overwrought, claustrophobic, plaintive;
clouds of dust invade the house to settle in layers.

The fisherman walks by the tower and waves,
Nancy, Nancy – Yorgos, where is he Nancy?
Look at this, look, what happens next, tell me?

– Our ridiculous government, those idiots in Athens.

Words rise like birds driven off shore
scattered over the dark economy rolling in,
a country pirated, an evident blue removed.

4

Of course after all that there's nothing left,
grounded and scattered in the wet wreckage
born with a memory of the end in darkness buried,
driven down the magnetic hole, epistulae ex Ponto.

I've landed here, head bouncing on the messy table,
bright signals from everywhere burn my face;
there's only one action, one principle to follow,
radio waves flood the upper air calling and calling.

By day I live above the One Gate, look east for news,
abandoned on this shore in the marram and sweet vipers;
I've turned the poetry inside out on a rusty banjo,
cranking up metaphors with their roots exposed.

The city bright gleaming stands and sinks,
the smoke of riot clears and the poor are poorer still;
no man a house of good stone nor a painted paradise,
τραπέζι τράπεζα try eating what's spread on that counter.

Work out the big names, Xerxes, Caesar, Goldman Sachs;
who can translate this lot for you, trace the etymology?
But the music in the air at night is real classical, the song
flowing backwards as it proceeds – and it's not made up.

*

For Eleni's baby at the taverna it's year zero,
imagine the life that sparks and fizzes in his mind;
we come in from the night and revere him in silence.
Dimitrios – may the light shine on him strong as his grip;
Dimitri – may it go well with you in the crashing storm.

What you're hearing passes for news in the sliding world,
clowns play the numbers, bounce the market oopa oopa
and tax the air for breathing in a fire sale for strangers;
let the sea roar and the wind bend the trees unreasonable,
the halo around your perfect waking face holds still.

Even as the TV screen flickers over the pit, all's well;
you'll not be abandoned on the hillside or the sea's margin,
those irrational, brutal practices we no longer follow;
no child, no generation is sacrificed to save the powerful;
we stand in a circle around you to tell you this.

Here's Eleni's baby, his hands reach out to everything,
his eyes track every move and his face lights up the world;
tomorrow we fly kites for Clean Monday, the green the red,
we'll go out with Archylus and discover aerodynamics,
the green, the red, the dancing, and send our messages up.

*

On the TV screen heads shout in stacked boxes,
the killer word – troika troika and a country shrinks;
and my waitress is doing her homework in silence,
intent as the ground disappears beneath her feet.

She is Greek blonde this girl, lifting her hair
to show a neck white enough for a swan to grasp,
her wide apart eyes flicker Europa departing;
thunder rolls in the gulf, booming off Taygetos.

I am researching Amelia Earhart, she was a pilot,
yes, ah, that word, a vi a trix I am learning it,
what she did when she was alive, no woman did;
I am learning English and German after school.

The village boys saunter by her table, look away,
swim in the light of her white waterfall;
– It is my ambition, I would like to be a pilot,
to fly the crowded waters of the Sea of Abduction.

Outside the yellow taverna the world turns to night,
hauling in the silver lines of flight the sky empties;
the black sea calls to the land people, come come
the sea calls, calibrates the heart and spits us out.

*

Saidona was once known as little Moscow,
staring down in mid-air to an opalescent sea;
this is the buzzing spring of greening trees
excited and wired birds swoop and call,
spreading flowers rise high into the mountain.

Saidona is quiet, far off a man hammers his roof,
the aconite, anemones and spilling daisies
dance at the base of the memorial's white wall,
an account, the many names, the lines by Ritsos;
and the sky opens endlessly to the whole world.

In Saidona stones speak where fathers hide,
at first from the wars, then from their children;
Eleas Noeas survived the death camp in Essen,
returned home to be executed in the civil war
and the doors open as if nothing happened here.

Ritsos was exiled and imprisoned on Lemnos,
Makronisos, Ayios Efstratios, Yiaros, Leros, Samos;
he thought wrongly, wrote wrongly and survived;
his voice sings out from Saidona, sings out from stone,
sings out in the vertigo of Spring on a perfect day.

*

Scent of orange blossom floods the ruins,
stones taken from the plain for the city;
what's left of Sparta to raise Mystras
a final stand to fall against the Ottoman.

In the cathedral of Agios Dimitrios
the marble slab beneath the dome
bears the Palaiologoi double-headed eagle,
talons extended to attack east and west.

Constantine stood there to be crowned,
last Byzantine emperor, boss of new Rome;
looking up he saw the great Pantocrator glare,
the roundabout of prophets spin over Sparta.

The small cathedral articulates a message,
flutings form knots, animals jump and hide;
Plethon grins and capers from the prothesis
a centaur in relief after popular conception.

In 1464 Malatesta turned up all aglitter,
took the lower town from the Turk
scooped up Plethon's bones for veneration
enshrined them in a hole in the wall Rimini.

*

The Paliatzis ο παλιατζής: The Used-Things Man

Most days of summer from the white furnace
the used-things man calls – ο παλιατζής ο παλιατζής
broken fridges, bikes, chairs, water tanks piled up;
village to village around Taygetos.

ο παλιατζής ο παλιατζής coming in closer,
bring out your junk, I can use it;
his face is dark wood, subtle,
he's made of sinew and dust.

Psychopomp in a wrecked Toyota,
the air has eaten holes in its wings;
his woman doesn't move, her eyes flicker,
she sits by him, draped, fluid, watching.

ο παλιατζής ο παλιατζής – give me your junk
bring out your bosses, banks, economics,
your big ideas – you can keep the politicians;
see everything disappear in waves of heat.

He looks at what's left of a stripped car,
an engine block in yellow weeds;
he looks, weighs it up and drives off
pursuing better junk in the next village.

    *

The road surface cracks after one summer,
a winter rain sluices down the mountain
takes its course and digs a trench
under the tower's slow turning shadow.

A black ship went by out there, close to shore,
dumbfounded men and a fat dolphin aboard;
we saw them, under full sail out of their minds
off Cape Tainaron and its good grazing.

The music on the water floated by,
we all heard their singing as one voice,

honeyed notes swam below the surface
the shining sea made calm to the edge.

From first annihilation to pressing word
they sang the song every turning hour;
interpretation would require a ritual,
an oracle, a whole troupe of exegetes.

They sat there, the wind drove them on
sailing back to morning, an unknown harbour,
their hands empty and idle, dispossessed
out of a clear sky: that was Apollo.

*

Bring to the table the glassy waters crash
the last run black bull in a wheel turning,
the war the poor will lose, the falling house
and the kingfisher zooming the harbour.

Bring animal heads set aside and grinning,
the withdrawal of international finance
and system collapse as a theory untested,
the first ear of wheat on a marble dish.

Bring to the table ghosted everywhere
a whisper imprinted on the chambered earth,
the empire of dust become an order of song
to salve the glamour burning our eyes.

Bring the vacant places the young abandon,
the light on the underside of wings leaving,
the dark window, the empty chair, the lost child,
the unimaginable mountains and sea untold.

Bring from the bloody ditch Ritsos the ghost
alive outside the bank in blue and white tatters,
bring the creatures from the passage underground
blinking in the light of common day restored.

*

Big morning steps down the mountain,
seeds cloud the air almost a substance
scattered everywhere to see atomised
Apollo of more than 130 names.

Over the sea's static and blue horizon
a litter of language laced the rocks,
bright silver then gold, a song rising
out of the meander of rubble and words.

To see the day lifting from darkness,
from the shadowed houses lives come
work the grain of the wood, the green wave,
a door handle made to fit the human hand.

Do you make music of the air kinetic,
send migrating light from afar,
tune your bees and release your birds,
set olive trees flashing high in the mountain?

They said if he paraded in the village square,
his attendants making shapes like thought;
he would change us, burning our shabby lives,
no-one would go about normal business after that.

*

Come sea wash lucent
over grainy wood wordless
wipe clean the slate
salt rot the stave
stain the cheap pine
sliding buoyant to
the unexplored shore
raise the ships of Oitylo
Ibrahim Pasha's fleet
the Don Juan the Spider
the bonny barque Ino
unpack our ignorance
in a deep bowl oblivion
over my knees knocking
over my frozen heart
drench my head
pour water words
O O into my mouth
talking and not talking
come sea wash lucent.

5

From this wooden ramp today
the sea like blue steel shines
a line of light on the edge of
day breaking on the harbour in 3D.

Water falling drawn into
a temporary white noise
song of the pebbles piling up
in every room of the house.

Make a mosaic of the air,
walk the stubborn tracks
the white stones, the leaf labyrinth
the light-invaded trees breathing.

Lady of the Way, Hodegetria
the inner knowledge
                                and the outer
show us the way   restore the city.

Today we have no petrol,
tomorrow we waste a crop of peaches;
roads blocked, post office gone, today
we have no times around the corner.

And then my neighbour called Helen
called, to speak about the troubles;
and it was a Greek morning for talk
and the history was hardly random.

     *

Waves break along the shore
packing crates, moulded polystyrene,
a red cap without a head.
Haul up.

Off that cape the deepest water,
invisible forest of blind depth
of bioluminescent forms.
Haul up.

Where Europa rides half sublime,
open-eyed with her darling bull
sparking little gods and goddesses.
Haul up.

Egyptians and the boys of
fifty towns, float open-mouthed
under a glassy shine.
Haul up.

*

Late in the year a second spring
the daisies and the mallow
that patch by the chicken coop
making a show of nothing gaudy.

All we need, tender song
a fortune at the window, there
across the way my neighbour
sees his garden dancing.

Abjure dread necessity,
occupied by beasts:

that light a beginning
the voice of the fire.

Boats out of the harbour
the sea rolls in a dark season,
wind from the south, 7 to 8
sea grey, sky a lifting distance.

House tidied for winter
papers squared away, table empty
for another, Yasmina clouds
the courtyard, perfumes every room.

Last night we noticed the children
everywhere, as Peter said of Bukovina,
on bikes racing, jumping the harbour wall
in *kafaneio* light, they flit door to door.

All over the place, the children
tip-toeing next to rolling darkness
spray flying crowns them, everywhere
look – it's you, it's you, it's you.

Facing West

The Abduction Zone

The Abduction Zone

After Argos Io really was in Egypt
sand in her mouth, sperm in her lap;
she took the wet with the dry
a preservative in the Nilotic oven.

She wasn't caught in another account,
unlike Helen of the different narratives;
she was there, she ran or was abducted
Greeks asserted as self-serving ambiguity.

Though the names have changed since then
you can go there, see the long lick of the river,
the deep horizon, cold stars, the bull of Apis,
hear the creak and splash of waterwheels.

Io didn't feel like a figure in myth,
a clause in the east-west see-saw shuffle,
no boustrophedonic ur-text girl;
she liked her nails and mouth neat and red.

I'm a king's daughter, she said,
give me what I want, I don't trade;
the tender little quail for dinner
and at night that one-string song.

*

Then the ancient world wavered
in the voice of Roza Eskenazi,
her volatile rhapsody might breach
the barriers of expectation.

A song circles the harbour wall,
Greek night blackens the village,
the little owls call, dogs die, new breeds run
and Roza my child sings on the edge.

Then the ancient world, who sailed by here?
Oh Cleopatra, that we perish, talk to him;
take our kind tender for the distant dead
their white selves walking against the sky.

Their unaccountable emotional quality,
their feet sliding on the waves;
illegible their names, the distant dead
come calling in an unimaginable tongue.

*

Theseus abandoned Ariadne on Naxos
by the harbour, to the rocks and swine;
the dancing god in bloody riot arrived
and she screamed her head off.

I can't stay here, counting village idiots,
smelling pig flop and that effeminate stranger
spraying the asphodel like a tomcat;
the sea blinds me, the sail-away sea gone sour.

I trip on the beating tide, sway like a tree,
there's no centre here, just rock and wind and salt;
I see the drowned temples of white forgetting
where nameless creatures feed and fuck.

Ariadne really couldn't live there,
so it ended in the olive grove on the hill;

she stepped off the dithyramb into thin air
the sea winking blue all around.

*

Where Ritsos fought and stood aside
where imprisonment drilled his brain,
they've built a monkey house
a monument to fake money and nepotism.

*

Europa swam into Ovid's arms
the sea's crowded and I can't get o'er
the sea surges flooding all the time
a girl wide-eyed as if it all just began.

*

Doctors redeployed to avoid the sick
a swimming pool tax for others,
the scabrous rash of shoddy houses
begins the rot as future option.

*

Reports all along the Pylos coast
last offerings gold scrap metal victims
ships from where? raiders? burning?
light beacons, mobilise, burning, stop.

*

So what are we doing now Potnia?
Do you see them at the foot of the hill

surrounding us, a flood, do you see them
through our transparent walls?

Slaves to an alien code, eyes shining,
mythographers bound and hungry:
will they come to care for purple robes?
Either way, at present, it's of no comfort.

May as well dance on sea glint
and expect to stay dry, return home,
prosper beyond the long shadow
occupied by courtyard stir only.

Lady we kept true to you
in the high places where light is born
and in the caves of bloody earth
breathing, we kept true to you.

*

A warm wind crosses the Hellespont
but subtle rather, a breeze hesitating
slips into the long reaches of the afternoon
and the blue margin between two worlds.

And I remember my submission to you;
it was always there, its slow message rides me,
an inclination in my limbs, just let go love,
then hurtling down hill at the tilt of your head.

You're out there now, a black dot above the splash;
the better swimmer cutting a V, will I ever catch you?
It's a large body of water and deep enough,
on the other side, in the dark village, we'll rest.

That's the trouble, she said, I breathe this element
but where do you start with a founding myth?
These waves absorb me, drown my secret names,
and the last thing I saw – a golden beast swimming.

*

With our expansion westward we found the Sicels,
not even peasants, primitives living in ditches;
what they'd do for some pottery and metalwork.

We mapped out the edges, the coastline and inlets,
never what we really did in there for diversion;
the silver sea to the ends of the earth tricked us.

There's an art to founding a city and an art to forgetting,
our music was in despair, ruined and irrelevant,
even the thought of song scattered to the rim of our lives.

*

So one day there you are out in the meadow
friends together collecting the pretty narcissi,
counting rows of cabbages down to the river;
you laugh and cast lots for sex, for business.

You wave at the coloured yachts gliding by,
Life's Promise, Bright Dawn, perfect names for fun;
and the little rowing boats like breathing
ascend mesmeric into the broad paths of heaven.

Then cataclysm – smashed face down in the dirt,
eye to eye with the roots of irrelevant plants,
their little white teeth snapping underground;
you see the hole in the dark heart of everything.

Of course this is Persephone's practiced song;
as the lights burn low in our buried gardens
and memory flits from gate to gate in rounds,
we're all singing – no we'll not come back again.

*

Hermes donned his cloak, primed his sandals
and lifted the baby onto his shoulders;
for the rest they were naked, at ease.

The baby reached for the cluster of grapes,
ready to drink a river and take possession;
but where were they going at such speed?

Though there was talk of escape and rescue,
looking at them you sensed the baby held sway,
a radiant beam trailing across the blue.

. . .

Hermes was rescuing the twice-born Dionysus from divine slaughter. Some of the dazzling wonder of Praxiteles' statue is the baby's innocence of this circumstance and of his own growing power. Compiling the various versions of their journey would make the sky look like an air traffic control screen at the height of summer. The flight is the point, and a youth rescuing a baby, a god always arriving – a double promise of life.

*

So another day, and there you are in the meadow,
not particularly aware of the archetypal frame,
again a flower picking scene, this time by the sea;
normality at rest in the shadow of father's house.

The white event tiptoed in suggesting dressage,
his mighty breath barely stirring the daisies;
oh feel his soft nose, his chains of dribble stiffening,
an electric shiver ignites his muscled flanks.

Hold on girl, he groaned, plunging up and down,
we might hit turbid water the way we're going;
see that island there floating free in the blue,
between Asia and your name we're surely bound.

Once on land Europa never looked back at all;
subsequent events proved she had a strong stomach
– and a good deal of curiosity: she became a queen,
eyes wide she surveyed the court and liked it.

*

Antiope

Four syllables you slug,
say it Ἀντιόπη An ti o pe
a voice at night opposed
could storm a city.

Antiope, her trickster
and their versions, a voice at night
a shower of arrows
razor confetti falling.

As always, this question
from the abduction zone
Did she go to him?
Did he steal her away?

*

a horse that runs in dreams

a find
        fields and fields
of votive horses
            sprightly black

*

She swore by the dark bed of Persephone
she'd had enough of village boys,
their dumb plucking on banjos.

Give me one who can move at speed
who looks like he can wear a haircut,
give me a horse that runs in dreams.

*

She would listen to country music driving home,
decisions made, hands steady, tuning in and out;
certain colours worked for her on the windscreen,
the headlights reaching forward into the future.

White – meaning blue of the familiar hills,
darkness rushes by like a bow wave forgotten;
from a capsule of dials and calibrated thought
she splashes home to open her mouth and speak.

I heard this song on the radio, I just
I thought it was but no, I don't know,
it filled my head, I just wanted to be here,
the road a lyric, like the wings of song.

Dionysus

Dionysus begins the action by walking on stage;
standing there, frank, androgynous, slender as a snake:
I am Dionysus – and they threw the stranger in prison.

I am Dionysus – and Thebes took off enraptured,
a seismic ripple rolled around like a boiling sea
stirring the poor out of town dressed in goatskin.

Everything went lopsided, the city walls, the women,
a thought tearing the air and the pines bending low,
foxes, dogs, horses blew trumpets and ran in mad circles.

Then Dionysus pursued the action in absolute terms,
light fingered the vine, agon, stop, kill a fool or two, over;
and the leaves clapped their varnished little hands.

At last the earth's many mouths gaped blood hungry,
dark song of smoke rose, pretty wing pretty wing;
her wreathed face held in the mind half a life.

*

We'll come to Cadmus arriving and departing,
as hard as ABC and the hierarchies of meaning
smack you in the face in yet another storm,
to find an account of the alphabet in waves;
ropes sing, big sail billows beating across the world,
and always, the sound the waves make shaping thought.

The wind hit them broadside, skidding on the water,
askew the elliptical grain, down into the glossy trough;
pulling the steering oar for endless correction

they sailed westward – and like a feature in experience,
his back fairing hand traced rounded circles and scratches,
at first light engraved a lexicon, trade routes and ascent.

Cadmus – what have you caught in your net?
Big trouble language and its aetiology,
buried sinews, a god and indifferent fish?
You'll sleep on bare salt-encrusted rock,
limbs stiff entangled, dream of artful speech
and the river running about the earth articulate.

*

Nonnos claims Harmonia was spoken to by her foster mother in a clever imitation of speech, an eastern mode of beckoning. She explained everything but the girl would not have the stranger. She was not mad about alphabet boy.

But there he stood, gold in his body, persuasion in his mouth. Desire licked at Harmonia and then bit and it changed her heart. She kissed her country's dust goodbye and one morning in the season of fair sailing, she went down to the sea with him. At this point, with her first step onto the unstable deck of the little ketch, she understood the nature of myth and volition. She was herself and not herself, the material of the deep song always sounding. Harmonia and her boy would have happily drowned themselves together.

The boat was a common trading vessel. It was full of strangers and crammed with the gifts of Sidon; a graven model of speaking silence, a notion of connected harmony and other goods – copper, wax and dye. These things, and a band of men, were needed to found a city and forget seafaring. Cadmus kept her untouched and they sailed for Hellas.

In their long life together she always thought of him walking out of the saffron valleys of Cilicia. This was before their time in Illyria as snakes in the underworld. And Harmonia would say – Hey Cadmus, do you hear our rhythm dah de dah de, our cart bouncing out of Thebes and the mounting waves of memory and forgetting, dah de dah de?

*

The war is perpetual but interrupted occasionally by peace or mere exhaustion and stand-off. I think it may have always been this way. Ten years of war and ten years to reach home, as preface to continuation. In *The Women of Troy* Euripides depicts the required murder of Andromache's infant son. Her husband is dead, Troy is gone in rubble and smoke, the women and children are enslaved – 'The Achaeans are carrying home their property.' The child is to be thrown from the battlements, lest he rise a future king against the Greeks. We understand this as a pre-emptive strike. Andromache says to her son, put your arms around my neck one last time and let me smell your sweet skin. This is a different order of reality beyond the ops room, the peace conference, the cockpit.

The young are slung by their clean little heels into the grinder. The slinging is largely a matter of ideology and the protagonists in charge agree how to set about this. There they go, the keen unblemished youth, whoosh like stars into the furnace. The pleasure in eviscerating the enemy isn't denied but is best enjoyed by proxy, by proclamation and broadcast. You survive by staying out of the lists and remote from prefabricated thought. Though the bloody dance is everywhere, spraying body parts centrifugally, writing the red words all over the shop from here to Timbuktu. Come little one, let me smell your sweet skin one last time.

*

I can find no account of Persephone's return from the underworld
it must have been on that first day the ground did not open for descent.

She walked in the Spring meadows of Hellas with no shadow in mind
alive in the total field to feel every blade of grass turn and flow and
soften.

The ripe cud of it invaded her hands and flooded her nerves in one wave,
light running like a river in every element of the field of the whole world.

*

Battened down in the house all week, buried
at night the wind roaring us into the waves,
thunder rattled the roof, rain blinded the windows
and in sonic troughs mountains collapsed.

The storm spoke darkness in our dreams,
blew thought to pieces, the season torn apart;
daybreak drained colour from the sky in holes
and the olive trees dance blasted a crop.

Slowly music infiltrated the air
returned the first experience of sound
the rules of the anthropometric world,
all distance washed away around the cape.

ο καιρός the meteorology of gods
dictates a climate of unusable terms,
all along the coast to Trachila,
the sea reclaims its default blue for blue.

*

I was in a light aircraft with my dead parents,
I think it was them, I could tell it was my mother,
the way she held herself, her look and dark hair.

I had a small rucksack with a parachute packed inside,
it kept changing, a cocktail umbrella, a delicate parasol
then a parachute again; timing matters here, I thought.

My mother said – *But you're always going away.*
I said – *I know but I really don't want to.*
Then out into the darkness all the way down.

On the tilting ground of roads and revealed borders,
I was staring up into the dark sky of the absent ones;
they circle the earth to spot us and we never see them.

*

There are crossing points and they belong to Artemis;
any journey is an accumulation of crossing points.

They are marked by shrines, hidden tunnels and entrances,
the trash of sacrifice embedded in the mass of fibrous roots.

From Argolid to Arcadia, from Messinia to the end of the land
we drive the empty post-crash roads of ruined commerce.

Through the deep catalogue of our dealings and mineral certainty,
Artemis, torch bearer, depicts the lot of us moving off.

The journey is never personal – and is always personal,
a hole tapped in the skull, a child curled by her mother.

Our actions autonomous, joined, as if by thermal imagery,
the heat conveys red purple red our dance on hollow ground.

The road takes a final turn to Matapan and the double sea,
enters the inhabited darkness dressed in beads of light.

*

Two old men talk dressed in fawn skins,
holding wands, ivy crowns their heads;
– But the very thought of dancing, cut and caper
makes me falter, it's not for me.

– Come on, let's get on with it, just a few steps,
up the mountain and show respect.
We think them old and foolish, twittering,
then the bloody fool enters and takes charge.

Up there on Cithaeron rivers run, women run
without memory and smiling confinement,
pines waver, animals feed, that song sounding;
come on, step up, show respect.

*

We're here for anthropomorphism to deliver its low blow
and see abstraction cartwheel across Arcadia;
but to stand aside, conducting the disquisition
abandons the figure of the journey and its meaning.

And without asking – what do we know and for how long?
the moment of our jangling limbs is certain, the journey fixed;
my girls walking ahead into the dark streets, baby in arms,
his bright face scanning the whole world for clues.

*

Ino took on her dead sister's baby, she had no choice,
the one unharmed by the thunderbolt that orphaned him.

Keep him safe, urged Hermes, as he landed out of the blue,
– You'll inherit the sea, the story of your sisters, Ino of the waters.

She kept him indoors, unseen by sun or moon,
those drones of spiteful gods plotting smoky vectors.

Dionysus, bright light, you beacon face darling, she sang;
the boy never slept, full of leaping life and hard to hide.

Later, driven to streaking madness by Hera, Ino ran,
her own son, tortured Melicestes, wrapped in her arms.

Under a spinning sky she saved him from her husband,
and mocked by her sister, hurtled the air into whiteness.

She curled her toes over the bite of volcanic rock,
took her dive and entered the deep as Leucothia.

Meanwhile Dionysus lounged in the fields of Lydia,
blossomed and swam in the rolling golden river.

Cushioned by roses and lilies on the dewy banks,
he auditioned his party friends for orgy and riot.

– Hang around, blow a flute, flick a drum, he said.
– Oh she's nice, he said, and the celebrity circus moved on.

Before, Ino had a hand in the dismemberment of Pentheus,
grasped and tore and danced the scatter dance in the meadow.

Ino meaning sinew, erotic prompt, the many versions manifest
but none of this is reliable, just dubious etymology, speculation.

As Leucothia she ran atop the white waves and found her name;
her life was in the sea, diving to save the drowned.

Under a spinning sky she hurtled pliant into whiteness,
ready for the dive, Ino of the waters, Leucothia of the deep.

*

Indeed Dionysus seems always on tour, rolling into town,
India, Thrace, Thebes, Crete, various islands, like a rumour;
leaving a trail of dead women discarded, as if in a ballad,
Dionysus with his village song and clodhoppers ascendant.

Dionysus is always arriving somewhere, hennaed, pissed,
his mouth in our mouths – sings, *let the vines grow over me;*
surrender, whether you surrender or no, the oyster his world,
what's not in his hands, made-up, comforting gibberish.

Dionysus, standing there, says – *water won't slake it,*
his middle dynamic like background hum ineluctable;
Lydia, Phrygia, Persia, Bactria and Arabia claim him,
launched from the Asian seaboard like a prick torpedo.

Orpheus/If I could

Morning of birds and sea sound
on three sides surrounds us,
the sun lays a path through milkwort and daphne;
barely on land at all, a ruined country at our backs
where some lives survive.

Morning of birds, pigeons of the tower,
bonny sparrows and various warblers
weave and chip the air of sea sounding;
to walk along the spit from the peninsula
face west, catch the literal song of spring.

*

Orpheus
      of the scattering
Orpheus
      of song
      of the power over beasts
Orpheus, wry-necked
      from the underworld.

Which is what we know
not the closed mouth mystery,
the torn sounds of song.

Separate scattered singing atoms
that blackbird this morning
and once I heard … gone.

There was a child in a garden,
once I heard that long note
was it the air in a long note?

Like the boundless young sky,
Or phe us
of the bloody spouting tree.

*

Son or pupil of Apollo,
husband to Eurydice,
son of the muse of epic poetry:
name of obscure origin.

Orphne: darkness or night;
his journey to the underworld,
his initiations conducted by night,
origin of the English word – orphan.*

*(Thus, for instance, Frank O'Hara
discovered his genius.

'If anyone was looking
for me I hid behind a
tree and cried out, *I am
an orphan.*'

And it's always crowded
behind those trees,
all of us orphans dancing
– and the trees dancing.)

*

Mycenaean tholoi tombs
stationed across the hills
radiant bones, gold, weapons.

An entrance, a passage, a chamber
ritual of crossing points,
ritual of what is done.

We went down into the fields
to talk the quiet word
to feed them and lay gifts.

*

Orpheus walked the dark path
through black trees arching,
their bloody roots like shadows
seeping deep entangled underground
where the light collapsed in stripes.

The earth gives way at every step,
foot sinks, birds stop singing;
in that silence Orpheus said to himself
– My heart's a stone, I cannot speak,
I don't know what I'm doing.

Worse than falling into a heavy sea,
worse than the biggest wave of the sea,
to be smashed down again and again,
face broken, head empty, staggering,
propelled into a wall of obsidian.

Hit the mantle, then fixed and dumb,
caught in the mineral density of loss;
katabasis to the core, the shadow zone
then turning, her hand on his shoulder
lighter than – gone, and then turning, gone.

*

If I could assemble the shadows and light
which lie in the folds of your discarded clothes,

the pink jacket with pearlised buttons,
the red jacket for work, the black dress like a wave;

their syntax would speak the life we hold in our hands,
show the shape of you I know and slow the running film.

If I were a lark and could rise to sing
I would write my love a letter we all might understand.

Awe fee us
       sing it
out of dancing darkness
       sing it.

*

From the garden we see the stars turning
and we're sure that these words won't fly;
I was thinking rather of the silver birch
sweet and limby reaching out in the night.

There it shows green again, green sparks,
I was thinking rather of you, your face
staring up steadily in the lit doorway
and the taste of you filling my mouth.

No man looks at me like you, you really look;
and there goes the song running for the exit,
the mystery dance slides us across the floor
flips the order of things in the inhabited world.

I see you with my hands, the colour of your stare
in dark rooms, eyes open, stroke by stroke aswim,
a night spent turning the day inside out,
late late writing the book of wonders.

Footnote to the above

Above the sparkling sea displayed
on the stone steps rising to the chapel
permanent black marker boxed in white
– FILIA KOK SUSTS –

From here the Messenian gulf receives
the meeting of the Aegean and middle sea;
a short way out the water is 4 miles deep,
unnamed bioluminescent forms thrive.

Under darkness village dogs bark in Greek,
dog counterpoint shreds the starry sky;
the waves turn and turn about, barely tidal,
barely tidal the stain on the harbour wall.

*

A black boat makes for the east,
a long slow wake opening a V
on water almost glutinous.

They sit fixed and unfixed in their story,
she stares back at the past of her past;
a man's face, a city of men, blanched.

The sky blazes and the sea boils red,
they breathe darkness into themselves
and can't keep their hands off one another.

That morning on the shallow indentations,
dazed and lolling, they scoop out each other
with no sense of what's solid, what liquid.

They don't talk but stare and scoop;
the coast recedes and bearings reverse,
the boat slides forward into the risen sun.

*

That night in the silent city
the gates closed and fires low
Helen walked around the horse.

She ran her hands on its flanks
stroked the charge and clicked an X-ray
of the crouching men patted into slaughter.

Her mouth brushing the grain of the wood
whispered their names in the voices of their wives
and they saw the shape her lips would make.

Old red horse, battered, flaking,
where are we now?
What whispers inside you?

We've crossed the Trojan plain,
rolled through the gate
let's do what we do.

*

We hang suspended above the city,
jigsaw pieces thrown into the air;
the islands and the sea, the Periclean hills,
the Parthenon and Syntagma Square unconstituted,
flicker and fall in bright array as time stops.

Those relationships of men and women turn over and over,
collapse into Saronic blue, the arms of the darkening coast
under the flood of stars over the Argolid and Arcadia;
falling and falling we fear nothing, only the end of thought,
to be layered in dust, seeing Phidias and the face of Athena.

*

Lydian luxury: the invention of coinage
sent seismic ripples pelagic,
electrum wrinkling the face of the Aegean
made the whole world a subduction zone.

Lydia on the caravan routes of the east,
flooding the Maiandros and Hermos Valleys,
whispered, *man is money* in Smryna,
ships head west on the old conditions dissolved

Unload debt slavery and economic facts,
the propensity for genocide on the borders,
a handsome stranger at the door ready to trade,
commodities rise and fall singing their own song.

Look what I've got, said Croesus, hands blazing,
my treasure house, my flashy power,
my lion and bull imprinted on your palm;
the abstract weight fits, shaping all you hold.

*

Eleanor at the taverna that night saying
– Of course the government has a plan B,
we run this business, even we have a plan B,
you see, they have a plan what to do, if if if.

People are tir/ed, years the money going,
how long now is this, not knowing what?
So now €200 is a lot, it was 500, but is a lot,
a lot more than nothing, people are tir/ed.

(Plan B) Dog poets of the Mani bark your lot,
send up your poem of despair unmeasured,
slung into the dome of night your distress flares
fall to the ground burning and you bark bark.

*

The David Lynch carpet squares the corridor
red and black out of sight to the lifts of crisis design.

The Euro Bank ATM in geometric shadow
flashes without a queue at 2 in the morning.

Stray cars, Periclean hills stripped bare, Solon gone
O City, suburb of Kifisia, the neighbourhood of power.

Think hard about what you angle for.

*

I saw an island on the mainland
trees by the waves, the south breathing
from Lebanon on Tyrian seas.

I saw the king of the wet drive his car
over soundless calm and the city of Cadmus
it looked like starry sex or Memphis.

He entered the women's apartments
sought the unguarded chamber of Europa,
she was long gone ferried to the west.

Fountains spouted and fell unattended
desire sprinkled over the earth
and Dionysus sang a hymn to himself.

The party over, why was he there at all?
There was a girl and he was lovesick,
the cestus cinched around his sticky heart.

Comeuppance had him saying anything
just to have her in the springy woods,
reproaching the sky and darling cedars.

I will give you Bacchants for your bridechamber
and satyrs for your chamberlains,
I will make my mind a parade dancing in the street.

Girl, you have the blood of Cypris,
I will I will – all the old jibber jabber,
rejected he left with a thought of Ariadne.

He quit Asia for the cities of Europe,
to rattle the palace of Pentheus
and ready another scatter dance.

Common Measure

Letter to Arov Manttir

1

I wanted to write though you're far away;
out here I'm stuck on this upturned bowl
walking the white bones of the peninsula
under a booming dome of blue.

I don't know the year the season the rhythm
but sense there's no linkage across the sky,
no route around the circuit of daily town
where cyclopean walls fell in the last tremor.

So we're laid open to the sea on three sides,
the wavering world crowds back and forth
lapping at the shore piecemeal and frigid,
and I dream myself anchored in capital certainty.

But the assurance of big knowing has run dry,
a-stutter on the narrow exegesis up the slippery hill
abandoned to the bespattering birds and beasts;
we're belated, spitting dust, scornful by default.

On this arid tongue of no tune nothing flows,
we dance up and down the mouth music scales
like a brittle ladder lofted into the night,
foot on the first rung you can't see the top.

Deserted by the advocates of desiccated speech
I'm embarrassed to say how meaning is spilt,
leaking corrosive in the streets for paddling youth
– but forgive me my fault, this is a night rant only.

Saying what you thought cost you everything,
your ingenious mouth sewn shut and buried;
an audience of white rocks arranged in a circle
night curving darker from island to island.

Pitched into silence I track the lighthouse sweep
in the undergrowth fauna glint and retreat;
the sea for which there's no fixed term
bears everything in the burden of its song.

2

I lay awake again last night
into the hours of don't look,
I remembered their cities
where you must wait and be still.

Power seeps from their houses
from their banks and commissions,
across the pretty night square
I saw you stand up a world away.

In the little drifts of autumn
you made ready the speaking forest
like Russian music on the march
against their rancid craft.

You made ready the speaking forest,
and in truth you said – dump the poetry.
Tell me Arov what's the thread here?
What matters in the end?

She stood in the light of the doorway,
she was still and I stepped through the door;

the rest of my life I heard the first song
and walked in the light of that street.

The first song we always hear
is the shape that language takes
around the charged earth referential,
a substance made in all we make.

A small boy sat on the forest floor,
the forest was in a foreign country
he didn't know that, he just sat there
and his heart was full.

In the drift of leaves falling
he looked up through tall trees,
the leaves fell to his hands a wonder
and his heart was full.

3

Thank you for the account of your situation
what you say of the single gate barring the way
suspended and locked to turn the click of exile,
the very ground cast in shadow confirms it all.

How the houses of power blaze long into the night
wrinkle the brown river upon which they sit;
there's a dark trick to authority like that
but here it's made manifest and unashamed.

Your two recent ballads strike home
Barbarians in the Capital and The Border Guard's Lament;
I can't decide which best states the case
against massive, predictable orchestration.

Imagine erosion of the terms of resistance,
the dismemberment of the ethical state;
our betters high on the hog of language drift
making milk and honey from the froth.

The shape of their power is not complex
but a matter of hidden tunnels and loyalties,
the occasional firework display or sticky pageant
bread catapulted over ramparts for plebs.

The second accounts for much of our history,
says who we are is a function of borders;
those others we jig back and forth with hot-foot
to dance the cognates recalling a greater world.

The Ballad is the dream of an objective poetry;
words shaped and weighed released to purpose
the sure steps to the door of the tower,
the door itself neatly fitted and easy to open.

Stepping inside you find the single instrument
set to sound the dream of an objective poetry,
the song of the well-made thing ready to hand
the singer on stage who happened to sing.

4

Arov if I have you right
these messages you send,
with the first snow at the window
and the forgotten song of the sea,
speak the stubborn joy of making.

If I read you right you say

The movement of water shapes
a surfacery lettering, inscribes arcs
and lines to record an intermittent blue,
a path of mineral accumulation
catching the sky over broken land.

If I read you right you say

There's nothing to fear in deep erosion,
the movement of water requires
a specific vocabulary at root;
in the dark heart of the river its metre
speaks of Spring in a different country.

*

Reports of your last whereabouts make no sense,
dead or out of your mind, holed up in a camp,
a reading man, befriended, writing letters for others.
Really, was that you, dropped at the last station,
the slow earth turning an uninhabited sea of grass?

You said – until you're ready to go, stay;
don't look out the door at the frozen tracks,
otherwise you'll never leave;
a scatter of rotting huts, ditches, a fence,
the inventive ways of men with cement.

Time crouching behind a barricade
staring from a wall of forest at the boundary
waiting for the next wave of barbarians;
the single thing that changes are their names.
The rule is ten lines only, the postcards lined.

Everyday you saw the sun decline
into the same trench, everyday you looked
to see there was nothing down there,
everyday the running music effaced.
The rule is ten lines only, the postcards lined.

5

Today the wind falls on the sea like a drunk
and the impossible blue of sky and water meet;
in the shelter of the garden every leaf, every stone
restores sight by doing nothing, and the white path
laid over granite and the bones of the dead is just so.

To see it merely as the edge of the land is a mistake,
forever unrecorded in the end, the descent
over stones, rockpools, beds of seaweed, takes no adept,
without even a dog-faced sceptic of a seal to see you fall
down into a signal-free zone where raging tides contend.

But here Arov I've translated your last message.

Perhaps it's poetry's lot to sing outside the walls
for all it's worth, for company – as if we make a thing
above ourselves in the air apparent as a flightpath;
come you cormorants, you tearing gulls, feed and leave,
we're laid open to the sea on every side.

You articulates of air, feed and leave
over the dark device on the horizon
carrying, timber, scrap, a final cargo? I don't know.
And those hired hands graft one country to another,
caught in what contract and conditions of the imagination?

Then nothing but a memory of the bonny gorse,
– and walking beneath the dome of scattered lights
then at last nothing but a memory of the gorse
– and I've no idea of the way, which turn to take
dancing both sides of the road into night.

Leipzig

Listen to Steve Reich's 'Music for 18 Musicians'
for the long, slow descent into Leipzig Halle
through the canopy of pan-European clouds
rucked and pinked across the plains of Saxony.

The first lights of town propose an exact location
of fields bound by roads, the Porsche Werke
and the lake pictures a darkening summer night;
double check dial light pilot, double up you players.

We see from the Stasi headquarters in the Runde Ecke
how Honecker made the state a poem in paranoia;
we see the people of Leipzig who took the streets
standing together, night after night to break an empire;
there the music of Bach rises up into the sky
an architecture of light transparent and exact.

*

Joseph Str 7, Leipzig

Lotrowsky the Jewish baker
of Joseph Strasse, his good bread
popular with his neighbours;
ran a fine bakery.

In Lindenau dreaming Zion
with banners unfurled, dreaming
refugees welcome in this country,
where ghosts trip on stumbling blocks.

An inscribed tile in the pavement
records that life and its ending;

a ruined house allowed to speak
and this was Isaac's garden.

His children played in the street
his wife's name was Ida,
*They marched us to the station
with nothing in our hands.*

Ida deported to Riga 1942
Anna left for Chile aged 19
Adolf to Brazil 1940
Joseph to Sachsenhausen.

    *

Even if I could hear nothing
and see in a spotlight nothing
but Tamamo Saito's bowing arm
surrounded by unending darkness
and the fingers of her left hand
flicker over the strings of running genius
nor hear a single note of Bach's Partita:
I would know beauty is made.

And then there's light and there's sound
rising on the air of the Nikolai Kirche
and Tamamo Saito's black hair a river
falling over her right shoulder dances
flowing through the intricate ciaconna;
a girl's hands remaking the whole world.

At the Hospital Doors

The sun shines on the Oncology Centre,
the red cars, the grey, the marked-out spaces;
workmen to the site office, patients to reception,
paces vary with purpose at the sliding doors.

Wind from the distant world sifts the borders
and the light lifts but there's no revelation here,
the working night turns into the working day,
deliveries arrive, innocent cells race deranged.

Pain seeps down into faults below ground,
grips the roots of trees with blackened fingers
sounds every note of diving bird song
and directs the shifting clouds not to speak.

Guided by certain hands and quiet talk,
around whose neck are these pearls arrayed?
Little aria little aria in the streets of dark town,
out in the hollows the air of Autumn sings.

*

*Three ghosts sing for life
from the white sheets of final care.*

I was born in 1920 – I married when?
and then the war, three sons I had, my boys,
my brother died when I was ten,
it grieves me still, that something unfinished.

Well that was me working on the farm,
me and my dad, up the hills, the best school;

though she left me, I love her even still
but oh my daughter's the pillar of my life.

The year? I don't remember. I'll ask Alan,
ah – no, I can't can I, he's gone now
but we had fun, hungry most of the war,
the Mediterranean, salt water out of the taps.

Two women and a man sing for life
moment by moment from their beating hearts,
the miracle of ordinary events recalled
– oh but I miss him, all gone I know.

*

We lie in common secluded, curtained for surgery,
paused on the threshold for time to be removed.

I hear a man close-by weighing his life thus far,
hear his words hit the cold pan of the scales.

Let the sincerity in his heart, lighter than a feather
open the doors from the light and from the dark.

Dream Journey

I fell asleep on the train speeding through a long tunnel,
under that mountain those invasive voices came in close
dedicated to their own preferment at every station.

I dreamt there was a Tory government and didn't know the place,
heard dictation from the mirage book of history in self-effacing chorus,
for instance: the nations we helped make are unmaking themselves.

They live in high towers above the river, sparky sparky they circulate
corporate ghost men and women spin spin in their golden circles,
from the centrifuge they measure the bounce in system collapse.

In the archaeology of long occupation the dust of fallen capitals
rises over our heads and shows how even Jerusalem fell upon itself,
Jerusalem the Golden made dumb with a mouthful of ash.

*

Zaventem is open this morning and the flights
come and go again above the suburbs of Brussels,
leaving empty places at the tables of the innocent.

The girl whose feet were severed by the blast,
the boy who saved his mother,
– *No no, stay here, there's always a second bomb.*

She is learning to walk without feet,
he is learning to carry what he saw;
when count is taken of those families nothing will suffice.

Beaming from a box of light Bruegel depicts the living
and Icarus kicks the sea; parachutes, parachutes said St. Michael,
though the landscape of ekphrasis makes no answer.

Ah, the traffic is heavy today, but no said the taxi driver,
I think there is a problem; gridlock, sirens, helicopters,
we sit in stationary cars, everyone looks at everyone else.

*

All morning I've waited on the terrace of this expensive hotel
reading about Mandelstam and the terror, the genius of Nadezhda;
I sit in the European sun as the Spring rain pools on the tables
to stare straight back at the rolling sky, in the air surrounded
by the genius of Nadezhda and the earth our boundless house.

I sit and work and see the planes come in one after another
arriving on an invisible cord, wheels down, ready for business;
the sun flickering their heraldry makes a dancing yellow,
guided in, their song descends from an expanse of blue,
a deepening tone to touchdown in another country.

Common Measure

I walked out one March morning
the wind chasing the sky about;
saw no future, spoke no claptrap
green Spring came up from below.

I kept the polished artefact of it
in a glass of water at the window
the red oxide ran like a river
in the temporary light of day.

Composed of Indo-European words
it would sink roots into the Earth,
the facets – field, king, village, house
washed all aglitter I saw.

    *

A Man Sings from the Bar and Beyond

Another night listening to Iranian Radio Traditional,
Sonati Reliability: Excellent Bit Rate: 12kbps
prompts the song to rise from an unknown world,
a sustained solo on the sandouri closes the distance.

What shape does the language substance take
surrounding the earth to make the shape of what we make?
Those particles of words as if thinking and speaking,
sonati – the fresh water river rolling around all our days.

It casts the news without meaningful captions,
sends children across the world alone, we know this happens;
I hear Peter Riley read from a CD, from a real town
a possible speech carrying its load lightly on the air.

Under a mortal sky medical conditions prevail,
my regular irregular heart beat patters on;
it's not significant Peter, I hear you in all that poetry,
the grand conversation – and snow is promised tomorrow.

*

Dear Sandeep

Sparta Egypt Troy triangulated
What does it take? Helen thought.
She understood something when the boat
hit the iceberg, the grinding nature of
the sound of desire shook everything.

Like the rumour of a golden girl in Sparta
flooded the villages and made men mad.
Seismic Poseidon – You jealous fuck,
let my thoughts dance, what does it take
for my body to follow? Helen sang.

Dear Sandeep, to your unanswered question,
Today Helen would be? Jack the sailor said,
'To make her into an artefact is to try to kill her.'
I don't know, I think she was already there,
we're predisposed and those men already mad.

It seems a harsh sentence and we're charged:
Helen a substance soft on my fingers
and before me above ground walking,
Melanie's vigil over me all night
talking me back to life, *talk, you must talk to me.*

Driven from hell through the body of air
Greek summer full-blown filled the car,

I saw a woman's eyes and moving mouth,
a way of going about the world, of deciding
what Helen would know and the shape she would take.

*

Melanie you gave me back my life when we met
and saved my life when I fell to the embolism spooks.

I think of you, the dark conspiracy of your body,
when you're gone I'm a stripped pale man who sleeps alone.

I hunger for you, that you are there, proportionate, complete;
if I could explain this it would be an irresistible music.

Sing those slow songs to me as night comes on
from your beautiful face, from your moving mouth.

As you in your life make decisions in the world
sing me those slow songs from your mouth.

*

Let's walk out in common measure
the fit of your hand in mine
the ground falls away at every step
the circuit of Spring unfolding.

Let's walk to the next turn,
you know that place we came to
where woven sound of sea and air
ballads the chambered ground.

A Greek Spring

The Costa NeoRomantica sits in Kalamata harbour
a brightly lit toppling wedding cake of eight decks
above the darkened immiserated town of the Peloponnese.

Sister to the Costa Concordia it carries the grey heads of Europe
to cruise the Mediterranean promising luxury and classical ruins,
that this ship floats at all seems improbable.

The passengers see the outline of the Taygetos on a clear night
and will sail to the Piraeus and the ancient capitals of the East,
they're not here to see where an economy has landed in cataclysm.

On the Costa NeoRomantica a crew of 622 serve 1,600 guests,
the public rooms are furnished in rare woods and Carrara marble
and the walls drip with original works of art worth millions of dollars.

Alcaeus, Sophocles, Aeschylus and Plato launched the metaphor
but may not have envisaged the ship of state cruising thus
and I don't reclaim it for the fleet of the Carnival Company plc.

*

Spring of fornicating pigeons hot-foot on the wires
back and forth to the tower of Captain Christeas,
they measure and clip the coming riot.

Spring of painting stones to protect the Oleander,
Yourgos paints his boat to make ready for summer
everything seen in the green haze rising from the earth.

At night lights low on the water set out in darkness,
three lights, a one-man fishing boat, a living;
and elsewhere on the other side of the same small sea

Pity those who take the 25 minute crossing,
pity those who make it and those who don't,
25 minutes, $1,500 sailing into darkness.

Spring of everything rising from the earth
Spring of everything drowning in sight of land
the air a chamber of birdsong wide as the sky.

*

Outside the plate glass windows of Country Burger on E65
the Spring sun lifts over the plains and valleys of the Argolid,
light flooding the green panorama of deep memory.

Agamemnon lies under that hill, Orestes runs the hidden pass
and the radio sings – you will find me, time after time
but there's no western music for this moment.

The Spring green inundation of the golden Argolid.

Lee Harwood 1939-2015

1

Lee in the high room, Ward 9A East
with a view of the Brighton Sea,
the sound of July's children playing
as a coastal breeze taps at the window.

I drove long tunnels of swaying trees
through Gloucestershire and Oxfordshire,
and walked the hospital maze to find him
through green underwater light made blind.

There quietly asleep, my friend and poet
who gave us space in which to breathe,
that poetry could be like this too;
I touched his arm – *Oh Kelvin you made it.*

Short of breath and *ah the names escape me
no matter,* he knew what was happening,
a handful of poets to keep and his children
he held them there like the pull of gravity.

*

Lee on the mountain, above Llŷn Ogwen say,
the mist parting, Paul's there and it's alright;
no rescue required, no Rope Boy at the ready,
just the clear view and the mountain at his feet.

Reading he casts his artful net,
where have we come, where is this?
I thought it was simple but here…
time has been folded and then let run.

Passing on the late train he waves,
sporting his official British Rail scarf;
the blue and red script of a better country
streams out like a banner across the Downs.

The light from the guards van recedes,
the train slips into a pocket of memory;
he's seeing the last passenger home,
making ready for the next shift.

2

The bees are heavy in the Polygala
and the sure-footed lizard climbs the wall,
the heat rolls slow waves off the sea
and abandons itself to layered silence
– he would have liked its colour, a Harwood blue.

The slightest breeze slips into the house
and my mind's made white for staring,
what I thought I wanted to say drifts and sinks,
the postcard sent too late, an old, blue, Greek lorry;
– Look it's me driving, where do you want to go?

To think of talking to him is like this now,
an unaddressed postcard sent into the world;
the stamp looked like toppling slices of melon,
he would have liked it, considered its provenance;
the people of Melonitsa singing late into the night.

The Melonitsans are poor and own next to nothing
but on festive days gather around the central square;
each citizen brings one precious thing to hold aloft,

then improvises a song, though the rules are strict;
if favoured all others sing a rousing chorus and cheer.

Lee, the bees are heavy in the Polygala
and the sure-footed lizard climbs the wall.

3

At breakfast in the high room at home
light playing across the ceiling,
in the street people walk by and talk.

The sea's just down the road to the right,
the white band of the sea and all the world
making its song for him to follow.

*Have you heard this CD? Rafe sent it, it's marvellous
and here's that book I was talking about*
and this is how I will think of you alive.

*

He stands under the dark tower now,
the sea drags its only word back and forth,
a dog barks half the night, a train approaches;
he waits, turns to listen, courteous to the living.

4

Drinking to the mighty dead in the arms of the queen,
the day rises sea-washed and fit for riding to the end,
with Botallack fallen into sea surge and the sky in ribbons
we're on the tilt, the frame the course was set by broken.

Hereabouts generations of men slipped underground,
the Bal Maidens above unsheltered, spalling the ore;
livings made and lives lost for mineral truth, for tin,
hereabouts the song runs into the earth, the hidden adit.

From below you hear the sea breaking on the shore,
a continuous muffled speech without meaning;
to picture the world from this sound is unthinkable,
the dust-filled air, the empty cup, only restate thirst.

Lee I object to your death – I object to death? How useless
to fight the dark apprenticeship with hands tied;
but drink to the mighty dead on a bright day in Botallack,
where the Atlantic rolls a chorus and gathers unbearable light.

*

Yesterday we walked from Zennor to Pendeen Watch,
tramped the white stones of the path and turfy moor;
two girls swam in the cove, a hovering kite for company,
for colour late foxgloves, seathrift and sea-wash changes.

We dropped into a pocket of silence below the clifftop,
then, step by step, the sound of the sea returned on the air
as we rose out of the hollow and distance laid its claim;
this would have done, it was just right for Lee to join us.

But his delight remains untaken, he'll not stand to see
the sunlit hill towards Morvah, Tor Noon and the Carn,
the exact detail of the Celtic fields green and yellow,
the blue curve of the moor, the band of light to the west.

So I can only imagine him at the kitchen window
up early, asking –*What do you think that bird is there?*

*

and always the sea and the
hills sloping down to the sea.

The sea drew that man into itself
into the formless body of water
through a brimming submarine zero.

We're all bound for Boston
so haul away boys, haul away
though I doubt we'll find him there.

Farewell the good man Harwood
farewell our fairest friend
come morning we'll see no land in sight.

Radio Archilochos

Ραδιόφωνο Αρχίλοχος

'Of the Greek poets of the seventh century BC
we know almost nothing and none of their
poems has come down to us entire.'
Guy Davenport

1

What am I doing here far from Paros,
as if I've fallen from radiant thought?
The whole place is out of season, buried,
the crested grey wave curls under a grey sky.

Thasos is always out of season, stuff it;
all the signs say how far it is to elsewhere
in a thickening Thracian jibber-jabber;
it's harder to find the unreachable here.

I would be a sober border guard, walk the line.
What border? A nest of rats squeaking – *mamma*.
No seriously, tell me what we are doing here?
A better source of nutritious nuts and pig meat?

I watch the waterfront; see the trade come and go,
sit with the washed-up and fashionably wasted;
they assume a witty commentary, make much of little,
their daughters and goods shipped out the back door.

*

Another cold night, the moon high, a small coin
tossed for a cheap scene over hills and sea;
an old woman shouts at the dogs by her door,
they bark and circle and she stops shouting,
and they bark: it's hardly the matter of elegy.

Yesterday a new boat arrived – Golden Dawn,
Shit Day followed by Fucked-Up Night, more like.
When we're gone, what will these Thasians do?
Fall on each other? Forget how to cultivate grapes?
Let the mines collapse and trouble the goats?

Isolated camps, a few hovels, smoke pours out;
spin my shield to your mates, I'll buy another;
that gap in the wall's not topped by my face.
It was a sweet night, the frogs set up their choir
and the sea all around us rolling in silver.

*

None of this is so,
just figures of air
for a theatre forgotten,
dust replaces ritual.

I did none of these things,
not even the sea rinses the mind
nor dancing on its sliding steps;
we're spume, froth, trappings.

In the dark heart of night
only regret is real.
I watch you sleep, the light
pools around your face.

*

These mainlanders, their Thracian cunning,
will adapt quite readily, smile and serve,
acquire new rhetoric, kill us when they can;
there's nothing broken in them
unlike the chippy trash at the harbour.

So much for strollers and playboys,
the clueless pimps of the academy.
In what sanctuary will his name sound,

before they debauch it with assignations
and let their dogs foul the floor?

We suffered the great provocation
of the greening of the season,
saw pictographs arranged by the leaves:
Gloukos is dead – what do I need now?
Grey slab; I write his name a final time.

*

On the morning air a film rises
by which all is made clear
a ghost I drift anacoluthon
tread the marble bones of Thasos.

Intricate white fingers articulate
a dense forest, shafts of light
fall deep in the pines to the sea floor
where the wavering world says naught.

At this turn of the path something
though there's no-one here,
the frayed air sifting shadows
and I walked the river of stones.

*

I saw today the river of stones
white and cursive under the sun, terraces
and the separate compartments of the gods,
such is our morning calendar.

We make ready, loiter, polish our kit,
look at us scrawny cats of the village;

mostly we wait, sleep and remember
licking our lips at mechanical birds.

When I was a boy running about the house,
he, my father, dreamt a thalassocracy,
looked at the sliding sea's crests and dark gaps
and came up with this, his master plan.

A Thasos of the mind, fat and ripe at the crossroads,
the Black Sea trade, Lydia, the young Greek states,
the gold mines of Mount Pangaeum, timber for ships;
and once I was a boy running about the house.

*

So I sit and drink the Thracian wine
before they export the life out of it;
a slow sunset stretches over half the sky,
in what broken mode behind those clouds?
I don't know, I skipped music lessons.

It looks like her arms and legs opening pink,
d d d delight I taste doesn't begin to say it.
Do you think I could have had a life at home,
unobserved content, she with beauty in her bones?
When I'm gone I would hover over such scenes.

The children of the harbour are like dust swirling,
sparrows skittering, happy and dirty as you like;
they scratch their names in our fortifications,
run and fetch until dark, then those with homes leave;
what the others do until morning I've no idea.

Here's a secret, we're smashed on Ismaric mesmeric
and in the bottom of every cup I find a poem waiting;

Exarchos I lead the dithyramb and climb the walls,
my friend in his old slippery dance calls from Paros,
he doesn't give a fig for me on the killing field.

So we fuck and fight rolling across the taverna floor,
though it might be the ceiling, the world's upside down,
a fine place to meet Lady Muse, dabbing her lips so cool;
the boys collapse in a circle, grinning and unmanned,
come on, I'll sing the lead, I know the words out of here.

*

Boys it's not the easiest number
to be favoured of the muses,
a lyre for the cow didn't please the old man,
he spelt it out in stripes across my arse
for all Apollo and the dancing ones might say.

So come, let's sing another song of home,
we dregs of the Aegean drained to Thasos,
a confluence of half-wits and brutes
it swills about our thighs in triple shit town;
the young wag up to his eyes, marked for death.

*

Do you make of me
the landless bastard son
fit only for the fighting
shelled versions of versions?

The aristocrat dilettante
with a taste for rough trade
and my smart name means
top dog of the squad?

I am The Man I am I claim
to please the boys in the clinch;
think all the dirty work we did
tropes cast in blank memory?

The sun shines, the day rises,
spear points are sharper still,
gold-bearing streams run to the sea;
how many voices, four, five, six?

*

Our settlement extended from the harbour
the new markets and fortified base;
we built sanctuaries to Dionysus and Poseidon,
an open-air precinct in the name of Artemis
for commerce of gods and keen men.

There was even, for some to step back in time,
a rock-cut relief of Pan piping to his goats,
floral honey from the high grasslands,
woodlarks, nightjars, birdsfoot trefoil,
pine, yew, prickly juniper and ash.

But Melkarth, seafarer, where were you?
Will we lose this taste for the wealth of others,
this voluptuous itch to have the unknown?
For answer: empire over empire to the horizon,
I saw a mountain turned upside down for gold.

*

Listen you priests and pretty virgins
arrayed in precious stones and gold,

our trade from the east is skinny girls,
stretched-out boys for business men to bore.

You need to know this so drop the shock,
this is the competition you'll face at home;
and there are family estates to settle
and the children of empire to make ready.

As for the thalassokratia blueprint
it was commanded from Delphi
found a new city far-seen, such advice costs;
but Delphi is a sound investment bank.

2

[papyrus   top right corner torn
three words remain
                wrappings Alexandria]

sparks in wheat
[   ] take
[   ] heart and what
you have
                too tattered to read

Thasos
calamitous city

*

even old men
        wanted them
Gloukos my boy
their cunts
                again papyrus torn
perfume [   ] for most part
conjecture
        from the shuttered house

*

Athena .. make me strong
come down   [un]surrounded   (embraced in battle?)
a sea of spears catch at
the sky … ? day (light)   (in holes, shreds?)
fields of corpses stink

*

. . my kingfisher
morning darling
she flatters my stump . .

*

from the shattered house [illegible] out
smoke   gone . . those kids
(in the mouths?) of Thracian dogs

*

. . little muse little muse
dancing on the table
on donkey humpback island

I see your eyes sliding
but will you come away
to Paros of the radiance?

*

the dead flat . . (lie in?)
         pools of shit
(and) don't choke [   ] skim slime   [left side torn vertically]
remember us   killing field
javelins out   earth
remember (us)

*

I in darkness thinking light
she [torn] of shadow (form of?)   (body of shadows?)
stepped out ...
         unarmed – night

           melting (her)
soft fig (pliant?)
               perfumed

*

call the shop for a new shield
I chucked mine in the hot scrap
ran for dear life on good legs
a treasure (ακριβώς ακριβός)

*

. . came to the dark shore
the one light/star/fire – she
burning   the one thing I know . .

3

When we first came to the village we were befriended by three children; Clea, Romana and Fiorella. The families, Albanian perhaps, rented a house at the back of the harbour. The girls would pester to play on our bikes and we gave in. They would circle the square, stretching for the pedals and then make off for hours. They broke the gears and punctured the tyres repeatedly. How? I don't know, I've no idea where they found an assault course of nails to ride over. Their mothers would say – thank you for letting them use the bikes, hand on heart, a slow nod. Our pleasure.

On New Year's Eve the girls lined up at our gate and sang to bless the house – for sweets. St. Basil with your alphabet of sticks, bless the house and a long life to all living there, the lady and the man. It's an old custom quickly learnt. As they grew older the village shrank around them and they're gone elsewhere. Clea, the brightest I think, was learning English, the ticket out. Clea, Romana and Fiorella young women now, somewhere in that other world. Cross the New Year's Cake with a knife. Cut the first piece for Christ and then for the poor, next the host, his wife and the family, beginning with the oldest.

*

That summer the reinvention of poverty was very apparent. The English woman running car hire in the next village agreed, there were fewer labourers around, fewer builders. For several decades Albanians have been the casual labour and skilled house builders in parts of rural Greece. She thought that most had left; Albania was a better prospect now. She shrugged and said – *Well, Greeks have always had slaves haven't they, they'll find some more.* This is an uncluttered, plain view of history. We were having this conversation in Messenia, the slave grounds for Sparta. An older, harder pattern has returned. The young are leaving. The surface style of mainstream European expectations is being effaced. Driving across the Peloponnese on the big, post-Olympic empty roads the towns looked like a war had rolled by and just stopped from exhaustion.

Late one night we heard rembetika, the Levantine blues, sneaking out of a narrow street. For drinks, two young men and an older man were performing outside a *kafaneio*. The old man was missing several fingers, a typical injury for fishermen who dynamite the fish to make catching them easier. The music had its sardonic growl, its bite, its pissed-offness and weary companionship. The young men and the old man all knew the same songs. We'd slipped back decades to earlier bad times; the population exchange in 1923, the war, the civil war. That the crisis is good for rembetika is no comfort to the newly poor. The bloody-minded singing, its mode of bitterness tells you about this dark continuity.

*

I saw a poster today, taped to a post. It was a picture of a politician, fair but with dark eyes and a dreamy look. He appeared almost feminine or perhaps a forgotten descendant of Atatürk. He had that smile; if snakes could smile it would be learnt from him. There were slogans in red print sending the blame elsewhere; anything will do to short circuit thought. Apparently to make things better, right to the top, we must pursue the policies which led us here. Those already at the top must stay put, for their expertise in getting us here. This is called the new way, a revolution in the halls of the capital. These posters come ready faded, soon tattered and the print bleeds.

*

Continuity runs deeply. We went late one night to a performance in the amphitheatre at Epidaurus. The play was *Heracles* by Euripides, and the acoustics are astonishing. From the centre spot of the circular orchestra you can hear the merest whisper to the top of the 54 tiers of seating and, perhaps, spreading out over the Argolid hills; the original psychorama to the plays themselves. The theatre has been there since the 4th century BC. The original capacity was 15,000. I think there were approximately 10,000 of us there that night.

The sky darkened, the play began and we became near silent. Heracles returns from his labours, releases his wife and children from captivity by the usurper Lycus. All's well. And then Heracles is made mad and slaughters his family – and by now it is very dark. Several moments in the play brought us back to present conditions. One in particular was well received. Amphitryon, father of Heracles, updates him on the situation in Thebes.

There's a large class of needy men, who make a show
Of being prosperous; Lycus has their strong support.
They raised the riots; they sold Thebes to slavery
In hope of lawless plunder, to redeem their own
Bankruptcy, caused by extravagance and idleness.

But the play is two and a half thousand years old, removed from us by translation and cultural specifics, and besides everything is different now.

*

A history of empire is reflected in the vulgarly attuned face of the patrician poster boy. You can't look into the drilled gaze of his eyes because there's nothing there; the thinking has already gone to the future. His introspection is about imitating and replacing the life deliberately destroyed and on the back of which he rises. A version of the good times, always in the past and always coming soon, is bundled on a handcart to market for people to buy, to reacquire what was taken from them in the first place. The old perish and the young leave to sing sad songs on scut wages in the very countries whose bankers burnt their homes and stole their economy.

*

After a night and day of storms, of a hot offshore wind at force 9 flattening the sea to hammered tin, scalping the pepper tree and littering most of the garden across the courtyard floor; the old women come out of their doors to talk. About what? Their business, the price of dog food, what goes on in Athens? Where's Yannis got to with the fish van? He's no good, like his uncle, the one who had the donkey. The dogs play fight under the tower and the woman across the square joins in the talk, laying it down. Andonis fiddles with his moped to get it going. The sea's roar is a murmur and the renewed sun picks out every leaf, every surface, every hovering insect.

4

Crossing a big sea (24)
in a toy boat
κατεστάθην.
I am restored
to the light of day.

                                      ἀμφικαπνίουσιν
                                      They will surround with smoke (89)
                                        blinded
                                        hacked at
                                        drained to
                                        feed the earth.

[θεσσάμενοι] γλυκερὸν νόστον
A sweet homecoming (8)
Paros open your arms
make soft your marble bed
night by night illuminated
spoon me your pleasures.

                                        ἀκόντων δοῦπον
                                        Thud of javelins (139)
                                        exhaled bone
                                        of white atoms
                                        a small cloud
                                        forms no word
                                        where you stood
                                        sucked backwards
                                        into black zero.

[Ὡς] κηρύλος
A kingfisher   (41)
flicks its wings
delight flutters
wrapped in her
nectar flows.

            γῆ φόνωι χλκ ονδενηεδ[
            The earth with blood   (91)
            the fields of the dead
            spread but nothing grows
            bones   slippery guts
            on which you build a town

Παρδακὸν δ' ἐπείσιον
Wet cunt   (40)
from the lord of moistness
I walk I swim drenched
the field entangled   she is
always blessed wet Dionysus.

            τί μοι μέλει ἀσπὶς ἐκείνη;
            Abandoned shield   (5)
            added mine
            to the big display
            growing on
            a pretty bush

γυναικῶν
Of women   (10)
of the water

of women
I drank.

        Ἐμοὶ τόθ' ἥδε γῆ χ[άνοι].
        May the earth [ ] for me   (220)
        gape wide
        χ[άνοι].)
        earth
        hold my tongue
        let go the sting
        earth
        my last vessel.

5

South then the circle island's candid calling,
a boatload of tumescent men going home
awash with it, steaming and propelled;
the girls of home flexible, keen from absence;
come on boys, Paros is worth a rash.

South then for the circle island's soft calling;
let's make two colours of the whole business,
the blue, the white, the joy of entering port;
the water churning transparent as thought
we shoot the fast channel for home.

*

I devised the elegiac couplet, iambic and trochaic meters,
dimeter to tetrameter, epodes and asinarteta;
I wrote I every day and coined the term reggae.

And yes I liked a good fight, Ares at my side;
it's true I had the hot sister, the lively younger one,
bragged on every chat show; swing Lycambes swing.

It's also true that critical reception has been mixed;
I was considered quarrelsome and foul-mouthed,
a lascivious, common bastard – or something like that.

It's a bright Spring morning, the air is scented and moist,
all around the little birds are fornicating;
the Naxian who will kill me is eating his breakfast.

*

That sense of something there in the charged air,
I think Apollo Hylates is curving the words to himself,
I think he's got the green eye on my stranger, my darling;
though he'll protect my name against the bad mouths.

The young get Dionysus of course, and don't need him,
possessed of riot, burning day and earth's pulse;
they don't need dancing gods or a presence in the trees,
their moment is unbearable, endlessly pursued, complete.

I built a temple here to the slippery one, sang him up,
sang him up from the streets dressed in iamb and elegy;
the sea like a thought lapping at the marble shore,
our days of figs and seafaring, of honey in the pot.

But unlike H I never had the big sweep,
that epic arrogance to make much of little
– ten years for one woman, come off it;
I rise and fall with sporadic song abounding.

Good spear strike home, cut to epode restored or no;
the tip is worked bronze, balanced, good for slashing,
one, two, fast as you like, opened face, point's made;
though I'd rather be an old dog dreaming in the sun.

Above all else I swear bad poetry will do for me,
the lickspittle decrepitude of our lolling tongue;
after invasion and the markets going yoyo mental
etymology alone counts, crooks make snot of words.

I keep faith in ellipses without reaching for proof
but I'm lost and nowhere between the songs,
a blindness of another kind, a different periplus,
an archipelago of girls in a milky sea.

*

In Candid Town where I was born
there was a young maid dwelling,
stroked for epode she caught my breath.

We knew her name, her father and all that,
not to see her was like death in the street
not to be looked at by her even worse.

In the hot maze of alleyways and markets
the light buds around her and feeds the earth,
step into this darkness darling, let's play gods.

We can cast the nets of pleasure all night,
a gentle pull, a touch here to ease the living thing,
it comes with many names and I know a few.

I only follow your lead, over the wall, into the meadow,
you choose I stumble after, unstrung but for your word;
from my thought you've already wiped all other women.

Even if the goddess were your sister I would be blind.
Shall we shoot the milky stars in the Parian night?
Come let me lay down my special cloak for you.

I have a memory of a girl in a field when I was a boy,
there's nothing like a girl in a spring meadow
tremulous as the April wind rippling her garden.

Your tender breasts, belly and dark cunt
shaping my tongue to our first language;
your eyes and mouth hesitant shed glory on the earth.

I would unravel from you, from your dewy skin
what will be wrapped around a rotted corpse;
papyrus girl, be unafraid, be untranslated.

All the flowers, their little faces dancing to the goddess,
and me, the fool in flood, losing it on the temple steps;
well, let me leave it as a tribute sweetheart.

Pressed against your shape, your colour it gives again;
you were always what I wanted and I'll come back for more,
that you are in the world answers the big question for me.

That you are in my arms slowly turning is even better,
head down on my steady hand, look at me you said
then you glanced over your shoulder and whispered – I need this.

*

From here the ways of Paros
and the sea where the sun goes
to the bounds of the inhabited world,
I keep my feet in the hearth.

What is out there I know,
sweet waters of Siris flow
those islands of furthest blue
waiting for their names.

What is out there I know;
Leophilos friend of the people
Leophilos shiny face all over the shop;
let me translate the future tense.

But I've no spear in my hand,
no swooping crow in my heart;
I'm done with all that, it appears
I reveal this to you here.

*

It's surely a joke that after Thasos, after everything,
I died on Paros at the hands of a Naxian?
Calondas you crow – what do crows eat for breakfast?
Do you see this letter postmarked Hades?

Well I have precedent there with Demeter;
so listen, this is what will happen to you:
my gods can strike the censorious limp,
make the bridegroom impotent and pale.

But you at Delphi will get the elbow from the god,
how does that taste as you flit down Parnassus?
It tastes like shit doesn't it – you fuck:
crows eat their own guts, eating kills them.

*

She held a flag of myrtle and the rose
and stepped softly from the shadows.

Do you know me? I said, and stared,
I'm the first person to write in the first person.

Really? Well the price is still the same,
for you and your friend, Exarchos or not.

*

Last night there was dancing,
thunder rattled down to the sea
and the local trio struck up.

One ancient granddad played the goat
step stop stop – pause, stop motion, shot
and sprang back into it like a boy.

The sinuous girls bending, steady-eyed,
untouchable, make the air a substance,
faces lit up and glistening.

Dionysus from our village dances,
and the music circulates intoxicated,
an enclave of light on the mountain.

*

Archilochos, his voice broken, sits collapsed,
legs splayed on the soft bed of summer dust;
a spear sticks out of his chest, its black length
rises and dips with his last breath and the next.

His last sight those grey stumpy olive trees
or figures of final truth paused by the track,
and below him lies all the geology of Paros
where young marble giants wait to take their form.

Get up, get up Archilochos we need your bite;
will you bring us the news, say who benefits this time?
Archilochos has gone to the rushing night, the dark sea,
he hovers one moment in the light over Antiparos.

Below This Level

Diagnosis

What the Birds Said

I sit by the window and read the poetry received.
I can smell smoke from a neighbour's garden,
hear a collared dove coo, a buried piano, a distant aircraft.
I can understand these things but in my reading
I lose track of the world in the would-be samizdat.

I'm sorry I can't say anything to the generous poet
I'm sorry light is draining from the sky,
that affective meaning has gone in darkness.
This is not a manifesto but longing for first inscription,
to run through the mortal trees with the fox and the rook.

To be saved by names on Rue des Hiboux and Zaventem
I run walk run over bars of light, snow is forecast,
a return to first things is forecast – I like that, said the rook,
I can pick at that, I might eat it and then take off into the sky.

Run Walk Run

Again I'm off in the morning down the track
stepping through the one-time bars of light with David Bowie;
I swing swing on the monkey bars and pull faces at the cemetery,
suspended above the tilting ground in diagnostic limbo.

Come out come out companions mine,
where are we now and do you have a word to say?
I saw a woman with a three-legged dog
and various corvids posing for Bruegel.

Here's a dawn song for Magnetic Resonance Imaging,
singing inside the tunnel of exploding stars
to make a dark picture from sound I don't want to see;
companions come out and fall come fall gentle rain.

*

Localised but not metastasised.

We will use all three approaches.

Surgery. Radiography. Hormone treatment.

Localised not metastasised.

Repeat after me.

No metastasis. No katabasis.

*

The track the trees run run walk
could be Spring that dampness

behind me the streets are clear
beggars in place, kids away to school.

This morning's text is from the Reverend Arthur Russell,
'Show me what the girl does to the boy, if you can get around to it.'

I'd say, don't wait around too long for the demo,
I'd say Melanie I remember you, dark girl in the high flat under
    the eaves,
the city a map of lights looking like the whole world spread out
    below us.
Over your shoulder you said, I need this, you said.

I'm down the sunken path with no understanding,
the dark passage of incomprehensible chemistry
and it could be almost greening Spring out there;
bring out the day, let me go.

*

This morning's darling chorus
a compilation of Glenn Gould's background humming,
his transponder signals from the Bachosphere
as if there are bearings to be found up there.

From which we can reconstruct the music,
the miracle pouring from his fingers
like the flightpaths of the plural world
ascending into depthless blue.

Over the white track through frosted grass
the flights arrive, wheels down, insignia on show,
sliding along a silver cord from everywhere,
easy on the pedals for that music, said Captain Glenn.

*

Avenue Reine Astrid, Kraainem is a long road
longer than a solo by Neil Young,
with Spring tipping over the Lego houses
and the sun warm enough to tempt the birds to sing.

It's a road as long as hope passing Rue des Tulipes,
keep to the path, don't cross against the lights,
walk boy, talk to Doctor Agneessens, weigh the odds,
carry them through the flatlands in early Spring.

*

Rain everywhere a thousand mirrors this morning
and with 18 musicians it's crowded on the track,
we bump along as best we can.

A cello rests for breath in the fork of a tree,
comes back in and we're off for Steve Reich racing
over dark holes in the path showing nothing.

Through the trees of the cemetery, a stage set of skips
yellow on red Soret Soret, for the disposal of symbolism;
Oh Soret, little lost thing in the trees, pick up the pace.

*

In the cool morning my neighbours walk their dogs,
mist pools around their revolving feet hiding the circuit;
Below this level there is none, the operator said
and Malcolm Mooney returned to sing the sun up.

I hang from the bar count 90 drop and turn
see the tunnel of light through the swaying trees;

below this level forget the poor soil, the lactic acid burn,
89 90 push the day uphill against katabasis.

*

I walked 100 houses and a fallow field
last lap step-by-step to Centre Medik
to catch corvids blown like rags.

Scant pickings birds, time waits
at the near boundary in falling light,
face like pedantic death.

The White Road

If I went back there would I hear her voice
and see those figures again, that side of the family
the other side of time folded in the blue and green hills
of the Slad Valley as evening falls under luminous distance
and they work out their lives, come and go,
turn that field to better use, raise children, stop?

There's a patch of light in the sky seems to pause
and shed a painterly quality on common nativity
picturing the practical, hard-bitten characters,
raising the fallen as if still walking long-legged
over hedges, brimming ditches, taking the road to town
with the blue green valley at their backs alight.
I see them come tramping over the fields,
catch the rough old songs beating in their hearts.

*

The boy dreamt of a white road,
night was all around but the white road shone;
he walked along thinking it was death
and everything said – no invention is allowed.

Poetry was buried in the mud and muck of the ditch,
he forgot its sound and wondered if it ever happened;
the black trees bore the names of the all the girls he'd known
and the spaces between the things making sense enlarged.

I would rather walk in the Atlantic light of Penwith,
the tilting perspective painted by Ben Nicholson
spilling us east and west into the slapping sea
as we teeter on Celtic fields, skate on granite hedges.

Day recalls that village to the left of the lane,
a bridge of sorts over the pell-mell stream and its aria.

*

In Europe now, in our city garden,
bats jinx the trees as the light goes
and we sit and talk and talk;
here you are, bright one in darkness.
I can lay out memories like a dance
the days the girls were born
you standing there in a lit doorway
and we walked into a new world.

The silver flightpaths flash above us,
arrival departure, arrival departure;
at the end of the garden is the unknown
and there's no talking there;
only chemistry counts, words fail
walking the damp steps underground.

Let's Leave

Captain of the turning sea,
do you know the sound a boat makes
hauled up a shingle beach,
do you count through white noise breakers?

I would swim the Picasso Sea,
swim with the women, fish and goats,
ride the bull dripping on the shore
to Paris, Madrid, Barcelona, Antibes.

Treatment

Surgery

Wheeled clueless down the white track,
time made absent, memory removed
by the kind surgeon.

*It went well, but I had to take more
when I saw inside I knew,
it went well but more than planned.*

Five incisions across the abdomen
for robotics and this for extraction,
it went well I hear through fog.

*

To return awake in the white room,
to see a block of window daylight
and listen to Sibelius
for the world to return over fields of snow,
a country risen in the air-bright score.

My conversation is with nurses
at 3 and 4 in the morning
from Romania, DRC, France and Holland.
My conversation is with the wall
awake all night the wall answers.

— *Thank you, you are very kind.*
— *Oh, it's my job.*
— *It's a very good job, I'm grateful.*
— *You're welcome, it's what I do.*

Uitgang, provisional

From the bedside by love's hand
the removal of clothes,
the removal of hair,
the removal of thought.

To surrender the beloved
to the care of bright strangers,
to render the body abstract
a creature of biometrics.

*

There but not, afloat like a baby
held in a net of catheters and lines,
dreaming a sky of sensors
in the constellation of data.

Poor Baby Blue in no space no time
hauled back shed a galaxy of blood.
Shovelled into a trench, worked on.
Vision dissolved in black holes.

Nine bright strangers fill the room;
the fabric of thought disintegrates,
a torn cloth stretched and discarded.
Nine bright strangers fill the room.

Voices call then stop and walk away.
What there is of you, next to nothing,
is entirely in the hands of others.
And I hear one voice – Melanie.

*

'The path is through perplexing ways, and when
The goal is gained, we die you know – and then?

What then? I do not know, no more do you,
And so good night.'

*

Two older nurses work the nightshift,
kind and capable, coaxing in their Flemish.
I think they are familiar, universal aunties.

— *Oh yah we are from the same village,*
— *we have our own language*
— *you have been a good boy, see the numbers.*

I heard them singing in the night
on kitchen chairs in the hospital garden,
taking a break and singing.

— *Oh no, you wouldn't want our singing.*
Of course there is no garden,
and there is a garden where apophenia blooms.

Radiotherapy

Every day we file under Leopold's triumphal arch
and the river of traffic lands me flat on the radiation table.
— *Bonjour monsieur, ça va? Come down a little, feet in there.*
No need to help – a hand on my hip exactly as before.
We leave you now – and the monobeat pop music persists.

Clouds drift to the east behind two tower cranes,
over the stripped trees and circuit of roads – *I love love love you.*
I think a city stands and corvids wing me to their plan,
if I hold my arms like this and stand like this, will I fly?
Melanie I didn't mean to lead you to this dry cave.

The satellite panels revolve, the red beams hum as before;
in space my eyes close, count parachute flares in the dark,
the drenched fox stares straight back from the drowned garden,
deep deep bioluminescent forms blossom.
Is there life on Mars? the radio asks.

Good Science

At night in the courtyard lost in irregular perspective
the dead gather for me and I know them all,
an apple tree rises in bright light, white blossom floods the scene
and my mother as a girl, laughs, reaches up to catch her brother.

If this is the last light, drown me in memory,
if this is the last meeting in the moment of seeing,
if this is the last of my name from Melanie nearby,
save me from chemistry, drown me in memory.

*

I count through space, through white noise
scooping out the bowl of language
good science burning my inside out,
good science, they sang in headlong flight.

St. Michael cast down the rebel angels,
every day they dance on Cinquantenaire;
Dr. Otte and Dr. Entezari unlocked the DNA in cells,
every day they dance at the hospital St Pierre.

At night when the chords descend
rinse my heart in wine
skin restraint from my tongue
and let my friends deny death.

We've brought your husband back to you, the doctor said.

Melanie I don't know how you stood by me,
how you helped make me ready for the surgeon,
shaved me and comforted me and left that evening
driving across the city in a capsule of light.

> Sitting on a collapsed marble column
> outside the room we rented in Naxos town,
> in the heat of the narrow streets of the chora
> looking straight at the camera, a beautiful girl.

How did you attend me as I floated off on the bloody bed?
I am dumb to the bone to say what I must say.
What did you do when I was reduced to flashing numbers?
What did you think in the white pauses of my absence?

> I see you on the ferry to Mull in a red jacket for the rain,
> I don't remember a word, just your face like a light;
> at the rail the sea and sky pitching behind your head,
> the horizon we were crossing over to Mull.

Melanie I don't know how you stood by me,
I was often not there it seems, will you tell me later?
I remember all that you did and all that you brought me
and we were there in that room standing together in flight.

Afterwards

To Ian, Recovering

People here are extraordinarily welcoming. 'Ye are welcome' they say. Feennone, the name of our house and the village, is a pastoral townland in the middle of highly marginal bog and upland and between the mountains and the sea, referred to as the village.

Dear Ian

I hope the steady progress continues. I love the picture of Gruff's childhood that you describe. Nine? I thought he was still a toddler, ridiculous of me. The school sounds tuned in – you would know otherwise. What a sweet setting for him, and for you too, on your feet, nearly? It sounds like a distinct world and that it's writing itself for you. Good.

The end of the unrepeatable radiotherapy treatment has been as hard as predicted, nasty but normal, and the good Dr Otte saw me through it. Again I'm humbled by the kindness and skill of the clinicians who have cared for me. I have a big thought, against the pessimistic tide, that we are an astonishing species.

I've tried to explain this to several friends. If I think of everything that has gone into my treatment during this year it is extraordinary – not just the medical expertise, the technology and smart bureaucracy but the sheer human kindness and ethical intention that it is all there and just given. There are thousands of people capable and willing to learn how to do all of this for others who they don't even know.

My amazement doesn't depend on finding out if I'm cured or not. How on earth does this all come about? It is morally extraordinary and we think of it as normal. I am in awe of it. I have been carried high in the arms of *philotomo*, that Greek term. Of course I do this for you, it is my obligation because we are all people, no? It is my pleasure, it makes us human. You're welcome.

I talked to the nurses at the time of the surgery and haemorrhage. One had just come back from the refugee camps on Lesvos, another was off to the UK to study English Literature because she loved it, and another who wanted to work in ICU all her life. We care for each other, and we're good at it and it astonishes me. To find you're welcome. Enough.

Below This Level

    As of
        today
                PSA
                      below
                            this
                                  level
                                        0.
                                          01
                                                there
                                                      is
                                                            none.

Arrival

At last we came to the first language
birds dropped the carved letters into our hands
calling all night to a pictured childhood,
death was not involved and we were all there.

Every meaning fluttered in the trees,
furled leaves disclosed an original morphology,
graphemes flashed on/off shot through with light
havering around the edge of knowing.

In the lost towns and invisible homelands
jaded clouds tore holes in the account
keeping us apart from our own interest
like slow semantic drift wrong footing thought.

Modes of seeing collapse and are replaced,
nowhere is fixed and the ground is rising up;
only the topographic reveals a sort of truth,
planes tilting around the sleeping houses.

Questions of perception in the village square
restored us step by step to the literal world,
showers of red, blue, white, black, drew the future,
tearing me from the earth that night.

Under such simple conditions
Vitebsk detached my head for dreaming,
we flew out of the bedecked room
X-ray snapped the sky and dissolved the window.

You were always there and I was with you.
Zesty, zesty – said the floating man and left.

Messages Coming In

Glenn Gould arrived today in the arms of J S Bach
from the garden of morning the aria took flight
over the sun-cracked quay and inclined greenery.
Roger Hilton back flipped a perfect arc – *Get me out of here.*
Where's my bloody boat and which way is the Côte d'Azur?

The advocates of Spring dig dig the spreading mulch,
dig the mud, the tubers, the building block sequence
to find the roots of their own ascendency,
at the edge of the turning world silver compounds
proclaiming delight in unlike forms.

Fingers in the soil, at first chthonic cold
rising to blood temperature for us to assume the literal.
I heard the sounds of the world enter all around,
taking shape the solid bodies transduced
by efflorescence, by intelligence into my empty hands.

Across the Square

Awake this morning to the literal world,
I see Nancy's house across the square in Agios Dimitrios,
dressed in black she hangs a blanket on a rail to air
and there's a freshly painted red box on the wall.

The sea sits on Nancy's left shoulder, light bathes,
and the scene is framed by oleander and a pine tree.
The sparrows and doves are in good voice for the rain
and the clouds stream in banners from the mountain.

I think Nancy's memory has holes in it,
- *You English, did you know my husband George?*
Yes we did, we knew George for eighteen years,
a retired merchant seaman who kept by the sea.

At first he drove the yellow school bus,
he fished in a good sized boat, the Alexandria,
he swam in the harbour and parked by the house after asking;
there's an enamelled picture of his younger face on his gravestone.

For years Nancy pretended to speak no English,
occasionally she sits on her veranda and plays the accordion.
- *Did you know my husband George who was here?*
The sparrows and doves add chorus to her playing.

George's boat is gone, his car is gone, his face is on his gravestone:
to enter the literal world is difficult, falling falling falling.
ο παλιατζής, cries the junk man in his wrecked pick-up,
ο παλιατζής, bring out your used-up things, I'll take them all.

He circles the square, leaves diesel fumes in the trees,
ο παλιατζής ο παλιατζής, Nancy Nancy, play that song.

Singing with Chagall

Borders of gold
              studs of silver
I will make
        a green bed
                cedar beams
                        fir rafters.

Your banner flies over me
your name fills the sky
my fair one come away.

I will go about the city
the streets and the broadways
and I will find you.

A fountain of gardens
a well of living waters
love is strong as death.

*

Caught in the pink rush of flying fish,
donkeys and goats – did I say that, see that?
Chagall singing up the swoosh of it.

Jerusalem Vitebsk the compass point swings
yellow gazelle blue gazelle a woman in flight
Bathsheba is flying to rest in his arms.

David sings, above his throne he hovers,
I will do a handstand and play the clarino for you,
I will show you a city on a hill and lie with you.

I will paint the darkness green and saturate the sky
and we will live under this canopy just as we choose,
I stray from the text but would not let you go.

The birds fly right side up, it's the world I've inverted,
they sing in single notes suspended to fashion meaning,
ice crystals like coins tossed ringing in the blue.

*

An unassuming man stands to one side
depicting olive trees, the brimming sea,
playing a fiddle to the drenched sparrows
as everyone comes and goes in the village square.

This morning the leaves have turned electric green,
the day comes rolling down the mountain hot-foot
over grottoes, aquifers, goats and gods;
we could just begin a civilisation here.

It could be Spring in another country transparent
that sweetness, across the stage of the square
the world makes an entrance at the end of waiting,
the fruit and veg man, the junk man, the living and the dead.

She rose up into depthless sky at first light,
cut a forward roll over the mountain and other acrobatics;
neighbours clapped and the children danced,
 – *This is the special dance we do to make everything grow.*

A voice from the well explains how it all turns;
hold your nerve birds, auguries are shot.
I'm on all fours, face down to earth's core
to hear the triumph of music in the world.

*

The sparrows have gathered in the trees
for chaos and their singing contest;
the sun is up, sing you birds of green vertigo.

Between the horizontal and vertical planes
the old woman we thought dead has returned,
she walks in her garden and lights a fire.

The visiting children step down to the shore,
light pours over the mountain at our back
and the sea puts on its cerulean.

Let this be the season of zero gravity
for relocated donkeys and talking myths
for flying fish and Melanie's gaze.

For Asclepios to dance us across the orchestra,
for the Dionysus Transportation Company
to carry us over the stony ground drenched in light.

The Republic of Song

To Write a Mythology

Rue des Hiboux

1

To write a mythology
      commensurate to an ignorant island
      is not difficult.
They were of that class of traitor
self-serving, unimaginative.

Their only skill
      to make the poor vote for poverty
      the preterite for abandonment.
Oh bury me quietly
      in Hardy's field.

*

I perch my head in a bare room
on Rue des Hiboux, dogs bark in French
Ash and Silver Birch talk all night.

Reynard at the rubbish
on the tree-darkened road
Europe at the corner.

His delicate step, his nose in filth
by comparison is noble
and not given to self-destruction.

*

– What in the shape of a cloud?
A cloud in the shape of a cloud

in the shape of an imagined country
adrift on the edge of a continent.

– Doubtful, we've moved on from that,
since meteorology usurped portents.
It disintegrates anyway, thin as air
snagged on a fault mid-Atlantic.

I like the high ones up there,
silver white capsules full of people
sun under their wings gliding the trade routes
rising to the world, the many.

2

To drill a hole in this wall is hard,
you need an extra-long bit to get through the granite
but then, task accomplished, you can pack in the charge
play the fool and bring the house down.

As if I might say – Jerusalem is fallen, lie down and weep;
a blunt truth, as if you might hear high-toned counterpoint
spinning in the eaves a social contract of forgotten triumph
turned to spite and Albion absurd.

3

Ironies are everywhere like roadworks on the pavement
and although I might not find the Supermarché,
my short-term memory shot, my sense of direction set at zero,
is as nothing compared to that country called England.

There the fields sing no more, the road taken buried in connivance
and time runs backwards to an empire of amnesia.
What is the name for the shade of green where the holloway leads,
where they travelled to follow the trade of their day?

Yes – the high ones up there zip zip like silver bullets,
there's a silver bullet and there are flightpaths above us,
they form and evaporate as we pass, there's a silver bullet,
the ones I like over the cities of Europe light the sky.

Biographies of the Brexiteers

The Quiet Man

Iain Guido Smith did make division and gather the spoils
plied his bonny craft the Centre for Social Justice far,
tacking across the lake of fire all the way to Betsygate.

Then setting fires in Baghdad and Washington and London,
his smug little face caressed by the claw of the Lady Margaret,
he conspired in the smoky arts of a sovereign nation once again.

The image which must enter through the image deserted him
his stand-up was only comical when he tried for gravitas
his mirage bucket for storing mirage history had a fuck hole in it.

As the girl Europa struggled all at sea, Guido looked on dreaming,
arranged the limbs of the drowned to spell Breakthrough Britain;
and gathered the spoils to build a new nation for old time's sake.

*

Twisting Michael of the Gove

The king sat in fair Witney Town
drinking the casual wine:
'Where can I find a good true knight
to keep the land for this clan of mine?'

'I will,' said the Gove, 'trust me,'
said Michael of the shifty border
with betrayal in his shrivelled heart,
the Gove across the water.

'You must call me minister
of speed-speak abjuring thought
and I will lead you backwards
into an England of last resort.'

He turned his coat again again
sporting repugnant on either side
a dark and double lie disclosed;
'Follow me follow me,' he cried.

A loud laugh laughed he
in a future fifty fathoms deep,
there lies the bad Michael
with the nation at his feet.

*

Boris Johnson and *Seventy Two Virgins*

I imagined there was a prime minister
and that he had written a comic novel
and it was called Seventy-Two Clichés;
a pile of stercus polished with huff-puff rags
which disclosed a steaming mind-set
at home in the ruling class for decades.

Cameron is an American research assistant,
she is a beautiful woman and available;
the British police are bumbling but kind;
the BBC is run by cunning liberal cowards;
and the main character, resembling the author,
ah, yes, right, bumbled into a leading role.

A fake Asian TV crew English flummery
the gun bucked a gargoyle's shoulder

the House of Sharmoota kingly lineage
a sharpshooter, Dean, Habib and Haroun
and spiteful Debbie from The Daily Mirror:
reconstruct the nonsense for yourself.

'Dog-fuckers and corpse-eaters and gloom-addicts
rule the future with excrement.'
> Odysseus Elytis, *The Axion Esti*,
> translated by Edmund Keeley and George Savidis

Radio Logos

1

Should I dance on the mouth music scales?
Meaning nothing, meaning valve dust.
Why taunt the dumb beast?

Well, this aside, you must listen to my morning broadcast
I've recharged the arcane batteries of Radio Logos
stroked the air and rewired the marvels of Hellas.

Do you like that tone? A little grandiose for you?
Certainly not a songbird in a cage eating its own droppings.
Lesson 1: don't be a hired mouth or pundit.

Lesson 2: you must remember only archaeology is true:
the invention of sailing, recall the beauty of trade routes
but the meaning of unread inscriptions can change everything.

Good: the valves are humming and the meters flicker,
the dust burns, I tap tap the microphone – you can hear me,
you can hear these words remade on waves of morning air.

2

Has the colour of the sea broken your heart yet,
the air in blue waves transformed your seeing,
the bronze mountains turned your head? Yes?

So there's hope for you then, listen. – Lesson 3:
'There is no history that does not relate to the present,'
we know this, we know the cities that once were mighty etc.

They're nothing now but decrepit dormitories
populated by the insular, the ignorant;
imagine a country shrinking into itself: terminal.

The meaning of an unread binary choice
has changed everything, a future unexamined;
picture an island slowly rowing to the America.

The Tinny Islands go trumpety-trump
and sink in a fog of self-absorption
as the princes pipe their old new tunes.

3

I sit here on the edge of time gazing out to sea;
if history is an account of semantic drift
it can be read backwards to the well of speaking.

That was lesson 4 – were you even listening?
Were you just smiling at the pretty dial light?
So here it is again – call it Terms of Resistance.

Lesson 4: you must trust the people, their erudition
from unlikely sources, from the stream of first meaning
from the mouths of all the people under the ringing sky.

As surprising as the beauty of recalled trade routes
the acquisition of obsidian, highland cedar and coral,
the expansion of ritual activity, the invention of sailing.

As surprising as the small pool of cool water
found high in the mountains, that bright ellipse
keeping a cold eye on the arching blue.

4

Their country has played itself out,
Eng-a-land has played itself out;
I landed there, loaded with memory.

It was a novelty dog show in the spring,
the sun made arrows of every blade of grass
the hills folded into themselves a miracle of green.

And here they come, the happy dog lovers
in their camper vans, Freedom, Odyssey, Rambler,
grinning and panting like dogs to a tilted field.

At the close they dive in to a sclerotic sea,
buried under a regular sunset, hardly making a splash,
taking the living with them: thanatocracy.

Your country has played itself out,
no, those feet did not – Freedom, Odyssey, Rambler;
this is the anti-Jerusalem.

Mr President's New Hat

'Genghis Khan loves his new mauve hat'
        (*Genghis Khan's hat.* Lee Harwood)

Mr President loves his new red hat;
go rally beyond its spinning shadow,
hear the music, see the pictures
and dance one step across the sea.

Shostakovich set light to Brussels that night
and the young cellist flew up to the ceiling.
I went six times to the Bruegel show,
saw good Doctor Williams and dreamt of Europe.

        Red cap rolls across the border down Sonora way,
        snagged on a prickly pear the desert does its business
        and the original legend is folded back and sullied,
        tattooed with sand ake arica eat aga.

By train to The Hague across the flatlands
open stretches of water like a second sky,
the masters of light are waiting in line,
to be as in life but with symbols displayed.

Young women look out from lavish interiors,
indicate oysters, a bowl of onions, red roses,
and she's there, that girl turning, a pearl,
a gaze as still as a sky of reflected water.

        Red cap rolls on further south and all around is desert
        and the desert of ideas; a jack rabbit takes a bite
        k am t ga a distracted coyote anoints a claim
        red cap yellowed comes to rest with bleached trash.

The point is an ordinary day before us
and the landscape of just what happens,
a city stands off in the painted distance
the ploughman's bent shoulders deny tragedy.

The dog attends, the shepherd looks away,
a wind fills the sail and Icarus kicks the sea;
a dead man feeds the root of thought
and there's ploughing to be done.

        Scorpion takes refuge in the engorged and tattered dome
        at aga ma all around lamentation sounds in darkness;
        empty red cap with flaccid peak dreams am ic gr e
        venomous and stealthy predators innocent by comparison.

The Near Distance

Now that I've recovered from the time of flat vision
all things do stack up in a way, for instance the clouds
above the moving trees behind the apartments opposite.

The ambition to make depth from the single plane returns,
unconfined by the immediate intricacy of leaf mosaic,
as if seeing hovers above the wet gardens and engulfed houses.

The vision machine runs in the heart of this civilisation
issues revelations, battlefields, boys in mud arranged in choirs
fly over Maastricht to circle the open city of Cologne.

To have regained the pleasure of layered vision unbound,
to have blood flow to those parts of the brain unrestricted,
means learning to see again out of a blank, blind zero.

There are suburban conifers here receding into the near distance,
closer, a silver birch, then a bank of deciduous trees I can't name,
staged alongside a raised road of a hedge under an open sky.

Light plays variously, turning the pale underside of leaves
as the wind moves everything together and apart,
the windows of seeing open and close in the shadowed transepts.

Conifers, silver birch, a young ash tree inclined, already there,
the full spectrum cast across the fields of Europe, the circuits of history;
risen light exacting every blade of grass, every recalled name.

The Sinking Colony Revisited
in the Days of Lee Harwood

A trail of bookmarks, a trail of postcards
I found around the house after you left
tic-tac-toe through the little labyrinth
a string of shining beads in a lost currency
and many different faces came and went
in the days of the days of Lee Harwood.

Poet most alive living nowhere now
clues come fluttering from the shelves,
late arrivals from not the full story,
that walk we never made across the Downs
Grasscut CD 1 inch ½ mile, map and voices
drilling holes in the discontinued calendar.

*

This was all so but from another time
the reminders kept arriving, the paths not taken beckoned,
that secluded bay in the heat of the afternoon
after the rains finished and a translucent curtain opened
across the whole vista of their other ways.
And though the scheme was for the benefit of all,
the metropolis and the dominions let's say,
there was a groundswell and unexpected events;
the radicalisation of the tennis club,
the close down of the baking circle,
the preference for autochthonic dance.

Your soft linen like a wing swept the veranda
analogous to the mystery of the rain-washed view,
another season of calculations, of glad-handing

the nabobs and salesmen, their butterfly wives.
At least the women set the air alight, a sort of flagrance
I never knew if it was sex or absent-mindedness,
lost deep in the intricacies of the local dialect
itself a version of an implacable, closed book,
it might as well have been shapes scratched on rock
or pitter-patter feet around the bay for all I grasped,
I just never knew and none of us saw it coming.
I like to think our expeditions were genuine,
were not always for cover but for pure geology.

Later I learnt Captain Harwood's reports were correct,
they predicted the whole thing – you just couldn't tell,
he was so unassuming, gentle in his detachments,
and the reports were filed in Government House,
under a heading of Fanciful Imaginings At Large.
I suppose the engine of the age can run on,
can drive every detail of our lives and loyalties
and we don't talk about it, we just don't see it
and I came to think that's because we're inside it
encompassed and blind, duty-bound, modern.
I still thought this when she left for England,
that she had failed, fallen into a character flaw,
and I lay there every night under vague imaginings
pretty ghosts circling the mosquito net, entwined
low susurrations of an erotic folk literature
released from their red mouths all night.

I must close, be done, you have been very patient,
there's no final account and the inventory continues,
a delivery of leather buckets for the collection of Yak milk,
wrongly dispatched, bullets of incorrect calibre,
non-regulation dubbing, polo mallets and hegemony cranks.
All I can do is wait for the cargo boat to arrive

let it edge its way into the bay without reprisal,
I doubt they even know the name of this place.

*

Trail of postcards to nowhere then, unaddressed
straight through the winding Platonic streets;
England crouches, its back turned on Europe
resentful, effaces history and dreams an America;
despite this you can see the sea from Brunswick Place
and poetry leaps at the high windows there,
you meet an old friend go to a bar and the stars appear.

Take the scenes connected over the years in turn,
each one designed by Donald Evans open, unresolved:
poet and old friend, the years relived in one night;
poet tackles bank robber, receives public acclaim;
poet in a foreign city at one, making himself at home;
poet in labyrinth turns, follows the sound of the sea;
poet scales the final mountain, everyone's there, it's ok.

The Republic of Song

Come Up Come Up

At night I think of the living and the dead
the Irish songs rise like light over Carrickfergus
and I lose my way on Grafton Street,
heading out for the Republic of Song.

In the Republic of Song we're all walking,
I see my father on the road from Wexford Town;
he survives the war and beats the drink,
I see him now on the black road turnabout.

*

Andy, let's walk along the cliffs, the turfy paths and rocks,
step high across the rumours, the old epiphanies spent,
and fling the whole lot into the uncased Atlantic air
with the Spring-dizzy fauna and every thought of art.

The raptor, the drone, the water streaming from the hill;
let all the music of earth figure by turns the path we walk;
let the Victor Freeman, twenty miles off Wolf Rock,
return safely to harbour and the sea settle its speech in the wake.

We saw Lee set off westward over the unlikely blue wave;
mountaineer, poet, friend, restored to all tenderness,
the good man Harwood, not waiting on pastoral rhapsody,
sees everything; the history of dead men singing underground,
the quick green one-time flash of the darting lizard
and the roll of the land overflowing to the final sea.

*

A History of the World in Twelve Maps
complete with a postcard from Lee;

2008, 'I'm setting out on a new stage.'
And this summer he's a year dead.

From the *oikumene* to map the whole world,
from the body to the hearth to the horizon;
the outer salt sea's no province for the living
though we walked the shoreline from your door.

The moon has made the sea milky,
opaque the memory of our commonweal,
that lost country where we once followed
a different life in the nation of now.

*

Spring landed in the small garden Brussels,
the day lost to Roy – and a glass of wine;
all the creatures go at it again, the fox stares,
various insects and assorted birds
glide their songs on the turning air.

Listen hard to the name they speak,
a dancing trio of notes – Roy Fisher, Roy Fisher;
there's a green plot, a thinking shade
where that hare, zig-zagging slowly
imprints its paw on poetry's field path.

Roy read as he wrote with no show, no pomp;
in Newcastle-under-Lyme twenty years ago
standing with Carl Rakosi and Gael Turnbull:
come up, come up my thinking shades,
see that hare 'zig-zagging slowly like the shadow of a hare.'

*

I thought I saw Robert Sheppard in the market
Place Dumon, Brussels, bright for business
wearing a leather fedora and a fine jacket,
looking for the language of the language of poetry.

He was smiling at the Coquilles St-Jacques,
smelling the hot waffles on the morning air:
Robert Robert, what do you have there?
– Ah yes, well, I've an appetite for all these things
and I'm thinking about Lee Harwood.

But Lee's a ghost now, a nothing, a film
turning uncast on the day, a thought
of the shadow platforms for the dancing trees
standing out like visions across the Downs
where the light infiltrates their leaves
for Spring in another country.

*

In the Republic of Song we're all walking
and you see us now on the black road turnabout.

Grahamland

The house where Graham lived
in Madron in the rain
is a shell of song to a light tenor
longing for Loch Thom.

Next door on Mount View Terrace
a satellite dish suspended
listens to the running streams
make ready the risen speech.

From his house of granite, house of words
the moor is flying blind
the black lane shining at the sky
for Penwith to silence babble.

The granite spiral staircase
from the Madron workhouse refit
lies broken up and buried
in the fields of Grahamland.

Treads worn smooth by the feet of the poor
ascending and descending
in the fields of Grahamland
where poetry takes its turn.

*

The second location of Grahamland can be found
at S 65° W 63°, country code AQ, population zero,
though names are disputed it's there, waiting for your step.

Using dog sleds and a de Havilland Fox Moth
we determined that Grahamland was a peninsula,
a white tenement in an unfixed magnetic field

Half-seen through the interference of the snow;
then the snow becomes the fabric of your breathing
and you hear high voices on the other side of blizzard.

The worst of it was settling down at night alone,
the ice song sounding from the deep-sea channels
sets the world atilt roaring at the broken door.

*

The last of Grahamland, listen back, listen back,
is the white tenement of memory and bare language,
the worst of it how the uninhabited names weather
– and this on a day of talk in the green wood of Madron.

And that would be the Graham Reel you join,
as if there ever was a choice, as the brimming tide
breaks in particles belonging as first light on Fore Street
launched even later there becoming a time.

– Do you know a poet called W S Graham lived here?
Yes, I do, there's a plaque up there on the wall – look,
see the day showing its colours, swaying to the sky
and see that large body of water sounding us out.

Launched even later there becoming a time.

BN

This is the Atlantic-washed radiant town
drenched in that light imagined again on the side of life.

In this way Ben Nicholson returned vision to the world,
that such things could be made from seeing.

In this unfixed landscape perceptual certainty is challenged
and you wake dousing your head in the western approaches.

In the arrangement of these shapes, these colours, this whiteness
pleasure is a sort of common sense of light and its geometry.

There you can totter all day on an inverted luminous bowl
augment the brimming world in the various planes of seeing.

Imagined again in Ticino, Paros and Rievaulx,
the pencil draws and carves, the stylus draws and carves.

Working through to the primer, to chase out something alive.

In the Hilton Memorial Garden

The garden is in motion all night
I've checked at 2.30, 4.00, and through the watches,
the agapanthus hovers, the sycamores bow.

Even in the dead of night light changes on the water
the decayed arch leans into further darkness,
the garden floods the house and I breathe Atlantic air.

The storm comes off the sea thrashing the land,
and you across the table, where are you from?
Where did you gather those looks Melanie?

The agapanthus hovers, the sycamores bow,
granite hedges and compact fields make dark divisions
under a vaulted sky – where are you from?

In the hollow night there's a spotted man flailing,
two monkeys in love, a grinning dog astride the sun
and a tipsy boat heading out below a snake horizon.

At some point, he says, I lost the liberty of words,
once it was tethered to the things of the world,
events, chemistry, the white road in the night.

I fell through a hole in the continual score,
hear me said the music before the music
in the echo landscape unvisited.

Nothing can be said of that music,
a garden, a stream of light, a coastline,
poetry only follows trailing pale ghost metaphor.

Over the hedge in the dispossessed field
I hear unseen animals breathe under stars,
set me free you cyphers for the rising descant.

Gebruiksaanwijzing der lyriek
Lyrical Poetry: Directions for Use

Having a Drink With Phil

Kunst, Traditie en Kwaliteit

*

Walking Don Van Vliet down Avenue Orban makes for a long road,
he's not easy company; leaping hedges, grinning at the Lego houses,
singing black ink mathematics into the sky as night comes down.

Bright capsules of everyone I've known glide by on grassy tracks
packed off to a different future, the girls wave wave and stroke their hair
shushed into the rolling darkness on route 39, 'Come out tonight,'
      sings Don.

In the black and white day night city I walk on and wait
in a moment of the Belgian Xylographic Renaissance,
the action freezes, the flags, the crowd, the girls stroking their hair.

Captain of Streetlights, Captain of Stars, give me a break;
I may as well implore you as another, Jesus Christ, my dead parents,
Paul Van Ostaijen, send me your directions for use of the lyric.

*

Leopold mounts his giant tricycle
pedals hard against the future
his white beard flaps like a fat tongue
– Oh where is my little Caroline?

*

'We all on earth have a commission to protect the weak from the strong.'

Leopold expelled us from the palace,
we left under chandeliers, exquisite taxidermy
through torture gardens and the human zoo Tervuren
saw the locals throw bananas at the exhibits in their pens.

We saw the Congolese paddle across the lakes
the park and lakes built in imitation of Versailles,
the World's Fair showcase around the colonial palace
and Expo 58, Kongorama under the Atomium.

Casement was standing off under the trees,
beard aglint, arms around his Congo Report;
I questioned the chief of the inner station
I met Conrad in Matadi, we talked through the night.

Our music – insects pinging off the iron roof,
our prospect – the trade of the dark river;
'He could tell you things. Things I have tried to forget.' said Conrad.
'We all on earth have a commission.' Casement replied.

*

Setting out for the Leopold Quarter I know the passengers,
all our heads sway together taking the bend on Orban;
Lee the inspector checks my ticket passing Mallaerts Ponds.

When do we get there? – 'Well, completion, I'm not keen,' Lee says.
The monochromatic city leans in, trees stripped, human scale shot,
St. Michael casts down the rebel angels on Cinquantenaire.

They caper and preen on the arch between two worlds;
we're bound for the always open Pavilion of Human Passions
for picnic tables and playgrounds, the wrong lesson in history.

Every day heavy objects and light move freely through the city,
some resemble ideas, others not, occasionally there's a collision,
our tram broadsides a car, the flow stops, then restarts at volume.

All this activity looks precise but it's not, at the point of stasis
it starts up again each morning, in other accounts like a dream,
the heads sway together, the ghost conductor, an explosion.

*

Leaving the gig we saw families bed down for the night,
parents, three infants, eyes over the edge of the blankets;
we walked through the new development of Bourse,
the smart pedestrianisation and shiny names of Bourse.

We saw Frans Masereel let the woodcut drawing
emerge from the cutting material itself;
the material is the city, the material is us, those children,
and night came down to blacken the page.

Leaving the gig we saw the apodictic principles of poetry,
Aristotle and Van Ostaijen stood by and pointed;
self-evident the vision the city affords, deep resonance and none,
we walked through the homeland of perfect knowledge.

*

The tram bound for Aporia passes,
driver Beckett gleams the Beckett gleam
lighting the track with his Angelus ding ding;
the routes are many and unpredictable.

Forget what Magritte would have you think,
the citizens of Brussels do not float in the sky,

they alight at random stops unsurprised
to live with unknown families for the night.

Beckett nods, waits for the green light click,
– I repeat, I've sentences to hammer out,
motley background static to channel,
the accounts of love to close at the terminus.

*

'It is at once chaotic and vague, bloated and pretentious, pompous
and empty.' *L'Art Moderne* 1890

So we set out for Le Pavillon des Passions Humaines in the fair May time,
the temple stands in Cinquantenaire Park close-by the Commission,
and there we found much writhing in marble though frozen in the act.

Owned at one time by King Faisal, along with the Grand Mosque;
we suffered Seduction Suicide Debauchery and Bacchanal in a pretty row,
closing at 4.45 in the summer, though how you enter is never apparent.

The 96 metre square bas-relief has a moral framework, of sorts;
the pleasures and sins overseen by Death, the Graces off to the side,
male and female principles meeting somewhere in the middle.

We arrived at the Pavilion of Human Passions in opening time,
the doors were locked and we sank to our knees at the peephole,
the interior glowed sepulchral and a cool draft stroked our faces.

In the park the trees blossomed massively and children scooted
      everywhere.

*

Phil, what are we talking about?
Novels. Empire. Beer. Gigs.
Instructions for the lyric.
Tram routes and Leopold.
The World's Fair of 1897.
The living and the dead.
The seven graves of Tervuren.
The full spectrum pavilion.

The Seven Graves of Tervuren

Leopold mounts his giant tricycle
his white beard flapping like a fat tongue,
pedals hard around the graves of Tervuren
gliding pneumatic on Congolese rubber.

Ekia, Gamba, Kitoukwa, M'Peia, Sambo,
Zao and Mibange, remain barely legible;
dumped in unconsecrated ground
their funeral procession booed.

For the World's Fair of 1897
in the model villages of the palace
these human exhibits died
costumed for the crowd.

Reburied in a row against the church wall
seven slabs lie at the side of the path;
we stood there and heard nothing – and heard
a song called A History of the World.

Seeing the City

Tower cranes conceptualise the city,
as if swung steel and an indecipherable script
articulated a theory of how it all came about
in a silver clattering language of the sky.

At the end of the working day, the golden hour,
a soft burr rises to the man in the lit cabin;
he sees the vulnerable network, various objects moving,
the configured pulse of light pause and ignite.

Then the moon is full flooding the gardens
a Masereel page empty of people,
the air still and the night more animal
settles about the darkened houses.

*

(Frans Masereel, *The City*)

A man with his back to us looks at the monochromatic city.
We see what he sees, no other view is presented;
industrial smoke drifts in one direction, a banner to the future.

By his density he appears superimposed on the scene,
at a distance he sees an abstract beauty to the tall city,
though clearly, we are meant to have doubts of the single plane.

Trains come and go at the station, blossoming more white smoke,
people come and go for the trains, gather in groups, pause mechanical,
then go about their business rather than admire the abstract beauty.

They diverge from one another until they see a fallen man;
only united by inaction, useless they stop and stare, do nothing.
History unfolds from here; in manic action, crowded isolation.

*

As if from the high cabin of a tower crane
Bruegel depicts a panorama of indifference;
floodlights, the world's traffic, a field of gibbets,
the charged circuit as ethical index unrefined.

An encyclopaedic composition is mapped;
pigs run loose in the wheat, *near het leven*
the wedding dance stamps on, children play,
a pedantic army advances in casual slaughter.

Mute mute the round mouths and blank faces,
a father holds his fingers to his child's mouth,
– *Hungry monsieur, hungry,*
bedded down outside the Bruegel show.

*

On Grand Champ across a square of gardens
I saw a Chinese ideogram crash from the sky,
the watercolour clouds of Shou lit by halogen charisma.

In another script a lopsided lower case *t* cuts an angle,
the horizontal extended brings it down to earth
gantries and ladders barely visible in the gloom.

A culture swings into place over the houses of the living;
in the delicacy of this engineering a city thrives, sings
packages of products and services for the home market.

If I climbed, strut by strut, in bare feet, eyes open,
up through the steel rib tunnel in high-vis orange
and hopped along the jib with plural flightpath birds,

tasting iron on my tongue, head lost in weather systems,
I would more keenly see the beauty laid out at night,
the spiralling lights and the fixed, the river of traffic, the fall.

John Berryman Played the Accordion

There was a choir later that night
alive the many voices anonymous.

John Berryman, grinning, played the accordion
approximately, something broken from youth.

Put the *Schlager* back in the box, John Berryman said,
I stand for difficulty, disclosure, rage.

Next time around I'll take up the accordion, he said,
his genius for accelerated feeling restored.

*

Later there were musicians in the street,
a young man, a young woman with mandolin and harp.

As if at first only imagined and unplaced,
morceaux traditionnels from many parts of Europe.

The song held the air and hovered in doorways
making a pause in terrestrial motion.

We walked to find the origin of the music within reach
and night came down gently like the end of time.

*

There are occasions in the world restored to precise experience
that perhaps were never there in the first place.

Though everything of saying says look, here at hand,
you can walk into the centre of the shape made by the sound.

There was a dark horizon of mountains across the water
and I heard the first song broadcast on Radio Apollon.

The ferry had left and there was nowhere else to go
and the waves ran under the quay in exact measure.

The bones of them are keeping

We climbed the kalderimi, Taygetos above,
let a yellow dog run and looked out for snakes,
the sea a bowl of light we're heading for.

Across the square in Agios Dimitrios a mulberry tree
catches the sunlight in its spreading branches
as if the light pours from the sprouting leaves.

Give me your unfurling hand, I would take your hand
in that dance, the opposite of dying,
as the vetch and daisies rise in a wave.

The sky opens to magnify the earth incandescent,
the sun a path of broken glass to the other shore,
a radiant scatter cast this way.

*

'Just beside, there is the Catholic church with the friends of Greece monument. In the crypt, the bones of them are keeping. Lord Byron was a real friend of this country. This is the reason we called our hostelry by his name.'

*

Tonight, a crowd fills the square in Nafplio for Good Friday,
the bower of white and purple flowers for Jesus held aloft
and purple banners for Jesus hanging from high windows;
priests, acolytes and bigwigs on stage and not a girl up there.

The silver band plays in death march to lead the parade,
Kyrie eleison
and there's a baby in pink rabbit costume on my shoulder,

Kyrie eleison
and for one moment everyone stops talking
Kyrie eleison
and the shops dim their lights for the parade to pass.

Let me join those families, lose me in that crowd,
the children grasp the strings of their ascendant balloons
the cartoon faces nod and genuflect above us all;
Ky rie e leis ON with a thump on the big drum.

Listening to Country Music

I'm sending you this from Agios Dimitrios,
October light on the sea as summer retreats,
the days strung out like amber beads of the turning world;
we can walk along the shore and see its radiance dissolve.

I can no more describe the light than walk on water
I hold everything, I hold nothing:
but on sighting the sea we shout Thalassa Thalassa
for the great enterprise; catastrophe tops the brim.

St. Dimitrios lives above the harbour they say,
I hear their singing, their octosyllabic miroloyia,
another lit photograph fixed to a headstone,
another grave to feed and water and talk to.

And the rain will be good for the olives,
straight-down spears of light falling on our heads,
the sound of its descent rising like inescapable thought
buoys us up in the layered distance of the mountains.

The island off shore is no bigger than a big rock,
there you find the bronze statues of the Discouri
standing a foot high in the open air of Pephnos,
the sea sweeps over in winter and never moves them.

A sparrow's two-tone chatter elevates the blue dome
over Taygetos and the gulf, the distance unimaginable.

*

I don't get Apollo, the far-seeing flash youth
but we were drunk listening to country music
attendant upon the god using women for target practice

and Jason Isbell sang – 'She smelt of cigarettes and wine,'
flitting back to Delphi in the blink of Spring.

The mist rolls in off the sea, leave the door open tonight,
Apollo the village boy walks out by the shore unencumbered,
– I've stopped thinking of the Indo-European question, he said,
of John Berryman's whiskey tears.
I'm Apollo, look, I'll show you my head full of light,
the human catalogue of irresistible actions,
lyres, vulvas, arrows in flight, ravens made black.

*

There's no account of Euripides' trek north to Macedon
slogging through The Valley of Tempe to voluntary exile,
writing *The Bacchae* on a tangent to Athenian reason;
snowblind, snowbound, Euripides evokes the stranger god.

Dionysus steps forward and announces himself,
'I am,' lisping, eyes of kohl shine insouciant liquefaction,
I am … is how a god would enter your life;
a figure of concealed and absolute concentration.

Here's a box of Bacchant tricks and fireworks,
fawn skin, thyrsus, bottle of beer, dancing shoes.
'Sweet fool, my toys burn holes in your piddling days.
If I landed my radiant gaze would melt your bones.'

'What do you imagine you have apart from me?
Think back, at first you knew what? There you go,
an alert body, hungry, ready to eat the whole world,
a figure of concealed and absolute concentration.'

*

(For musicians Sam Bailey and Jack Hues)

Down here below the glass of waves
I hear no music, no chordal tides,
no Brad Mehldau, no Christian Scott.

Jack, Jack – can you hear me?
Sam, my ears are full of the turning sea;
for just one song I would come back.

I would come back and walk down your street
of foolish things, of Sam at the piano
playing the whole world open-eyed.

Jack pitch an opera at the lowering sky
sound out the tones to change the climate,
let the music play us like swimming.

*

Nina Simone lived in the Republic of Song,
she married there several times and on occasion was happy;
once she arrived in the Republic from Montreux 1976.

Her earliest point of entry was that first recital
in the library Tryon, North Carolina, at ten years old
to raise money to continue her musical training.

She refused to play until her parents were restored to the front row.
'Daddy you can do what you like but I won't play until,'
years later, 'I sing from intelligence,' said Nina Simone.

*

Sam Plays Sam Speaks

A mythology of playing and speaking
I said from my mouth from my fingers.

From my mouth from my fingers
to beat the logos out of thinking.

Sam said from the tipping edge of thought
I don't know what I'm saying Sam said.

Why bother with the prefabricated
any fool can fill bloated museums.

(Sam now say 6 things that come to your mind, tell me and I'll write them back to you. Perhaps you include even the present statement).

1

2

3

4

5

6

My life as a DJ didn't work out.

Why taunt the dumb beast?

First broadcast of the day.

To beat the logos out of speaking.

Back to the stream of first meaning.

From the mouths of all the people.

*

There's a single point of light on the mountain,
the air between here and there is a substance, an intoxication.
I know the village, the steep road, the houses rising in terraces;
there's music there tonight, two sinuous old men singing
throw the economy on the fire – we all know these songs, always have.

We sing up and the year rolls forward against the odds;
by such means springs erupt, the wind drinks pine tree resin
and the sweep of the valley presents a map of itself.
A boy steps forward to dance before his family,
the faltering 9/4 measure jigs the Zeibekiko bones.

Subterranean the music tilts the kalderimi to the sea,
disintegrates the squared stones of the village walls,
breaks our contracts rattling bolts in the night
and makes us beasts clamour and dream,
monosyllabic and simple on the chambered ground.

*

If you are a big tree I am a small axe sings Orpheus
his lyre cocked – and carved from the tree addressed,
strings of air stretched and tuned to magical numbers,
a question of long division and sweet intervals.

'If I'm what?' said the tree, panicking the whole forest,
a single wave of sound crashing mountains, valleys, cities.

The ratio of matter anti-matter means something said Orpheus,
1:10,000,000,000 for instance means the world's congealed song.

Ughh, the mass of it, gibbering, unformed, the anti-poem;
that's why I have to chop some life into it, right into the grain.
It's not easy, you try it, harvesting by acoustics only;
my voice, my juice right into it, notch by notch, note by note.

*

There is another version of Orpheus going to hell for Eurydice. In this other version Orpheus must not say Eurydice's name because this, rather than turning to see if she is following him, will abandon her to that no place of shadows. He must not even shape the sound of her name.

It could be represented like this:

must not speak
walk she follows
must not speak
you rid he see
you you you rid
rid see sea seed
Eurydice Eurydice Eurydice
her hand on my shoulder
its warmth lighter than
and then turning gone
in song set hell spinning.

It could be represented like this:
I know the name I say in darkness.

I hold everything, I hold nothing;
the distance unimaginable.

A Revision of Jack Spicer's *Helen: A Revision*

Everything is known about Helen but her voice,
setting fires as a history of conflagration in the culture
even over the icy sea echoing in your ear,
even further north over the white shelf of falling.

For history I went to the North Pole Helen,
the magnetic music sought us out, made us naked;
it was nothing like a vision, just orders from above.
For history I went to the North Pole Helen.

Daddy Zeus President was there, squalling and whining;
he feared Helen was on her way,
he feared he did not exist, blah blah blah;
most of us wished that was the case.

His voice is like that because the sky enfolds him:
the sky, contrails, flightpaths, satellites – is boss.
They are not signs but items in the big emporium,
and below he drills holes in the fourth wall for immunity.

I won't do the ghost walk pelted with soft fruit, he said.
On the battlefield with the real dead of the new old world
you can choose to name the smashed-up plants and people
but know there's a simple opera rolling in the grass.

Finally Helen was in transit, her make-up sent on to Egypt.
There are particular insects in the desert, to be kept from the eyes;
Helen's eyes brighter than bright dehydrated the heart,
no artefact could do this, her presence runs in the nerves.

In your name my love I break off to write to you,
the space between us a matter of low resistance parabasis.

I can imagine you in Egypt, in Troy but not returning,
after much slaughter, to down-home Sparti.

If we harvest black ghosts starvation follows,
seeds of dust smeared on the faces of friends,
dumb and unable to grasp their own interest;
reckless love 754 miles off, from Sparti to Troy.

You must go there to set the poem aside.
They know everything about Helen there.

The Pleats of the Sun

We were in the air listening to the song about Icarus
holding the silver thread of morning like a tune,
turbulence flipped the flight attendant on all fours.
Icarus thought it funny until he touched the silver thread;
fizzing in the air like a firework, his first and last morning,
he saw a picture of the world turning and forgetting.

The olive trees swayed as one, clapped their little hands,
– 'There's no conspiracy on Earth,' Aeolis said, just gravity,
but given what you know about human nature…
We fell towards the sea, assumed the diving position,
the blue and grey perfection suddenly less abstract;
the captain sang the song about Icarus over and over.

*

I sit in the last corner of courtyard sunlight,
see the shadow plot diurnal, clouds resist quotation
drifting high across the shadowed mountains.

We step, we talk according to Homeric measure,
it's a matter of time gone deep, uncounted;
we've been inventing the song for generations.

My neighbours gather in the olive groves and high meadows,
bodies passing seen in the intervals of leaves,
I mean, they seem like drifting confetti of light.

Nothing is more beautiful than this temporary coruscation,
the refrain, the pause for thought, the contact made;
it secures nothing but sings the epic of a shared breath.

*

The roadside *kafaneio* is a stage set lit by a summer morning. Old men sit off to the side in the shade for a first drink. Variously garlanded figures assemble. Working men before work pull up for a coffee and a smoke. The young women, made-up, hair done, dressed ready, run the place, tease and serve. The backdrop through the big windows behind the counter is a huge sweep of sea fit to break your heart like a world of endless blue, endless promise. The men load up, come and go. The women attend and smile.
– 'Maria you are as fresh as morning.'
– 'What do you want Petro?' And tickles the palm of his extended hand.
– 'What I want is a break, and you.'

*

'the terrace is full
of salty murmurs
the dress and even
the pleats of the sun'
('Chanson Dada', Tristan Tzara, translated Lee Harwood.)

The days are columns of light
let them go in the unexplored grove
to stand apparent in the open air
an unfixed cartography surrounds them.

Those voyages unforgotten as bright shards
scattered trace another coast
after the submerged marble gardens
comes the first smell of the land.

Leaving the house I'm caught
that moment of evening, the wind in the pine,
the colour shift of earth, bronze mountains.
Lee, that moment you would know.

The Museum of the Sea

The Museum of the Sea

Setting out, the sun a risen fire
launched a day of promise
set to breakers
cutting the wave of the unknown.

1

He cut the motor at the exact point to glide and
slot the boat in place in one continuous movement
rope slung and tied stepped from deck to quay
six strides to the moped, one kick, turnover and gone.

An art accomplished for a box of small fry, unseen by tourists;
of the sea, of the harbour, made invisible to them,
lethargic in sports casuals seeking the real, the photogenic.
'What you want today? How much? Γεια σας κύριε. Look what I got.'

Transparent he moved across the light
rolling from deep time over the harbour wall,
just going about his business, occupied
the world of gods, the porch of ghosts, Ithaka of rock.

I watch the boats come and go, the spare catch
splashed silver on zinc tables splinter morning;
'How much you pay me today? What you want today?
Look what I got. Sardeles. Gavros. Gopas.'

I want the fleets of Pharis, Sparta, Messe to return
the friends of former days to come by,
to see that company, night on their shoulders
stepping over the harbour wall into yellow light.

The face absent at the table gone to remittance work,
to Europe and the America, the commerce
of the first ports lost like thought in a salt medium,
the spark they struck burning in a dark sea.

That year, land blown, they took to the ships,
some from poverty, others from chemical fire;
to find the poor season, the thin time of strawmen,
to find a clue, a song in a village adrift by the sea:

Little red queen, little red queen seated in her barge,
smacked-mouth lips and curly crown aglow;
attendants dip and bow, display their scarlet values,
their hearts and their vulvas like pretty purple roses.

And it was the same loading, the same departure,
by generation, processional of those taken,
all the traffic of the lives of men and women
bound in the trailing waves of abduction.

I watch the boats come, I watch the boats go; out there,
at the point of failing vision, the day shows promise
and the world turns for a line of light to advance
reaching to the absent and talk of the work in hand.

Little red queen, little red queen
your attendants dip and bow.

They sailed the upper sea of the setting sun,
for the pebble cut to resemble a woman
250,000 years ago at Berekhat Ram;
I would hold her in my hand.

Little red queen, little red queen.

2

The ladder into the sea made of rusted alloy
shifts with each step taken,
rung by rung the body submerges
surrounded by the rising coolness of time.

Keep to the left leaving the harbour
see the water pales in the shallows,
a fatal turquoise surrounds us, slow slow,
the wind's almost absent.

In an ABS plastic shell of 158 kilograms
afloat on a sea 4 miles down,
the silence deep enough overwhelms talk,
the village quit from sight, faces forgotten.

Go low on the water to find acceptance,
to find where the fresh water streams emerge,
swim in the cold eye of the sea
the still ellipses glassy on the surface.

Only the slow accumulation of detail
will keep you safe, keep you above the waves,
will have you come back one day, just to see
if you're remembered by the village girls.

Say goodbye to the bar for the glassy-eyed
the taverna for the lost,
the strophe antistrophe of a comedy
called Sunseeker Self-Congratulation.

The light breaks in a line advancing
and with morning the point stands clear

away from the business of the land
the white surfaces rise and fall aside.

You can swim into the caves of Kato Figi
and all the acoustic caves of the sea,
at any turn sink below the rising truth
sound the shape of descent in pretty song.

Swifts dart indifferent into the blue,
emit a net of signals scored in air;
we crawl under roots, over copper streams,
deeper into snake-dark, air-still silence.

Descend through words, pictures, obliteration
below white dots punched in grey rock
picturing a pistol like a diving dolphin;
the war continues and the earth makes no answer.

P. Pterneas
A. Strateas
A. Manoleas
S. Christeas
Panayotis Petreas

and above 1881
and above 2-8-43
         1946
and above
the war makes another war
blue on ochre stained
the rising coolness of time.

*

As if from nowhere, there was lapis lazuli,
stone splashed with water shone brightest blue.
Lapis lazuli, the mouth saying it, – from where?
And you the lapis lazuli girl in your estate.

Even the name unknown until then,
lapis lazuli goddess you processed.
It was as if everything, the whole world
fell into the arms of the harbour.

Seventy miles by sea took a day and night,
a day and night to shrink the world to market:
obsidian, seashell, carved chlorite bowls,
bitumen – to stick together the bricks of Babylon.

Obsidian, good for butchery, good for war,
good for scarification and shaping marble;
pots decorated, their temples teeming,
a riot of boats, vulvas, fish and stars.

Out from the islands the captains came,
gliding over a sea of gods, raiding the divine,
opening the sea lanes to the unknown.
Shamash – comfort us at sea, let us not fear the waves.

They say she gave birth to a bull,
they were the people of the goddess
and the host sat around in a circle,
and the goddess gave birth to a bull.

Weapons, tools and jewellery
items for trade, diplomacy and war
from seven different countries, empires and states,
for beauty and for slaughter.

3

Nation by nation they fall upon the meadows of Asia;
ships the hardware dictated by the muses – listen,
so packed their oars clattering sing on the water
the men, strung flesh only, febrile, a horde.

And you mean to set this lot against that city?
Boiotians 50 ships, Minyans 30, Phokians 40.
It goes on and on, nation by nation they come;
I make this 1,186 ships, I make this unthinkable.

Odysseus and his Ithakans only 30 ships
grinning dogs for the most part
the man a fleet of cunning on his own,
the whispering self of many selves, twisting.

If anyone wants an account I'll tell them,
wine dark vile sea swallowed us
the waves fucked us every way up,
delivered us to one hole or another.

Sucking the beauty out of slaughter
I lost my taste for the tang of the ditch,
old men and young men scattered like trash
on the altar of the plain.

Smoke ascending in endless blue – futile,
blood descending in the purple fosse,
just limbs, organs, offal – futile
nation by nation they fall.

Down the no-return tunnel from the west,
we lay down on the meadows of Asia

dreamt a war and a return nation by nation;
noise travelling over water to silence.

*

So they come and go at the water's edge
site a bearing, mark by mark choose a course
that headland say, then set out across rolling blank,
recalling the sound of a remark barely heard.

Ghosted periplus of a nameless land drawn,
unrecorded on any chart, the captain's book;
and at every turn to contend with sweet *himeros,*
the way that track climbs the remembered hill.

Well you best forget most everything else,
it might do boys, once harvesting the sea begins
and you've taken the spoil of others,
but forget the land that only rarely tilted.

*

I sit and see it all, they come and go, the living the dead;
I sit because I can't do anything else, shipped up, caked in salt,
against this harbour wall, whitewash lifting, pockmarked,
you wouldn't see me if I didn't move, and I don't much.

I remember a morning we set out in the black ships,
I remember her face, how she turned and spoke – and the light.
What I see is vision, I mean it's there, and below the water too
but the ground is uncertain with items unretrieved.

They're the things recalled before the final deal
the objects made subject to aqueous corrosion,

how she stood in the doorway, the garden floating
and how the turning world came sailing in.

The harbour opens to the little sea gates of memory
but thought on that tide is borne at a cost, then washed away.
I see everything as on a screen, though the surface is unfixed,
my eyes transparent from seeing – and what's the use of that?

Then as now, the tide washed over, and I'm as glass under water;
my thalassocracy at my feet, a snapped oar, frayed rope, an empty tin.
Salute the king of sea rubbish, sea scrap, the ships unreturned,
the big fish eaten by little fish, their bones picked clean on the seabed.

My absolute vision runs on the waves, here's an account if you like;
ships – burning towers – a woman. Enough? Add this: the war
       continues.
I remember a morning when those black ships set out
leaving a white trail sparkling to the edge of the known.

And falling over that horizon, a single boat makes easy passage
from Marathonisi under cover through the museum of the sea.

4

'Set sail without fear, for though I lost myself to the sea, others who sailed the same day put safely into harbour.'

No-one takes to the sea lightly,
you starve or sail or both,
so farewell my little ones.
There's no music sad enough.

                350 copper ingots (10 tons)
                1 ton of tin, thus 11 tons of bronze

We couldn't make sheltered water,
the sound of cliff-wash faded;
smell of thyme, fennel on the air
from the land we couldn't reach.

                1 metric ton of terebinth resin
                2 dozen ebony logs from Nubia

            Himeros
If you sail beyond Cape Malea
forget your homeland
there's no return   *Himeros.*

In time we're all bound
for the heartless body of water,
washed-up, washed-out, bleached bones.
There's no music then.

                200 ingots of raw glass from Mesopotamia
                dark blue, light blue, purple, honey and amber

Under the breaking wave
white borne on the blue
beauty steps ashore.
There's no music sad enough.

                pottery from Cyprus and Caanan, oil lamps,
                bowls, jugs, jars, scarabs and cylinder seals

*

At night lights low on the water set out in darkness,
three lights, a one-man fishing boat, a living;
and elsewhere on the other side of the same small sea.

Pity those who take the 25 minute crossing,
pity those who make it and those who don't,
25 minutes, $1,500 sailing into darkness.

                      swords, daggers from Italy and Greece
                      a stone sceptre-mace from the Balkans

Spring of everything rising from the earth
Spring of everything drowning in sight of land
the air a chamber of birdsong wide as the sky.

*   24 stone anchors

We all went sucked into the salt mouth
not at the sea gates in blue light running,
nor dancing the bow wave whisper;
the sleeping stone cast and never retrieved.

A fouled hull scours the soft flesh
the face, the genitals and suchlike,
the water's red but no memory remains,
below a blue ellipse closing.

                14 pieces of hippopotamus ivory, 1 elephant tusk
                statue of Canaanite deity, bronze overlaid in gold

We suffered the vision of closest things
everything drowned to support bees,
to house the pretty sea slug, the lichen spirals,
the crab waiting to loosen our sinews.

                      remains of grapes, pomegranates, figs,
                      coriander, sumac and other spices

*

His name was Alan Kurdi
a small body in the water
he was three years old.

      gold jewellery, pendants, a gold chalice,
      duck-shaped ivory cosmetic containers

Out of the arms of his mother
out of the arms of his father
they will never hold him again.

Out of the arms of his mother
out of the arms of his father
they will never smell him again.

      a yellow baseball cap, a black headscarf
      a map of Europe, two rucksacks

*

We sang hymns
to Lord Wethead
Sir Teeming Waters
King Rolling Waves
God Streaming Locks
himself Poseidon
but he's a mean cunt.

Comfort yourself
sail without fear
the Great Green Sea
the Sea of Joppa
the Middle Sea
the White Sea
churning hope.

Press on press on
without fear
the Lampedusa route
the Lesbos route.
Make ready a riot
a flood a troop
nation by nation.

*

From seven countries, empires and states
weapons, tools and jewellery,
items for trade, diplomacy and war,
for a vision of furthest things.

Bejewel my hand, armour my heart
for beauty and for slaughter,
drop the world at my door
and set in gold its raw taste.

5

What you want today? Look what I got.
Out of the big sea I had this thought, OK,
stranger, out of the big sea turning backward.
Do you think my hands don't tell the story?
Do you think I've not always been here?

You see there's an Ithaka and a wife
the pleasure of my eyes and hands,
out there somewhere in the echoscape
before I took to the dealings of the world
before the pull of this island or another.

The sea's roar will drill a hole in your head
and leave you with nothing, companions lost,
memory shot, what you have is what you catch
and what you will see you will see in one light
and at the end there's a clearing, held then gone.

Tell the rhapsode sing or else, tell the rhapsode,
song the only harbour to gain at the close;
I see my island, up from the port to my house
this path I know, these white rocks I know
and the sea all around a vertiginous blue of air.

On all fours in the waves I remembered
I dreamt I was climbing that path, that other story
of the trick of my return, Telemachus, Penelope;
and I dreamt the great restoration,
that the ground might quit rolling under my feet.

I might stop here, scoop a handful of earth.
Look, they said, look at that old man crawling,
he's piss wet, he looks like a dog.
Where the hell's he come from?
Look at him burrow in the ground.

I tell you, if Helen was an appearance on the walls
a seeming woman, ghost queen of the bloody plain,
then I never returned, Ithaka a name only,
the slaughter futile and nothing
and nothing the going out and return.

*

Little red queen, little red queen,
we sing for you far off – What you want today?
Did we serve you true? Launch your boat aright?

Do you hold us in your heart?
Little red queen, little red queen, riding on the sea.

What is it that we do as the sky darkens
and talk submits to the slow sound of the sea?
A nocturnal hierarchy returns, a bat flits a signal
an old woman talks kindly to a dog,
and owls weave mortal wires into dawn.

Night falls and the bronze hills turn pink,
a fishing boat sets out against the odds
outboard drones a bow wave whisper,
the moon rises over cloud above Taygetos
making a terrestrial bed of light.

Village voices engulfed drift to an ending,
the harbour wall retains the heat of a long history;
radiant click of Ares, the honey of Helen's mouth;
the sea is dark, the night is dark, we are free,
the boat's there, sits easy on the water, let's leave.

Above Ground

As if Auguries

City Garden

As currencies crashed and markets burned
I was feeding avocado and haloumi
to the foxes at the bottom of the garden
and thick blood to the jaunty magpies.
The trees were dancing and deep in the garden
there was radium, cobalt, spiralling light.

I noticed the city was full of birdsong
and that the birds had insistent business with one another,
over the garden squares pooled in darkness
over the empty roads of the lost, blueprint town,
the overlaid sound, as if a score for the unknown,
the clouds looked fixed but drifted, the air ferrous.

*

After the event whenever on the street or in a market,
she would look for places to hide, to get down, covered.
This could be prompted by a plane soaring, a shout,
a door slamming – to begin the roar of ritual slaughter.
Don't run from the first explosion into the second,
this is a design feature of such events to be refused.

In orbit – a child's sunglasses with white stars, silence,
various body parts, hats without heads, unmatched shoes,
and the dead man alight who flew to fall on the girl.
In orbit the impossibility of encompassing the act,
the quality of the stone, the lettering on the monument;
all of this before anything can land and the light return.

*

Melanie is driving home through the city and its priorities,
through the seven tunnels in the moment of renaming,
the moment for the little poets and big poets at their desks
to go shopping and wash the shopping, expunge the fear juice,
scourge the wax and death from under their nails
and consider the weather, default grey, dark as a trench.

Melanie, outside the glow of dial light touching your face
floating forwards in the various world, nothing exists.
I know there's a casting outward here, a reaching out let's say,
implausibly beyond the writ of the poem over nothing, over
a dry river bed, the blown avenues of the financial district,
the stream of lights gliding in every form of address.

As if Auguries

The jay hit a low trajectory through the garden
scanning along a beam of light, my flashy killer
left a rumour of blue-black sparks and feathers.

Illusive in the maze of suburban hedges
to reappear on the back of the bench
head cocked at window whiteface.

*

Grey sky lit around the horizon through cloud
as if waiting for the barrage to begin;
to the right the city Grande Bretagne leaving.

To the left Flanders, beyond scrubby fields,
the old horror poisons the soil still,
open trenches for fools to fall in.

*

In Place Dumon at the hour of first darkness
people would head home from work
shops stayed open, light fell on bright faces.

I liked this moment, and the earlier time
when kids ran home from school calling,
voices echoing the mortal hour of bright faces.

Light retreats from the sky
and the trees are silent, still
the boundaries made invisible.

The lights of houses appear to signal
night has come across town
as if a dark hand rests like kindness.

*

It was said that by the second week of the crisis
the animals began to appear and speak,
the pretty fox in the garden outstared the light
the jay ate his fill and came back for more.

I watched the magpies flip black and white
write their cursive message – satis verborum;
later the leafless trees resembled mad scribble,
a determined script scratched on the clouds.

The rattling branches and empty spaces of light
made a network of exits twisting in the wind,
a green and deeper green invasion, a common speech
remote from panic asserts, you knew this would come.

Crow and a Footnote

In front of me as I freewheeled
the rain-washed road down hill
the shadow of a crow kept pace
wings opening and closing overhead.

Passing the Chapel of our Lady and Centre Medik
beyond the suburban fields of maize
under an untethered sky out of town,
wings opening and closing, head poised.

*

There are implications arising here that I question, unthought habits of superstitious thought from the medieval torture chamber anxious for poetic effect. I meant rather the coincidence of the crow flying steadily in the same direction and at the same speed as I cycled down the road. I meant principally the sun in just the right position to cast the shadow of the bird gliding along in front of me with the sky washed clean enough after rain to make the road surface glisten.

The image of the crow's shadow guiding me, the wings opening and closing, may have prompted the ominous details from the utilitarian landscape, some of which were innocent. The journey out of town. The sickly coloured Mary in the enclave of the chapel's wall. The medical centre where I'd had conversations on the lines of – Well, this could kill me then?

It would be more useful to have better knowledge of the intelligence of corvids, something on their navigational behaviour for instance. The crow was following the long, straight road, and because it was wet and the sun was reflected, presumably the surface was shining up to the bird as a pointer. Or was it using a capacity for internal navigation? Whichever, it followed the road all the way above me. Presumably it was not much interested in the thing moving along below and its passing thoughts? Am I just potential carrion? The mortal maggot wriggling foetal in the brain. Click. X-rayed by the crow's eye. It is useful to call things what they are.

Of the Crows

Of the crows which fell into Helen's Garden
from a Brabantine-blue sky that day,
one flew off and one stayed
to tackle the catflap and befriend big dog.

Two crows fell into Helen's Garden exhausted
black Xs to rewrite corvid lore,
black wings refusing flight, beady-eyed
intelligence from flightpaths of knowing.

We know grief is locked in our bones,
we know we will fall in the same way;
loss is endless; Helen's hand drawing
a hawk on her father's coffin is love.

As if in a glacier or seen through opaque plastic
a crow, the image of a crow at the catflap tapping.
Feed me, the beak tattooed in crow exegesis,
– *I know my Hegel, the master servant trick, try me.*

Big dog and crow sat above the garden
taking the air from the green pocket of earth;
absent crow was absent but these two were at rest
on the metal steps above the submerged flora.

One day two crows fell into Helen's Garden.

The Correspondence of Objects

'Tween what we see, what be,
is blinds. Them blinds on fire.'

*

On the cover of the Faber edition of *The Dream Songs*
John Berryman's face stares out from a rectangle,
heavily bearded and wearing boxy glasses.

A look not improved by the empty wine glass I sat on it,
a magnifying glass on tiny stilts used by document forgers,
admitting a bright shaft of light on a life form trapped.

The process here, back and forth, between unfixed persons;
a glistening pearl stares back, blinks and flickers transformed
and the scientists run from the lab screaming – *What the…*

His father was a master maker of banjos – old school;
HH con banjo cranked out a lifelong aria on rusty strings,
hands shaking with beauty, spilling every other drop.

His, the laparoscopic vision on the far side of the bar,
the twists and turns he'd take like a long slow road snaking its way
      out of Oklahoma.

*

Against the window I can see the drop of saline,
a bead of sky falling into the tubular reservoir
adding to the pool of light every seven seconds.

The entire sky rolling westward descends in that bead,
over the towers and satellite dishes of Anderlecht
aerial aerial aerial – there is a correspondence of objects.

I would open that prosaic door and walk in;
at the edge of the garden blackbirds are calling,
they sing – when there's nothing to say, say nothing.

And those long stemmed small white flowers
– what do you call those Melanie? floating like stars,
and far off, understated, the city traffic whisper.

The falling saline drop an image of mortality in flight:
tremble tremble bright bead of light.

*

Walking the track to the parks and lakes
the hour of going home sounds on the air;
deep on both sides leaf mould leaf rot,
deep enough to bury me, already occupied.

Craik craik said the metal rooks drilling the sky,
light thickened and the ground took a seasonal tilt;
high in the trees the rooks passed through the screen,
in and out of holes of the sky of sporadic vision.

There was a message – You're not done with Orpheus yet,
music begins and ends in the body and constitutes the body,
which is why we Maenads tore the warbler to pieces,
looking for the music, elbow deep, glutinous, bespattered.

Keep walking, see the four companionable foxes trot by,
see them sit and stare, to disappear when the dogs arrive.

*

Unfinished, incomplete, unresolved.

The burning blinds at some point catch both sides.

The space between what is and what we see – a conflagration.

At some point a scatter of ash, a shadow language reassembled.

An audible sifting, a first music without pause.

Tremble tremble bright bead of light.

Ten Tall Youths

For a fire alarm practice
all the students are on the school field,
when planes pass for Zaventem
the Ukrainian children lie on the ground.

When the sun comes out 5-year-old Vlad
hides under the table,
– When sunny bombs come
    to kill my daddy, clouds they don't come.

*

In the park in the heart of the capital
there's an abandoned crazy golf course,
surrounded by trees coming into leaf,
bunkers, slit trenches, seeded with landmines.

Cartoon characters mouths open красивая krasivaya
point the way for you to shoot,
the fake fairway of empire calls,
the whole place clogged, smelling of rot.

To see this site of lapsed pastime fun
as a model of Putin's war in Ukraine
is of course ridiculous, unavoidable and present,
as no metaphor can convey the brutality.

*

My name is Marko. My name is Maksym. My name is Alina.
My family is mother grandmother two cats
and not here my…

What is phylum? What is function? You say?
Above his head a picture of Descartes,
on the classroom wall scientists, writers
and by the door an account of the Nansen passport.

Ten tall youths listen, quiet and precise,
Kyril says – I want to go back to fight.
Outside small children dive into a hedge
and show each other how to shake a sapling.

My name is Marko. My name is Kyril. My name is Milana.
My family is mother grandmother two cats
and not here my…

Singers

Ian Partridge sings Finzi's aria 'A Farewell to Arms'
sunlight on the avenue of trees running to fresh graves.

What has happened to my country?

The leaves of reinvented green catch the light lifting
from the west falling for history to be buried.

*

Lorraine Hunt Lieberson is singing Mahler
'I Am Lost to the World', live in 1998;
the cadences rise and fall in the order of things,
her voice comes walking to us and everything is changed.

Lorraine Hunt Lieberson is dead now
as will be some others from that concert;
they are all there behind an invisible wall
as that voice comes walking to us on boundless air.

*

In this world the word Haydn translates
as reason, as light, as anthropometric song,
the transparent houses and streets, life by life
slip into the common air allegro spirituoso.

*

To Toccata Prima written by Claudio Merulo in 1598,
light is splintering at the window spinning from the sky
touching the white table, the bright instruments of morning,

aglitter it goes through the open door to the nurse's station;
light for the mind to touch and run.

*

At the Gaelic Mod on Islay the unassuming man who was working in the café on the ferry coming across is now standing on the edge of the stage in a village hall and is singing a song in a language for which I don't have a single word and the song is fit to break your heart and is known to the audience who take up the chorus and the woman next to me explains that it is about our land and why there are so few of us on it.

*

For the applause Andrea Buccarella stood by the harpsichord,
bowed to the audience, pointed to the Goldberg score held aloft.

Bach's perfect geometry dances in the air above our heads,
that chord – Bonae Artis Cultorem Habeas, ascendant.

From Chagall

After the train through the night heading south
flew over green plains and blue hills
the wind off the sea blew up the hill and dropped us
at the Musée National Marc Chagall to swoon.

*

He was born dead, was reanimated
full of Chagall pictures.
He saw a trough, was dipped in water,
a fire broke out in Vitebsk right then.

A little reading, a bout of staring
will set this straight for you.

*

'Russia was almost covered with ice. Lenin turned it
upside down the way I turn my pictures.'

A cold morning for such business, frost on roofs, windscreens
but the sky lightens, flights arrive and the air rings,
you don't need to imagine sleigh bells and girls ululating.

There was a moment when the battalions flooding Europe stopped
and we were just shoeless peasants, a few uncertificated Jews
but there was a pause, Chagall said.

I saw Bella above the village, I saw the intelligence of beasts
in the band of stars glittering like the psalms the cantor sang.
I saw all this in Belorussia of the earth, back at the very beginning.

*

The coloured wind lifted every animate object
spinning like love and death about Vitebsk,
all the animals looked and the stars flickered
around the painter at work standing to the side.

Let me fly just once across the sky, said the cow,
look in my doleful eye before you eat me up,
just one time over the crazy houses and church
there is a life, a line between us, you know.

And the fiddler winked, stamped his foot
scraped out a popular tune for dancing;
and from the Feast of the Tabernacles
we shared again our temporary canvas home.

As if a blue-faced cow might carry a parasol
and a wedding dress rocket into the Tree of Life.
Can you believe this, even before Paris,
even before the big circus and the falling angel?

The floating lovers rise in an arc of revelation,
men go by working themselves to death,
the cattle dealer barely escapes early Cubism
and Bella stands above the garden of the world in a white collar.

Preparations

Priti Patel has determined that refugees should drown, I mean children and their parents. The exact physiological mechanisms of drowning are complex, progressing through skin cooling to hypothermia and death by way of disorientation, amnesia, cardiac arrhythmias and ventricular fibrillation. The temperature of the water of the English Channel ranges between 20 and 5 degrees centigrade. In water below 28C the heart may spontaneously stop. How long it takes to drown also depends on the size of the body and the volume of its fat insulation. Immersion in water at 5C can result in drowning between 30 and 60 minutes.

A small child would drown sooner,
in that narrow band of water
tightened to choke a nation.

*

Pavarotti is singing from Modena. Pavarotti has removed all the stops. Love, death and poverty, poets fainting in the arms of lovers – as is life. Puccini has abandoned recitative in the sustained charge of the music, a song of songs pours forth. Experiences come, one after another, and then more, and irresistible as if music, the stops removed, no recitative.

*

Sunlight patters through the market of Place Dumon,
arrayed on the gleaming fish, the fruit, vegetables and flowers.
At the Börek stall, the Japanese wife, toddler in arms,
pats the just arrived Japanese husband on the backside.

And he replies – *Bonjour Madame*, and the child, stars in her hair,
runs in circles whilst busking Eric Clapton busks about heaven.
And the eyes of the Turkish woman look like morning,
like the sun rising in another country.

*

A mantle of black feathers fell on my shoulders,
keep it plain here I thought, corvid feathers in soft layers
of deepest darkness whispering flight from small pockets of air.

The adornment was matt or gloss in relation to how I turned
as if a state of mind made inescapable in the world,
as simple as the way you move in the light without thinking.

By then I expected the removal of parts of the body
rather than this sort of addition, its meaning unknown,
a soft mantle of feathers, flickering like electricity at every step.

*

Robert Hass is questioning a boundless poetics – 'any poetics, any making, is bounded.' And he talks of the energy and importance of gesture embodied in the work of art, finite but ongoing. It was like breathing fresh air, restored and setting out over open fields.

Then I did take a walk along the track to the park and lakes in the heart of the city. The first air of Autumn all around and the slow turning of the season already known in northern Europe. That night was a Magritte sky and an almost full moon rising over the tall houses and dark gardens. The scene was just given, just there, for a moment magnetic.

I remembered walking in Cornwall, in the compact fields, knowing where there were gaps and styles in the boundary hedges. These stone hedges are Neolithic and still in use. They are built of two sides of stone blocks with small interlocking stones and packed with subsoil. Grass and bushes grow on the top to be battered by the wind. The fields and hedges hold and step onwards to the sea on the edge.

*

The Nansen passport was used by 450,000 refugees from 1922 onwards. It allowed the displaced of the Russian civil war and Armenian genocide to cross borders and escape the threat of deportation. Nansen stamps were required to renew the passport, the charge for which provided funds for refugee relief.

Ongoing. Included in that 450,000 – ongoing:

Stravinsky
Anna Pavlova
Nabokov
Robert Cappa
Chagall

Flying, flying over the village.

*

And there's a fruit fly, (there's always an and,
the world's at it, with or without you sweetheart,)
flickers around the open O of the Sainte Victoire.

Chords ascend, Bach processed as 32 minutes
of country soul, and it's moving, that limited voice:
Showtunes, a voice, O, not an instruction, beautiful.

I would not have my friends go before me;
there are children in the house and fresh cognates
first conversations and fields green again.

What is that light rises anew, writing a poem drunk to music?
O light of little knowing, there's a secret river
and a slow current for all of us to swim one day.

Another Country

When Blake Returned

When Blake set foot on Albion's shore
he found little changed and was shaken by the sight;
the same princes spaffed blood up palace walls
made new the same dark song of entitlement.

*

After Elohim

According to Ustad Fareed Ayaz and William Blake
the day Adam's soul was to enter his body
it was ordered to enter but refused.

It refused until it heard the voice of David singing
Enter – and it entered.
This is an example of sensory transduction.

The music of that voice became biochemical impulses
in the mind's order of astonishment
and gently lifted the roof, elevating Adam's head.

Everything was alive in the sky.
She stepped ashore, everything begins here
is another example of the same process.

*

30 January 2020

In the hotel opposite the lift goes up the lift goes down,
a crown of blue lights through smoked glass, up down;
and the Thames conveys its chartered business
to the sea where the ports have names for empire.

River traffic trails brown eddies in its wake
to the lower reaches, to Marlow on the glistening tide,
and William Blake walked across Lambeth Bridge
casting a passionate clarity on everything about him.

In a constructed future, hovering at a distance,
those houses and towers of Westminster
stand planted here immovably on your heads:
bow down you crowds and hold them up.

There are rewards for the gulls guarding mudbanks
and rewards for shrinking the definition of us;
morning light blinks and gathers on the water,
cormorants track their own shadows and leave.

Seeing England

Driving across England out of the tunnel into the day,
a single dot flashes heading west on empty roads;
folded in green of Salisbury Plain, a calendar of stones
fixes Hardy's vision of time passing to one end;
wind combs the fields with light, each blade of grass alive.

We swung by the pivot, recruited, bound to history,
our unseeing eyes crammed with grit,
saw the minister of speed-speak let flop on the compass.
Daisy, Ermintrude and Buttercup – hup hup my girls,
the near Neolithic algorithm will do for this lot.

They fall asleep in a country falling asleep,
surrounded by magnetic hills, the old money fretwork,
the sing-song verse from these southern downlands
proclaims they're done with courting abroad,
will sleepwalk an imagined nation into a ditch.

Are we there yet? Look, a land made invisible to itself
hurtling backwards to a supposed point of origin;
the princes of chartered vagrancy scour the place,
what matter Wordsworth, Shelley, Blake turned this field,
about them now the day falters in Atlantic darkness.

The Nansen Passport

The Nansen passport promised that the above-named person
may freely traverse and leave the state of Anomie
and enter the regions of immediacy with their pockets of air,
their turns of rain and the life of planned streets and apartments.

The Nansen passport promised that after chemical events
and last kind words, you could walk away above ground
through the failing light, the unfamiliar trees – that music
of the stateless multitude sleeping nowhere restored.

The Book of Journeys was written on transparent paper,
opening on green paths and half-buried tracks
as if suspended just below the surface of the page,
the known and unknown destinations mapped.

Even now it begins with a lost view from home,
the hill encircled and the word riverine in my mouth,
the proposition that everyone is there just one step away,
gathered in a living room as empty as the sky.

The floating poetry of the dark corridors
was once the condition of others, their voices
riding the air and falling, that we are all there,
one failing body released in bright song.

In that moment he thought of the well of forgetting
and the well of remembering, of blank night at the window
the empty screen of nothing; only a fool would remember,
and only a fool would forget.

The white noise of the city rose like a wave
around the apartments and separate lives

of that invisible choir, who now and then at night
would hear each other and call in one voice.

There is a bearing away from such events but no end,
there are the towers and quiet streets,
the parks and forgotten water meadows,
an uncovered river running to a memory of the sea.

Another Country

Feed me no Moly, let me not forget
above ground walking, the bright day.

Let the wind rock the house.
Where would you pitch your voice
from the North Atlantic fault
from Iceland's black shore?

Bells ring below the waves off-key;
through the watches of the night – stand down,
you could just stand down
for the slow rotation into day.

The clouds appear anchored
but drift at ease over the moor
through the empty hymn of the sky,
the uncased air about to launch.

In that quarter over the sea
the sky a bowl of light
surrounding the peninsula
with deep and endless blue of day.

*

And now and then with night coming on they would settle to talking,
the two of them. And now and then, the other figure he had not become,
would, as if passing outside the window, look in, unable to touch but
longing to see those mortal faces to which he was entirely absent in that
prosaic, yellow light; remembering the taste of food, a tone of voice and
she returning to the house a garden in her hands.

*

In the early hours rain is falling. Rain is falling into the garden around the house, on the small fields down to the sea, over the Penwith moorland and the hills and the road to Zennor. There is no light anywhere, not a smear and the only sound is rain falling and your breathing and I can picture you without seeing you, your face turned up, sleeping, each breath drawing the Atlantic air of morning.

*

With the day falling to the west
a murmuration swirled over our heads
rolling over the fields down to the sea.

A dancing wave folding and unfolding
fills the air with the sound of wings
and the sky breathing all around us.

*

Above an inlet by the abandoned hard rock mines
where children grubbed for arsenic and other minerals
their hands wrapped in rags, where copper stains the cliffs
leaching into the rolling waves, a mass of seagulls glide.

They glide like a single living thing wingtip to wingtip
without a flicker, as beautiful as calculus in flight,
vectors in prismatic air, an intaglio of flightpaths on nothing
to suspend a tracery of serrated blue, heads poised, searching.

*

The sky paused and the Celtic fields stared
the day before the storm made still
the air drawn into the coming chaos.

I abseiled on a thin chord into a dark zawn
to take soundings with the tide rising like time,
down into the rage of white surf with no return.

Streams fell musical to the sea and memory followed,
that would be a granite cliff topped with heather and sky:
somewhere, out there, is the perfect abstract art.

*

Dark the sea tilts westward without end,
I could step off the edge of the world here
seeing magnetic light over water I could

Step away from the net of yellow days
floating in the trees of the last road at the corner,
seeing lights of resilient lives turning to hear

What might be the music of everything,
the abstract art of singing through the night
when she looked around and said – I'm OK now.

This was the moment of the little rafts of light
taking to the sea, one, another, almost a fleet,
to make a constellation of the rolling deep.

Drinking Songs

My father worked part-time in a pub,
The Oddfellows Arms off the Square;
these scenes arrive and make no story
assuming their meaning decades later.

A pub for working men after work
packed at night and thick with smoke;
he collected glasses and was paid in drinks
and drank the dregs of the glasses collected.

He bought beer bottle caps home for me,
I set them out as static armies on carpet land
– Guinness v. Mackeson v. Flowers in futile ranks,
rank the smell, like the dosshouse in which he died.

I walked by the pub at night, inside
the roar of voices liquid convivial;
the memory like broken glass in the street,
bottles thrown unseen, shatter on impact.

*

I think these songs rise at night, not bound for story
they write themselves, and after time – when time is called
– the feelings are gone or not, make nothing of them
I don't know   there is   perhaps   I think

a hierarchy of loss unrecorded
                              ascending in an arc of glittering glass
hurtling a moment over the streetlights
                              of the rain-wet Square
spangling the familiar darkness of the night above.

I liked the Guinness bottle caps best
black and gold like coins of unknown currency,
the serrated circumference of the underside
imprinted a red crown in your palm.

There's no account to settle in that currency,
these songs set out from nowhere, recall even less;
the crown cut in the palm of your hand
like a pass to a different country.

*

Melanie sleeps as if floating in the white bed
and moonlight fills the garden like still water.
The city, an unrealised plan, is quiet,
sets out around us a proposal nearly visible.

I mean the houses and gardens, the streets
and the contracts of the day, drift far off
into an unthinkable depth of translation
bordered by the silent trees of the park.

My daughters and their children are asleep
away from here in cities to the east.
The risen architecture of morning
comes flickering across a continent.

Seamarks

Dave

Your watercolour 'Seamarks' prompted these poems and gave me a sense of what I might be doing. The picture is of eight small seascapes depicting eight different seamarks, though the seamarks are all distant and submerged in the prevailing conditions. I know these bearings will disappear before the journey is done yet will still plot the course by them. I know I'm subjecting your picture to a vague poetic interpretation here but press on in the prevailing conditions without much choice, reaching still for these absent back bearings at the point of departure to those islands in the middle of the sea.

i

On the dark sea off to the left a white tower,
further still, almost hidden, a darker spire.
The sky has taken the colour of the great green
and your channel conceals a series of rocks.

What ships sailed here have gone into pockets of air,
this place only remains in the minds of those who survived;
others trusted seamarks, they had no charts,
vision was poor, opened the door to disaster.

ii

That inlet might mean positive erosion
and the white tower direct a battle home,
and I'm seeing what's not there, clear and bright,
another history like a rising tide of denial.

I was waiting on the pier, we all waited,
the sun on the hills made it hard to see;

everyone reduced to the point of disappearance,
not even reflected on the water, over and out.

iii

First explorers, then charts,
then traders and ordnance
on the good ship Imperial,
raise these seamarks boys.

Sea full of money, sea full of bodies;
headcount the black and shiny coins below.
How many survived this time?
Plenty for you and me Captain.

iv

Lee, I know this is not the Brighton Sea
and you're not here and neither can we talk like this.
The sky wheels above the sparkling blue as always,
and the gulls post-modern make space in their song.

I remember from your hospital bed the sky
and the high window opened a little,
far below the tide rolls back and forth
but this is just one-way, though not a word lost.

v

Force 10 winds left our sails in tatters,
water poured in the smashed window,
the water rising and the wind roaring
adrift two miles offshore.

The girl said, – My uncle's in the RNLI
he's saved people at sea.
I know all the types of boats,
the Shannon's my favourite.

vi

That other shore, I've been there;
the light fails, and the return, if it happens,
a matter of medical competence and chemistry,
arrives in a white coat, free of metaphor.

From the other shore the view shifts,
you look and wonder – am I in that film?
Is that the seamark? Leading where?
Lighthouse, lighthouse, swing your beam.

vii

Lighthouse, swing your beam
show me Alan out there still,
Alan of the precise word
singing for William Blake.

New arrival on the other shore
I'm calling you, over,
radio waves rise and fall;
silence silence, the sea replied.

viii

Are those the houses of the living
low on the shore falling over the edge?
I remember fields down to a river
and boats drifting slowly out to sea.

There the days spiral in the green
and pillars of light twist and turn all sense;
I never knew then what would happen next,
moment by moment waves breaking on the day.

About the Sea

At a Distance Count the Crises

'…poetry is the only place where the power of numbers proves to be nothing.'
Odysseus Elytis, *In the Name of Luminosity and Transparency*, 1979.

('Well, you know, sometimes a crisis can be productive?' ed.)

At a distance across the inlet
the cars move as if with purpose,
there's no sound, just the appearance of order
the other side of the arm of the sea.

Tuesday – church bells ripple at speed,
this I think is for Constantinople
the fall of the city, Tuesday an omen
sounds out to the mountains and Mystras.

The conditional – as if – hovers around
the uncased air is a wonder
and Aegean blue for Byzantium
pervades the ruins of then and now.

Sleek private cruisers, super yachts
state their case (What do you call such boats?)
Security men stare, military grade comms,
darkened windows on every rising deck.

Everywhere, abhorrence and wonder,
as if one permits the other;
the pretty child begging at the taverna
allowed by the waiters last night.

*

Attica burning Arcadia burning,
terraces the colour of smoke;
fire streams in the valleys of Arcadia,
grey smoke snakes over Attica.

47C in the village that afternoon,
55C recorded at ground level Athens;
waterbomb helicopters buzz Arcadia,
– you have to take the old road today.

At night above Koroni across the gulf
fires cover the hills, burn red on the water;
pine tree resin popping around the house,
– I mean inside the trunk and boughs, popping.

*

Waking up in ICU in Bordet, Brussels, reanimated after the haemorrhage, I read *Don Juan*. Byron's wit set against the bleeping machines, the biometric readouts and the taste of iron and salt trickling down my throat. Byron kept me going. The doctors kept me going. Floating there I knew absence spoke for itself endlessly and had nothing to say.

We've bought your husband back to you, the doctor said to Melanie. Even as a smashed-up bloody mess I was in the world again, seeing you standing there.

Later I was trying out breathing – Sa Ta Na Ma, just quietly trying. The young Indian guy visiting his Polish fiancée in the next bay appeared through the curtains smiling. – *I know what you're doing man. It's good you know. Come on get up, you've got to get up, I've seen your wife in the corridor, the men are lining up for her.* – I was hardly a contender just then but it helped.

*

We drove through the mountains westward,
dilapidated Sparti behind us, the plain a floating heat haze,
the Laconic air thick as honey reducing speech.

The story here is of near abandoned tractor towns,
two for one poverty traps in plastic and glass showrooms
left as ruins as the tide recedes around Tegea.

Spartans took to these passes to enslave Messenians,
Maniots resisted the Ottoman and defied the Nazis;
and suddenly we're miles from anywhere in silence.

We came to a sheer wall cracked and gouged with gullies,
perfect chaos suspended and incised over us
then descended through saintly villages to the sea.

*

Ten years ago, I was made temporarily blind by a stroke.
There was only darkness and I knew nothing at all;
there was a man shouting – Tell that fucking man to stop shouting,
and it was only me shouting, and kicking out and screaming.

Then a complete calm descended and surrounded me.
I thought this is not human and I've been wrong about everything,
and I gave in to a huge and intensely kind, powerful presence;
it was all around me, breathing on my face and I surrendered to it.

Melanie sat with me through that night, doctors came and went;
months later I told her about this experience when it came back to me.
She said – I think that was when they gave you the morphine.
I've written about this before and can't let it go – the god Morphine.

*

The afternoon softens with its pleasures,
as if there's a way of thinking
with the slow iamb of the sea.

And the wind tries its rhythm in the pine
finding the dark shape of you there like that,
night pools in the hollows of the mountain.

*

(Everything Takes a Literal Turn)

The satellite dish pointing at Yannis' has fallen out of the pine
and with next to no connection I'm sunk, adrift or free,
tap tapping away on this stupid phone Excommunicado.

On a telegraph pole by the house there's an old message,
painted on an arrow-shaped slat tilting downward – Aphrodite,
and the garden is in riot, the sea a soft submission.

Cicadas saw at the nerves, doves swoop and coo in quotation,
the wooded hill rises like a proposal to the mountain – tap tap,
banks of oleander and hibiscus and mulberry seduce me.

Across the square Maria of the tower is sharing a soap opera,
rapid fire Greek counterpoint to slow emotion and music;
for twenty years Maria of the Captain's Tower, alone, abandoned.

Entirely outside my invention or any expected trope, it's her life;
in such dramas a man always returns from long absence at sea,
this is shown by seaweed draped across his face and graphic wounds.

Or by a chance sign – Aphrodite pointing, tap tap.

That Night

That night of Spring in Delphi stands
snow falling out of mountain darkness,
running from the taverna to the room
snow falling to fill the centre of the world.

As if the transponder signals – here we are;
as if two eagles on a shared trajectory
released from opposite ends of the earth
might meet to fix the co-ordinates of zero.

The wind makes a tuning fork of the passes,
the sky sounding the one note in everything;
we ran into the snow like a breaking wave.

And I saw your face turning towards me,
through the fabulous vectors of snow
in Delphi in the spring of the world.

*

Other nights stand – in Kato Zakros,
the silver jackal curious at the bins
frogs calling in the cisterns of the palace.

Thalassa Mavri young Greeks sing
from the edge of the Libyan Sea
Hale Bopp coruscating upper darkness.

Folded in sleep and awake
to the perfect tension of your skin
the colour of you on the air.

*

The midnight choir woke us at 2 a.m.
singing for the Panagiya on Tinos of the Orthodox.

Their voices rose to the balcony like waves
washing through stone streets after the festival.

Lady of the Way, the inner knowledge and the outer,
show us the way, restore the City.

Men in darkness walking home in song
the past unforgotten rising before them.

Sounding out the single note in everything
to find and abandon the co-ordinates of zero.

Orpheus Asymmetric

The Singing Head

The singing head of Orpheus
washed up on Lesvos
amidst dead orphans and wreckage
to claim its etymology.

A glassy swirl on the screen then gone
headscarves, inflatables, Disney armbands,
at $1,500 a 25-minute trip
over the divide in the world.

To cross just water, just sand,
Orpheus gave everything to song,
against those who know
and execute power by rote.

My singing head proclaims
common truth from Lesvos
his name was Alan Kurdi
he was three years old.

Out of the arms of his mother
out of the arms of his father
they will never hold him again
they will never smell him again.

*

The Off Season

Yanni, I hope the family is well
and the olive harvest was good.

We will see you again in the spring
in the high meadows of new electricity.

*

All night in the off season by the house in Agios Dimitrios
Orpheus cuts a frame from the sycamore, hollows out tortoise shells
and the sound breathes a music before music to the sea.

The muse is an axe cutting clean wood, said Orpheus,
a tortoise shell and a length of sheep gut from that meadow,
the labour undertaken for the release of light.

*

Although we're not there we set foot on the kalderimi
the sea behind us and below, Taygetos above and before.

Already the new growth makes a mosaic of the path
a circuit of green light threading the worn stones.

The first snakes take the morning sun
the air is an open window of the sky unconfined.

*

Themuseisa 1

(Ekphrasis exhibition, Bruno Corà, Boghossian Foundation, Brussels 2019.)

The Muse is an installation by Fred Eerdekens. The word *muse* in lower case, with slight deterioration of the surface of the letters, is projected into the shadow of the crown of leaves of a young laurel. The slender trunk standing in a ceramic pot topped with pale grey pebbles reaches up into the light. Propped against the pot is a sign in three languages

– Please Do Not Touch. The sign is missing from the catalogue photograph. About three quarters of the leaves are in shadow, the upper leaves are lit. On the wall there are patches of light around the white word MUSE silhouetted in shadow. The light is filtering through the density of the leaves. Every element of the installation is still, though everything suggests a young girl caught in a dance, unselfconscious, skittish.

Please do not touch the muse is good advice.

*

Barry MacSweeney rode a motorbike into a poetry reading.
Barry MacSweeney rode a motorbike into poetry.

He carried the commission from Orpheus on his back
and Pearl dismounted in a borage grove to say thank you.

We're lost in music said Sister Sledge to Mark E Smith said to
Orpheus said to Aniruddh D Patel of *Music Language and the Brain*.

'There's no turnin' back' – You're telling me, said Orpheus,
his hands held nothing, his face borne into pentatonic night.

*

Hamayoun Shajarian sings and his voice spirals – Avaz,
up up in the endless blue over the Zagros Mountains,
an eagle swooping to leave no shadow on the border.

There Rumi circles the sun and we fall silent;
Hamayoun Shajarian's voice finds its perfect acoustic
as the single notes of the tanbur drop like water – Avaz.

*

Mandelstam served Orpheus without restraint.
He would hear a humming in a language before language
striking at the noise, brushing it off for days.

From this the poem would come
and Nadezhda would memorise it exactly
so that it could not be taken by the NKVD.

Lobbed into the Neva Mandelstam's head
went singing all the way to Armenia,
Armenia is landlocked, but this is what happened.

As poetry moves trees, rocks and even men
Mandelstam loved Armenia; his senses opened, he breathed;
Lake Sevan shone, the days like spheres shone.

*

Themuseisa 2

The muse is a cruel fuck
makes fools of us all,
you think this archaic, inept;
good, you see what I mean.

With your face to the wall,
she's hollow night, the last attendant
dancing empty-headed articulate as air,
devout as a fridge magnet.

Her gaze peels numbers from the chart,
dumps you on Avenue Aphasia
abandoned to rage and fibrillation,
gratitude gasped with each breath.

From the first, a sound for 40 years,
sucking the life out of everything,
beyond the blue hills, the river running;
pretty mouth saying all you want to hear.

Into the room she slipped
after step step in out at the door,
her laughter like summer;
her smell is on my fingers still.

*

Echo Location

Descending the cliffs at Cape Tainaron
Orpheus sees the sea foaming in hollows below,
he sees inside another isolated moment
unending, disconnected in rolling waves.

First, he drinks from the well of forgetting
and she was never there, just someone away elsewhere;
then he drinks from the well of remembering
and she is there from the start like a question answered.

Flat to the rock set to zero in the spray zone
he sees a pattern to it all and his next move;
the submarine cave roaring is the way in,
hands shredded, face skinned is the way in.

He sees the landscape torn down in vertical stripes,
the narrow path, the olive trees and the blue inlet,
the stone bridge, broken gate and absent villagers,
tattooed on black banners driven into the ground.

By echo location Orpheus turned in the dark wood,
the sea sounding above his head like sleep;
as if the hollowness of a name filled his mouth,
as if village dogs howling ripped apart red night.

Or as when fingers pressed to his shoulder,
he sees a familiar hand and a mythology of pleasure
a pale imprint fading to mere skin, moment
by moment, the blood suffusing over and over.

Her name sounds on the air and then does not,
its meaning falls into a silent pitch over and over,
catacoustic night compressing even the name's shape:
Orpheus turned in the dark wood.

*

Themuseisa 3

Murder Ballad
(Many songs are murder ballads.)

First, we remove his innards, then we stop his mouth,
you can push his face into the wall, like this, OK?
We twist the head off the neck, the sequence is strict,
he'll have a lot to say after that.

The Muses the Maenads are one and the same,
the fool singer never knows this until the end.
It looks like this   the Muses
                   the Maenads   but he doesn't get it.

A bloody mess the lyric life.

The fisherman explained to the crowd
that when he found the head it was still singing,
the sea had not corrupted it, the blood was fresh
and the world followed accordingly.

*

'…a crowd worth joining.'

For Peter Riley

The muses: the Maenads the same – in a different mode;
if this formula is right then we're all finished,
the temporary entertainment made meat
flung like song over the trees to hang in the air.

Taking a step into the unknown, into darkness,
I wanted to line up and recruit my poets,
MacSweeney, Mandelstam and Lee remembered,
but the clamour was a wave overwhelming conceit.

Against all that I am thinking of those in other places
across the open and closed borders of the turning world;
a mind moving to the next line, a single pool of light
holds steady on the page and all about is various earth.

A crowd worth joining, the lights out there flicker,
float above ground, a cartography in endless night.

*

The Origin of Music

Orpheus stood in the asymmetrical scale
looking both ways the song rose and fell
the ground parted and a fault split the Earth.

Everything began there in that moment.

Of Tainaron and katabasis, absent in the garden
of the snake flickering at her ankle.

Of song in the mouth of decapitation
Orpheus tangled in the roots of orphan.

On this red-painted vase Orpheus is nothing but a voice,
the shape of the sound of that voice remains on the air.

*

Like Looking at Pictures

The sea made us dance in an arc
but not the village square way it was
as if there were words under us, turning

Of an oar, a fiddle, a body, a head as if
alive elsewhere rising to fall
in the basin of the blood-dark sea.

I am crouching ready to jump
I am dancing with my family
I am possessed by that music.

Who gave us that song
tore it to pieces, tore us to pieces
like the boat, around us then nowhere.

The undertow took us down
the music before music filled our mouths
but there's no life without it.

They threw everything overboard
the arc turned into a grin
and out of it came lamentation *furens*.

If I could picture what happened it would be this
and the sea's slow unpicking and dismemberment
I would make this picture to tell you.

Some were suspended in watery space
and the words in the water did not save them
as useless as poetry dissolving.

Forget Phlebas, forget five fathoms,
Orpheus launched from Lesvos,
the words did not save them.

You in love with the sea
bear safe by lights on shore:
listen, hands tap the hull at night.

Lay that body down, it is illegible,
small enough for one pair of hands to carry,
count the orphans, lay that body down.

About the Sea

'Having fallen in love and resided centuries in the sea I learned writing and reading'
    ('The Wall-Painting', Odysseus Elytis,
      translated by Jeffrey Carson and Nikos Sarris.)

1

From here you can see it all, the past draws back to return
what is not there as the light through the water raises the deep,
the surface itself a reflection of merging blue unplaced.

Shipped up here, spat out by those waves, a fat mouth
spewing transparent talk I might swim through one day,
a mess of limbs and possessions scattering flotilla memory.

This green turf is soft, springy and will not drown me,
I could raise an oar here – washed-up, winnow, lost, dumb,
with no idea but marine light all around inscribed.

I could step off the shore, fit medium for drowning
glistening the first song of the luminous rolling deep
where Ino might sling a lifejacket still.

Even from the high meadows, from home recalled,
my eyes were always on the sea, away there, the blue
– and just so you know, the sea is not the land.

There is nothing behind the sea, it's not a screen
and its intangibility will seduce you, wreck you,
send your empty head afloat singing on the water.

That white mark far off over the darkening wave
– I think night comes on though the sky resists,
a moment then gone, an island buried, unnamed.

So, to be clear, the sea is not the land,
it is as unfixed as the past falling away
over the ridge of risen light.

Whatever river of ocean you name,
you steer by seamarks no longer there
cutting through transparent waves.

But she is always there, that dark girl
turning in the chambers of the sea
turning to me and away to melt my bones.

And outside the light of her gaze – nothing.

*

The sea we walk to is 40 seconds from the house. It's just there behind the Maniot tower of Captain Christeas, warlord and liberator of Kalamata. You walk to the right of the tower, down the broken steps, along the edge of the garden with various head-high scrub and gorse. The unmade path slopes down and then you see it, blue above and below across the Messenian Gulf to Koroni. And there aren't enough words for blue. Look at the sea with the Taygetos at your back, to the right, north I think, at the top of the gulf is Kalamata. To the left, south, is the end of the peninsula, Cape Matapan and the confluence of the Aegean and the Mediterranean. Stories abound. Rounding Cape Maleas westward you've already left the known world behind.

2

I was Pytheas the autoptic, when autopsy meant to look for yourself.
So, I went and looked for myself – and for the merchants of Massalia.
I saw tides, currents, the Islands of Tin and the frigid amber shore,
I looked through the fog of fixed thought and calculated latitude.

But here by the harbour wall I don't move.
I see the boats come and go, the children grow tall and leave,
I smell rotten fish, see broken pots and discarded rope,
I hear sails flapping like braggart mouths that make no sense.

Polos gnomon etc

to establish latitude

recalled forgotten

the freezing wind

of the amber shore

found the route of

the metal trade

and tin island Iktis

knucklebones of tin

Britons in wicker boats

about the headland of

Belerion far-off etc.

Back in Massalia I could not empty my head of the sea,
my eyes on Tin Islands, amber shore, Ultima Thule.
I saw the world falling off the edge of the world
I was adrift and the harbour filled with silence.

I had followed a miraculous periplus of scraps,
made an unmatched poetry of reference
and scattered all former certainties in waves.
So much for a poor man, thank you Polybius.

When the Carthaginians lost the western sea lanes.
I slipped through the gap, I understood Gadir,
the pivot in the trade between two seas.

*

The sea we walk to is 40 seconds from the house. There's a weathered concrete platform, broken at the edges and discoloured by the water. The surface is rough like small, shattered pebbles. The rockpools around it fill with salt. In the summer a neighbour fixes an aluminium ladder to the side of the platform. Though there's very little tidal variation, when the water is low you see the rocks shallow in the water to be avoided when you swim out. These rocks are sharp and uneven and look like suspended explosions. The rocks immediately on shore look the same. They are variously grey or pinkish with different coloured stones embedded in them. The Taygetos mountains before you, if you look back from the sea, form an abrupt wall raised by tectonic forces.

3

I listened to the sea all night, every passage washed away;
the sea retrieves its voices, as if the music of thought returns
in quarter tones from the east in the ululation of the waves.

When the light is up, I'll check for progress, location,
I'll send in my report, it begins at the end of the tunnel of sound,
white the waveform geometry, white the risen world.

But if this is home, the hill above the harbour, the quick river,
the hidden lane behind the row of houses,
then it is not what it was and only strangers live there now.

I went back once and there was no-one there;
what we thought we knew made the tangible unfamiliar.
Bearings on what then, charts of dust mapping nothing?

It begins – there are not words enough for blue
and the white lines of the sea roll in unreadable,
as if all talk is an echo from a forgotten thalamos.

*

The sea has a lot to say this morning
pale ribbons of light embossed delineate a conspiracy of blue
placid over unbelievable depths to the horizon.

Whitecap syntax broken washed ashore,
as if innocent of drowning, wreckage and trade
deposited an alphabet like 24 packets of flotsam.

Víkingur Ólafsson plays Debussy to the doves fornicating in the pine,
the choir of various birds and humans improvise,
meaning restored under the mimosa, Víkingur listens and plays on.

And the sea falls gently gently on the morning.

*

Pephnos the islet, outcrop, is a short swim. According to Pausanias Helen's brothers as bronze statues stood here, unmoved by the crashing waves. Yannis had told us that it was from this harbour that Helen left with Paris, not on the other side of the Taygetos from Marathonisi, as Homer would have it. The bronze statues are long gone. An artist has laid a large white concrete egg, on Pephnos; the shape of which contradicts the shape of everything around it and every element of the seascape and mountains.

*

Here we sit like birds in the earthquake zone.

The sea trench running off Cape Matapan
is 4,600 metres deep, deep enough to upend Olympus
and drown all the twittering gods – to start over again,
we could just start over again on a silent sea.

Though Orpheus swam that trench for Eurydice,
we could just rewrite the whole thing,
one backward glance deep in darkness undone
everything lost left in an underwater cave.

Or just walking in that olive grove
waiting on the sea one morning,
the chance meeting in the village
or when you stepped into the room.

And the room tilted – we could.

*

Further west on the other side of the cape of the next peninsula the Calypso Deep is part of the Hellenic Arc and is the deepest water in the Mediterranean – over 3.27 miles deep. Out on his boat one summer Yannis showed us the various depths of the water on a small sonar screen. The African tectonic plate edges north here and collides with the Eurasian plate. Out snorkelling here is enough. The seafloor drops away steeply near to the shore and leaves you suspended, arms and legs spread, looking down in slow motion on the new depth as if from the sky.

4

Where am I washed up now? said the trickster,
smashed in the rolling blue white blue.

He held the transponder in his hand
shot the red signal like an arrow to Ino.

A monologue from underwater … — …
If my foot is on the last of the land /signal break/
where meaning /break/ is unfixed, churning
my toes over the edge of zero dance.

In sight of Ithaka he sinks swims sees
close to the end of everything and nothing,
to wake on the sands of Phorkys
and find the path, the way it turns under Neriton.

To wake from landfalls and sinkings uncounted,
the raid on Troy, a business proposition, exchange
of wine, oil, gum and violence, the pulse of blood
through a narrow channel of the sea for grain.

And after Maleas at some point blown westward
for 9 days with no bearings, no seamarks
like a blueprint laid down for the unknown,
you tell me we ate the lotus – well I recall none of it.

I remember the toredo worm, the pitch melted
and black the pine and the lake of pitch;
the one-eyed giant, a thug stinking of goat,
a stupid oculus painted smack on his forehead.

She said the turnaround wind will turn you around,
Aeolus, not a big surprise, it turned us around;
and after slaughter by rote, I remembered her,
the pillars of Melkarth and the stream of ocean.

She made pillows of my heart, woman of changes,
the passing pleasure of her streams of lotion;

I forget all of it, even the one who kept me hidden,
all those years, Calypso Deep, staring at the sea.

Gone the sirens song and the whole tour,
only the dark gates of furthest west remain
and the trench I dug for the transparent dead,
a hungry crowd beyond even polytropos me.

My detachment over I saw Ithaka,
at last, I saw that stony path
I knew the turn it takes under Neriton.
and where it would lead.

Slaughter by rote? There's always more,
we make it new, like in the old songs;
an improvised composition in performance
to scatter the homeless across the sea.

5

Print block sea cut from salt
an impression of the sky.

This morning I found a packing case
wedged in the rocks of Pephnos
shedding blue polystyrene grains
as I swam back to the shore.

From first light the sea is unpaintable
the impossible surface scalloped
shallow pockets of sky dancing
and at night the darkness pooled – unpaintable.

Print block sea cut from salt,
this morning I found as if laid out to dry

a torn inflatable, clothes, a rucksack,
the nurse who went to Lesvos to help.

She spoke about the camps
about what could be done and not done
the children who never looked at the sea
the mothers unable to talk.

It's as simple as song
to explain what happened on Kythira,
the boats crashed on the rocks
people climbed the rocks to escape.

All the locals went down to the harbour
to help in darkness and high winds
lowering ropes from the cliffs,
pull pull together in darkness and high winds.

The first decision determines all others
the rest is rhetoric, advantage, ambition;
and those strangers survive or die,
the first decision determines all others.

Print block sea cut from salt
shredding lives as I swam to the shore.

6

It's quiet in the summer. A few boats go by, small fishing boats and pleasure boats in the season. The days drift by like the pleasure boats, unburdened, unanchored. The fishing boats go out in the early hours, the fading burr of their motors almost engulfed by the sound of the waves as they ply the darkness in a diminishing song. Usually later in the afternoon the waves will kick up and can roll you over a stone beach. If you go out in a small boat and the wind drops you sit and fry.

Drifting into the mouth of a cave is an immersion in glinting reflections and delicate acoustics Finding the freshwater ellipses which emerge from subterranean streams and still the waves is like an original pause in time. In the winter the sea is very different, nothing stays still. I've seen the harbour wall dismantled by storms in January and the coastal roads buried in sand. By Spring beaches have often changed shape with rearranged surfaces of sand or stone. May – the month of fair sailing – makes sense.

There were days when we heard
'the secret conversation among things',
saw the kingfisher flash from the sea cave
skim the water of the visible
and the endless depth clearing over Taygetos,
we saw the sea turtle surface to ponder
before turning to disappear in the distance abstracted.

A mistake – to think any of this lacked meaning,
to think any of this required interpretation;
there were days in the summer when
a wind would tear down from the mountain passes
flatten the sea and bend the trees to the ground;
the next hour calm, just puddles, fresh mud,
the birds chattering, and we would swim in air.

7

Ritsos called in last night and said nothing,
said nothing of the knowledge of the end;
he came over Taygetos from Monemvasia
from Limnos, Makronisos, Leros, Samos,
through the bonfire of Epitaphios – nothing.

He stood in a yellow circle under a tin shade,
the sea turned its shoulder on him like Odysseus

rolled him on the rocks and opened his side for the fish.
I remember home, the causeway, one way in and out,
if I had a raft to sail, I would take to that sea again.

I would speak to the Greeks, their fancy goods awash
griffin heads, bronze flagons and that alphabet device;
such living they have as they swim through marble gardens
out from Naxos to see Ariadne unabandoned, breathing
those unnamed voices of the sea, a labyrinth of light.

If I had a flag to raise, I would raise it – *uniform kilo victor*,
and my banner would say – don't forget you're just a singer
landing on the other side of metaphor, in the chemistry
of the print block sea cut from salt, the matter of time,
a last impression of the sky – uniform kilo victor.

8

The world goes by, a pleasure boat for Athenians,
a fisherman returns – and then nothing;
a fish skims the water, the light recasts itself
from an unfixed screen set to zero.

Ritsos swam by deep in conversation
cutting elegant strokes for miles
above the sunken poetry schools closed for the season
deep and unreachable for Elytis to cast off theory.

For the fauna of the shoreline to take it up
for the waves to say here, here is enough
and the light gloss each rivulet at your feet
– dance little crab on the lip of the deep.

Dance little crab, stony grey and black
aglitter in the spray zone

genius of the broken rocks
dance on the brink of the deep.

Tonight, the sea will be as warm as the air;
our bodies suspended, outlines blurred,
and we will walk into the water
rising inch by inch to cover us.

In the mind just two bodies
floating, and I see you there;
the seafloor falls away
and I hold the shape of you.

The sea will be as warm as the air
and the air itself a fabric
and we will walk into the water
breathing darkness laid out under stars.

Afterword

The poems collected here were written and published from 1985 to 2023. Almost all of this poetry was written in sequences or entire books rather than as separate poems. I've aimed to keep that feature, with some trimming. I've excluded some early work in order to avoid repetition, and omitted the books written in collaboration with the late Alan Halsey, precisely because they are collaborations and not my work alone. One day I would like to collect all those books in one volume in order to restate the lasting pleasure of having worked with Alan.

In compiling these poems I've kept in mind Jane Harrison's remarks in *Epilegomena to the Study of Greek Religion*, that poetry has, according to Aristotle, two forms; praise and celebration, blame and satire. I hope both qualities are here in plenty.

Standing firmly in the list for praise are those who have published me across the human spectrum of enthusiastic support to amused tolerance and curiosity. At the head of this list is Tony Frazer, founder and dynamo of Shearsman Books.

In particular my thanks go to:

Robert Vas Dias	Robert Sheppard and Penny Bailey
Peter Hodgkiss	The late Richard Caddel
Peterjon Skelt	Ken Edwards
The late Alan Halsey	Simon Smith
David Rees	Alan Baker
Brian Lewis	Peter Hughes
Andy Brown	Alec Newman
Jon Thompson	

My thanks go to Bo Hilton for permission to use the gouache by Roger Hilton, *Untitled 1975*, and to Michael Gaca and Richard Blackborow of The Belgrave Gallery, St. Ives, for their help and advice in this, and to Carrie Stacchini for her photographic expertise.

Notes

When Suzy Was

The preface is Robert Parker 'Greek States and Greek Oracles' in P.A. Cartledge and F.D. Harvey *Crux: Essays in Greek History*, 1985. Parker referring to Herodotus as probably apologetic fiction on this point.

The question, *You may say to yourself, well how did I get here?* is from a David Byrne song 'Once in a Lifetime'.

For the third stanza of the third poem under that title see Shelley's *Homer's Hymn to the Sun*.

The second part of the poem *When Suzy Was* refers to a *Danse Macabre* of 1499 by Matthias Hus, the earliest known illustration of a printing press.

The unattributed lines in the third poem of *The Roadside Shrine* are Clement of Alexandria and P. Evdokimov in Timothy Ware *The Orthodox Church*, 1993.

The fifteenth Catalogue poem quotes de Quincey and the nineteenth W.S. Graham.

Backward Turning Sea

Jenkyns is a translator of Sappho.

Roza is Roza Eskenazi, rebetika singer in the Smyrna style.

The epigraph 'Over the calm, clear shining water...' is an anonymous fragment in *Greek Lyric Poetry* by M.L. West. There are also versions of Alcman and Archilocus here. See also Pritchard, *The Ancient Near East*.

Roger Hilton's Sugar
'Night Letters', Roger Hilton, 1980
'Roger Hilton', Adrian Lewis, 2003
'The Last Days of Hilton', Adrian Lewis, 1996
'Roger Hilton', The South Bank Centre, 1993
'Roger Hilton – Drawings', Jonathan Clark Fine Art, 2001
'Oi Yoi Yoi Roger Hilton', Jonathan Clark Fine Art, 2000
'Roger Hilton: An Instrument of Truth', Tate St. Ives, 1997
'Roger Hilton', Chris Stephens, 2006
'Into Seeing New: The Art of Roger Hilton', Tate St. Ives, 2006
The questions in 'From Botallack Out' are distortions of Merleau-Ponty.

Alexiares
'My Journey to Euripides': Alexiares, the speaker, is my invention; the name means one who is opposed. See Pausanias, Thucydides, Euripides, Kerenyi on Dionysus and Jane Harrison on ritual. After defeat the Athenian soldiers were imprisoned on Sicily in the marble quarries. Reciting a few lines of poetry could win freedom.

'Odes of Alexiares': for the questions in part 3 see Griffin: *The 9/11 Commission Report: Omissions and Distortions*, 2005.

'Alexiares in Exile': Martin Bernal is the author of *Black Athena: The Afroasiatic Roots of Classical Civilisation*, 1987. See Ovid's poems of exile. Nicos Xylouris was a Cretan singer. Songs by Theodorakis were banned during the Greek colonels' dictatorship.

'From Alexiares's Separate Notebooks': for *Kanun*, the law of blood feud, the canon of Lek, see Edith Durham's.

Ulysses in the Car
'From the Holiday Inn Athens': the third stanza of part 2 is Paul Merchant in 'Some Business of Affinity', the introduction to a translation of Aeschylus.

'Outside rain rains in this room' takes a line from Laurie Duggan – 'the people I sing to are dead.'

'The investigation remains live' see *Report of the Official Account of the Bombings in London on 7 July 2006*.

'Nameless on the water': an onos would be fitted to a woman's leg for purposes of carding the wool ready for the loom.

'Coda': in part this poem is derived from very badly mishearing the lyrics in Offenbach's *Orpheus in the Underworld* – When I was the King of the Boeotians, which made it sound more interesting than it turned out to be.

Hotel Shadow

'From Where Song Comes'
See Hugh MacDiarmid 'In Memoriam James Joyce', Maurice Bowra *Primitive Song* and John Blacking *How Musical Is Man*.

'Reading *The Cantos*'
Morritt who reports on the generosity of Captain Christeas is J.B.S. Morritt in *A Grand Tour: Letters and Journeys 1794–96*.

'From the Hen-Roost': The epigraph is from Ezra Pound.

'A Thesis on the Ballad': The quotation in 'The Truth' is from M.J.C. Hodgart, *The Ballads*.

'News of Aristomenes'
The only sustained source for the figure of Aristomenes, scourge of the Spartans, is Pausanias. See also Daniel Ogden *Aristomenes of Messene: Legends of Sparta's Nemesis*. With thanks to Alistair Noon.

'The Family Carnival'
Some of the carnival songs can be found on the CD *Carnival Songs: The Sacred in the Profane* from The Greek Folk Music Association.

'Byron's Karagiozis'
The idea that Byron was used as sexual bait for Ali Pasha, to win allegiance to the British cause in the conflict with Napoleon, can be found in Ian Gilmour's *The Making of the Poets: Byron and Shelley in Their Time*.

'Epicurus Is My Neighbour'
Anything remotely to do with Epicurus in this poem comes from Eugene O'Connor's translation *The Essential Epicurus: Letters, Principal Doctrines, Vatican Sayings, and Fragments*.

'On the Xenophone Label'
Sources include J. H. Lesher: *Xenophanes of Colophon: Fragments: A Text and Translation with Commentary*; George Thompson: *The First Philosophers: Studies in Ancient Greek Society* and Sherod Santos: *Greek Lyric Poetry*.

Sea Table

'Words Through a Hole Where Once There Was a Chimpanzee's Face'
For the opening poem see William Carlos Williams, 'The Descent'.

'He stared at death. Death stared straight back.' See John Berryman's *The Dream Songs* number 45, 'He stared at ruin. Ruin stared straight back.'

'A Short History of Song Set to Music and Abandoned'

'Thomas Hardy On Tour.' See Hardy's 'Poems of Pilgrimage.'

'All the Poets.' The italicised line is from Lou Reed's 'Sweet Jane.'

Peter Riley's poem 'How To Read Poetry' is in *XIV PIECES*. Longbarrow Press, 2012.

The music for the final poem is a transcription of the end of an improvisation played by pianist Sam Bailey before a reading by Kelvin Corcoran on 9th February 2012 at the Free Range series of music, film and poetry events in Canterbury, Kent, UK. A recording of the performance can be found here, the section of the music that has been transcribed can be heard from 11.30 on the recording. http://soundcloud.com/free-range/piano-set-9th-feb-2012

Glenn Gould and Everything
There is an account of Alberto Guerrero's teaching technique of tapping in *Wondrous Strange: The Life and Art of Glenn Gould* by Kevin Bazzana, 2004.

'Producing everything from one thing.' Schoenberg on Bach.

Sea Table
Parts 2 and 4 of the poem loosely allude to a ceramic of twenty small engraved tiles in a frame by Robert Wilcox. In part 4 the reference is increasingly allusive and abstract. See http://www.stivesonlineshop.co.uk/bob_wilcox.htm

The first poem in part 4, 'With usura hath no man a house of good stone', see Pound's Canto XLV.

The fourth poem in part 4. In Saidona, Messenia, the memorial for the Second World War and the Greek civil war carries an inscription from the poem 'Greekness' by Yannis Ritsos. Thank you to Maria Pavlidou, Yannis Voulimeneas and Lorna McFarland for their patient help in translating those lines and also for helping me find out what happened in the village.

> For years besieged from land and sea
> everyone is hungry, everyone killed but no-one dies,
> from the high lookout their eyes burn
> the big flag and the deep-red fire,
> and every dawn from their hands a thousand doves
> fly out to the four doors of the horizon.

Facing West

'The Abduction Zone'
Helen whispering to the Greeks inside the Trojan horse see *The Odyssey*, IV, 277–289.

'Common Measure'
In Leipzig *The Stumbling Block* project memorialises victims of the Holocaust. Their names are written on small brass tiles embedded in the pavement near their former homes.

In the second part of the poem 'Common Measure' I'm talking to two poems by Peter Riley, 'The Little Watercolour at Sligo' and 'That Grand Conversation Was Under the Rose' from *Passing Measures*, 2000. In the third part I'm addressing Sandeep Parmar and her book *Eidolon*, 2015. 'To make her into an artefact is to try to kill her' is from Jack Spicer's poem 'Helen: A Revision.'

The quotation in the final part of 'Lee Harwood 1939–2015' is from Lee Harwood, *Boston-Brighton*, 1977.

Radio Archilochos
For the ten archaic Greek terms from Archilochos in part 4, and for his generous and expert guidance, many thanks to Paschalis Nikolaou of the Ionian University. The numbers in this part of the poem refer to the fragments of Archilochos in *Greek Iambic Poetry*, edited and translated by Douglas E. Gerber, Loeb Classical Library, 1999.

What we know about Archilochos is found in the fragments of his poetry which remain. He came from Paros and lived from c.680–c.640 BC, possibly. His father, Telesicles, led the Parian colonisation of Thasos. *Possibly* hovers over every assertion about Archilochos. He was either the son of this influential family or an illegitimate mercenary; either way he saw military service on Thasos. He is credited with several poetic innovations and is renowned for his use of what could be autobiographical experience; or possibly not, as such details could just as well be the formal moves in a set of aesthetic conventions unknown to us. He may well have played a key role in the cult of Dionysus on Paros. Archilochos was killed by a Naxian whose name meant crow; the circumstances of this act are unknown.

Below This Level

Below This Level is for my wife Melanie.
With thanks to Dr. Agneessens, Dr. Entezari and Dr. Otte.

The title *Below This Level* is from the song 'Below This Level (Patient's Song)' by Can on the album *Rite Time*; the singer is Malcolm Mooney. References are made to various musicians. Arthur Russell was not a Reverend. 'Get Around

To It' is a song by him on *Calling Out of Context*. In 'Uitgang, provisional' the quotation is from *Don Juan*, Canto 1, stanzas 133 and 134. In the third part of *Below This Level* liberal use is made of paintings by Marc Chagall and of memoirs by him and his wife Bella.

The Republic of Song

Several of the poems in 'To Write A Mythology' have appeared in earlier versions; *Article 50*, Longbarrow Press 2018. *Twitters for a Lark: Poetry of The European Union of Imaginary Writers*, as Eua Ionnu, Shearsman, 2017. My thanks go to Brian Lewis and Robert Sheppard.

'The Sinking Colony Revisited in the Days of Lee Harwood' began life in *Winterreisen*, a collaboration with Alan Halsey, published by Knives Forks and Spoons Press. Although these are my parts from the collaborative poem much is owed to Alan. I'm also grateful to him for the title of the poem and his naming of the figure Iain Guido Smith.

Several poems from *The Republic of Song* were published in *The Fortnightly Review*, with thanks to the editor Peter Riley. 'Grahamland' was first published in *The Caught Habits of Language*, Donut Press, 2018, edited by Rachael Boast, Andy Ching and Nathan Hamilton.

The poem for Roy Fisher (1930–2017) first appeared in *Molly Bloom*, edited by Aidan Semmens. An earlier version of 'I'm sending you this from Agios Dimitrios' for Denise Riley was published in *The World Speaking Back*, Boiler House Press, 2018, edited by Ágnes Lehóczky and Zoë Skoulding. My thanks go to all of these editors.

'Radio Logos' part 2. 'There is no history that does not relate to the present,' Louis Gernet quoted in *The Mediterranean in the Ancient World*, Fernand Braudel, 2002.

'The Sinking Colony Revisited in the Days of Lee Harwood'. See *The Sinking Colony*, 1970, Lee Harwood 1939–2015.

'Come Up Come Up'. *A History of the World in Twelve Maps*, Jerry Brotton, 2014.

Roy Fisher, 1930–2017, 'zig-zagging like the shadow of a hare', from *Wonders of Obligation*.

'Grahamland'. The line 'Launched even later there becoming a time.' is culled from *The Seven Journeys,* W. S. Graham, 1944, and takes the first word from the first line of each of the seven poems, more or less.

'BN'. See *Ben Nicholson: 'chasing out something alive' drawings and painted reliefs 1950–75,* Peter Khoroche, 2002.

'In the Hilton Memorial Garden'. Roger Hilton, 1911–1975, painter.

'Having a Drink with Phil'. The essay *Lyrical Poetry: Directions for Use* by Paul Van Ostaijen can be found in *The First Book of Schmoll,* Paul Van Ostaijen translated by Theo Hermans, James S. Holmes and Peter Nijmeijer, 2015. The phrase, 'the homeland of perfect knowledge' is from that essay. For material relating to Roger Casement, Joseph Conrad and Leopold II see *King Leopold's Ghost,* Adam Hochschild, 2006; *Roger Casement,* Brian Inglis, 1973; *The King Incorporated,* Neal Ascherson, 1963 and *The Eyes of Another Race: Roger Casement's Congo Report and 1903 Diary,* edited by Séamas Ó Síocháin and Michael O'Sullivan, 2003.

'Listening to Country Music'. The Jason Isbell song quoted is *Cigarettes and Wine* from *Jason Isbell And The 400 Unit.*

'If you are a big tree, I am a small axe.' *Small Axe* written by Bob Marley, sung by U Roy.

'Helen: A Revision'. Jack Spicer in *My Vocabulary Did This To Me: The Collected Poetry of Jack Spicer,* edited by Peter Gizzi and Kevin Killian, 2008.

'The Museum of the Sea'. 'Set sail without fear...' Theodorides quoted in *The Making of the Middle Sea,* Cyprian Broodbank, 2013.

Above Ground

Several poems from *Above Ground* have been published in the magazines *Osiris, Word/For Word, Litter, Blackbox Manifold and Free Verse.* With thanks to the editors: Andrea Moorhead, Jonathan Minton, Alan Baker, Alex Houen and Adam Piette, Simon Smith, Dorothy Lehane, David Herd and Nancy Gaffield.

'The Correspondence of Objects'. See *The Dream Songs,* 'Song 64'.

'Preparations'. See Robert Hass, *Summer Snow,* 'Notes on the Notion of a Boundless Poetics'.

For 'a crowd worth joining', see Peter Riley, *Truth, Justice, and the Companionship of Owls,* 'poem xii'.

Comments on Kelvin Corcoran's work

"'Greece', Kelvin Corcoran has said, 'writes itself for me.' If so, Greece is a gifted poet indeed. While the country and its culture has been the poet's central passion for many years, through several books, he has written broadly about many places, people and concerns, personal and political, with feeling and sophistication.

Corcoran has as wide a range and as rich a vocabulary as any poet now writing. He possesses a flawless ear, a fresh eye for image and detail, penetrating analysis and a storyteller's gift. He can shift registers suddenly, from lyric to formal mode to common speech, and even a snatch of song. 'The starting point / is ordinary language and this / a claim from Gemistos / yes we have no bananas.' Gemistos alerts to Corcoran's thorough study of classical Greece, its history, mythology, philosophy and literature, which underlies so much of his poetry, complemented by his sensory alertness, mastery of form, wit, and strong feeling for nature; 'that night snow fell softly / then morning walked on white mountains.' He can move from Homer to the goings on in a village square with ease.

At heart here is the sea, 'the museum of the sea,' surface and depth, at whose edge is the line between going and coming, adventure and home, life and death. And the land, mountains, forests, orchards, 'where the wind drinks pine tree resin' and 'olive trees blown white in the wind.' The poetry is lovely. It works at a high yet human level, accounting for both 'beauty' and 'slaughter' of time, bringing together Odysseus, Helen, Byron and the poet's personal friends. The music, the poetry, are everywhere. And somewhere, the day ends: 'an old woman talks kindly to her dog / and owls weave mortal wires into dawn.' A human touch, and a line of pure magic.

Kelvin Corcoran is one of the rare true poets. Reading him is a privilege and a pleasure, a new awareness." —David Wevill

"Much of Corcoran's later work explores the possibility of being saved; this of course, is a reworking of the idea of elegy, as if he is standing in the same place, but looking firmly in the opposite direction…. Corcoran's austere, 1980s style embodied the politics of the left under siege – it was full of anxiety and anger. The more recent works … change the focus without losing conviction. They celebrate the possibility of utopia…"
—Charles Bainbridge, *The Guardian*

"Despite the denatured surface, much of Corcoran's poetry is extremely

emotional, and the accumulation of evidence of the outside world just involves us more firmly in his emotions about politics, love and family tragedy. What we may be seeing is a fundamental renewal of rhetoric – answering to a new generation with new expectations of artistic syntax, genre rules, and connectedness."
—Andrew Duncan, *The Failure of Conservatism in Modern British Poetry*

"Corcoran's *Helen Mania* is an ambitious modern re-working of the Greek myth with emotional depth and consistency. There is an effort-less lyrical narrative flow to this novella in verse, a simplicity and succinctness belied by the lush picturesque quality of his imagery." —*Poetry Book Society Bulletin*

"Kelvin Corcoran's translations of the seventh-century BC lyric poet and satirist, Archilochos, hit with such vigour, such confident strident voicing, such Villonesque bravura and candour and braggadocio, that one is absolutely taken in. These must be careful renderings of this obscure poet. The more one finds out of Archilochos, however, the more perfect these translacings are. Archilochos only survives in the form of fragments, yet he was considered an absolute master by all poets afterwards, especially admired for the power of his invective (which was supposed to have driven a family to suicide), for his inventiveness as a poet (he was believed to have invented iambic measure, the elegy, etc.), and for having been the first poet to have used a recognizably first person address: all the more reason to regret the lack of whole poems.

[…] Many of the fragments explain why Corcoran is drawn to him: he is both satirist and lyric poet, working in these modes nearly as far back as Homer: so appealing to the satirist-lyrical Corcoran and his sustained championing of the Greece of the pre-state 'ritual' period (see Peter Riley's extraordinarily good account of all this in his magisterial essay on Greece and Corcoran in the equally ground-breaking Reader edited by Andy Brown, *The Writing Occurs as Song: A Kelvin Corcoran Reader* [Shearsman, 2014]). He appeals, too, because of the burly way Archilochos mocked Sparta and its fascist war-cult; Sparta figures in Corcoran's Greek work as equivalent to the Anglo-American war machine. He appeals, too, because of the extraordinary verve and loving eroticism of the lyrics, especially the only relatively recently (1970s) discovered whole poem translated by Guy Davenport, affectionately titled 'P. Colon. 7511' or 'Fragment 18'. It was found, Davenport tells us in his introduction to his translations, *7 Greeks*, used by Corcoran for his epigraph (New Directions, 1995), available on a papyrus mummy wrapping, and is breathtakingly and happily obscene, unlike anything else in Greek literature.

This appeals to the Roger Hilton in Corcoran, the relish of frank sexual desire and love of the other's body. Across the airwaves of time and space, then, come the sounds of sexually explicit satirical lyric, on Radio Archilochos, and the renderings are quite simply unsurpassably superb.

Superb as all these versions are, they are *not* translations, but translacings out from the fragments, a dramatic monologue fusing with lyrical sequence recreation. Davenport reminds us that Archilochos only exists in bits and pieces of text: 'the tattered version we have of Archilochos, some three hundred fragments and about forty paraphrases and indirect quotations in the Budé edition'. From those fragments, Kelvin Corcoran has summoned up a real, true ghost, made the dead man speak: a quite astonishing achievement." —Adam Piette, *Blackbox Manifold*

"Kelvin Corcoran's recent work inhabits the imagination as a distinct sphere of abundance, drawn from reality as a celebration of the true scope of the mind. And the instrument of this is a written eloquence which takes in the past of poetry and of the spirit as a freshly lived condition, which the self occupies at its most impassioned and most sincere. So, it cannot be easy, or singular, though it is full of direct statements, simplicities and particular events." —Peter Riley, *PN Review*

"There is a clear sad music playing right through this book of answers, steady and unmistakable. Against it, the urges of friendship, love and harsh judgements move sharp and bright with their own turbulences … If Corcoran takes himself into a timeless Greece, it's not with the intention of fooling himself: he's an honest visitor to the oracle." —Roy Fisher on *When Suzy Was*

"Corcoran emerged into view around 1985, with the piquantly entitled *Robin Hood in the Dark Ages,* and has produced consistently ever since – something which is true of no other individual. It is this strength and calm which have made him a giant figure of the middle generation…"
—Andrew Duncan, *Poetry Salzburg*

"The poems in *For the Greek Spring*, written over the past 30 years, drift in and out of conversation with Homer and Xenophanes, but they also register, with equal care, the cultural pressures of modern Greek life, in

which one sees 'the newly immiserated / in procession under the Parthenon' and Albanian refugees who sell stolen iPads on the beach. Corcoran is a superbly skilled lyricist. He celebrates Greece's coastlines, meadows and mountains – the tangible, visible surfaces from which its most enduring mythologies are drawn – in passages of bucolic immediacy."
—Frances Leviston, *The Guardian*

"The poet's news comes so swift and sharp and fresh that it really is immediate, present; not loud. The magic of it, Cheltenham delivering, morning intelligence not subscribed to the delusions of higher paranoia, spooks and eavesdroppers. A world where you can still hope to 'slice a tomato and smell it', before some clown goes on television to fudge the plural vision."
—Iain Sinclair on *Melanie's Book*

"Corcoran is so skilled with his line and subject matter, he can help us wake up through his writing: he sweeps from the ancient to the contemporary and back again, often in the same short stanza ... His work is linguistically complex yet, emotionally, socially, politically and, above all, poetically (musically) alive." —Andy Brown, *Stride Magazine*.

Kelvin Corcoran's poetry of Greece has two sides to it, constantly engaged with each other. One is the relaxation of the northerner in the Mediterranean climate zone: heat, light, sea, stone, wine, music, dozing in the courtyard with a glass of ouzo... and all the rest of that (i.e., Now). The other is the whole of Greek culture: mythology, drama, poetry, ritual, religion, drama, philosophy, legend, history... (i.e. Then). The first of these is rational, the second irrational, but they get on very well together, in fact each normally implies the other. The Now is enhanced and dignified by the Then; the Then becomes visible through the Now and the whole spectrum announces sightings of the extended real. I fear that in a period of drives towards poetical austerity and purity such as we have had in the last 20 years or so in Britain and America, these forms of attention will be dismissed as some kind of indulgence or avoidance, which I don't think they are. Modernist zones might be sympathetic to the poetry in memory of founding fathers, but even here the implied fullness is likely to be disallowed unless contracted into politicised aesthetic inversion, or reduced to a question of language.
—Peter Riley, 'Kelvin Corcoran and Greece' from *The Writing Occurs As Song: A Kelvin Corcoran Reader*, edited by Andy Brown, 2014

www.ingramcontent.com/pod-product-compliance
Lightning Source LLC
Chambersburg PA
CBHW020053020526
44112CB00031B/63